STRATEGY AND PERFORMANCE OF FOREIGN COMPANIES IN JAPAN

STRATEGY AND PERFORMANCE OF FOREIGN COMPANIES IN JAPAN

Sikander Khan
Hideki Yoshihara

Q

QUORUM BOOKS
Westport, Connecticut • London

Library of Congress Cataloging-in-Publication Data

Khan, Sikander.
    Strategy and performance of foreign companies in Japan / Sikander
Khan, Hideki Yoshihara.
      p. cm.
    Includes bibliographical references and index.
    ISBN 0–89930–899–6
    1. Corporations, Foreign—Japan. 2. Japan—Economic
conditions—1989– . I. Yoshihara, Hideki. II. Title.
HD2907.K474   1994
338.8′8852—dc20   93–49034

British Library Cataloguing in Publication Data is available.

Library of Congress Catalog Card Number: 93–49034
ISBN: 0–89930–899–6

First published in 1994

Quorum Books, 88 Post Road West, Westport, CT 06881
An imprint of Greenwood Publishing Group, Inc.

Printed in the United States of America

The paper used in this book complies with the
Permanent Paper Standard issued by the National
Information Standards Organization (Z39.48–1984).

10 9 8 7 6 5 4 3 2 1

To Elisabeth and Salomon
Sikander Khan

To Fusako, Fumiki, and Hanako
Hideki Yoshihara

CONTENTS

ILLUSTRATIONS

FIGURES

TABLES

APPENDIX B

PREFACE

The idea for writing this book surfaced during Dr. Khan's one-year stay from 1987 to 1988 at Nihon University in Tokyo, where he was preparing his book Success and Failure of Japanese Companies' Export Ventures in High-Tech Industries. At that time, we had the opportunity to discuss the strategies, management, and performance of foreign companies in Japan, particularly in terms of the Japanese market being the most competitive in the world, at a time when the yen was rapidly appreciating, the Japanese trade surplus and outward FDI was soaring, and Japan was increasingly being accused of being a market closed to foreign investment. Simultaneously, we observed that there were weaknesses in the FDI and traditional international trade theories, which did not take into account the reverse flow of technology and know-how from a foreign subsidiary to its parent company, a phenomenon that was in fact taking place at the subsidiaries of foreign companies in Japan. Considering this area as vital and in need of further investigation, we formulated the research project that led to this book.

We were also baffled by the fact that most of the research on foreign companies in Japan was confined either to desk studies or journalistic accounts with limited empirical data. Furthermore, the bookstore shelves were filled with stereotypical advice on how to succeed in Japan, from such trivial examples as possessing a proper Japanese name card to having adequate connections with influential personalities.

Professor Yoshihara invited Dr. Khan to jointly carry out the book. Subsequently, Dr. Khan was able to obtain a three-year leave of absence from Stockholm University from 1991 to 1994, and we were able to commence the challenging work on this book at the Research Institute for Economics and Business Administration, Kobe University. A study group on foreign companies in Japan consisting of five members was formed in June 1991. The other three members were Associate Professor Dr. L. Huang, Otaru University of Commerce; Associate Professor P. Debroux, University of Okayama and University of Brussels; and Associate Professor S. Iwata, Kagawa University.

Professor Yoshihara was the Project Coordinator for the book. He played a vital role in formulating a conceptual framework and provided valuable comments on the entire book, which was written and prepared by Dr. Khan.

ACKNOWLEDGMENTS

We would like to give our very special thanks to the Research Institute for Economics and Business Administration, Kobe University, for providing full assistance, including research assistants and office and computer facilities, to successfully carry out the work on this book. Moreover, we are grateful to the Japanese Ministry of Education for providing research funds for the field study and for offering Dr. Khan a regular post as a Japanese Associate Professor of International Business at Kobe University during his three-year stay in Japan. We are deeply grateful for the funds for the field research provided by the Murata Science Foundation. Our thanks also go to Ezaki Glico Co., Ltd., for providing research funds.

We were fortunate enough to have had the opportunity to present the preliminary research results at a number of seminars in Tokyo and Osaka, which were attended by a large number of ministry officials, trade representatives, and representatives of foreign companies, banks, foreign and Japanese chambers of commerce, and others. We would like to thank all the participants at these seminars and conferences for their valuable comments.

Our special thanks go to the following sponsors of seminars: the Ministry of International Trade and Industry (MITI), Japan External Trade Organization (JETRO), Japan Development Bank (JDB), European Business Community (EBC), Sanno College, Osaka Chamber of Commerce and Industry, Center for Japan-US Exchange in the Humanities and Social Sciences, Swedish Chamber of Commerce and Industry, and the Commercial Office of the Embassy of Sweden. We also thank the American Chamber of Commerce in Japan (ACCJ), EBC, and the Commercial Office of the Embassy of Sweden for providing excellent letters of introduction, which were attached with our questionnaire mailed to their member companies in Japan.

The empirical data on which a large part of this book is based could not have been gathered without the cooperation of several hundred executives who generously contributed their time and expertise and supplied confidential data. We sincerely regret that confidentiality prevents individual acknowledgments, but we do wish to make a general statement of our appreciation for the full cooperation of the 436 responding foreign companies in Japan, including banks, ministries, universities, industrial associations and federations, and research institutes. (For a list of companies and organizations, see Appendix C.) We also wish to express our appreciation to those interviewees and their companies whose names do not appear in Appendix C due to their request for confidentiality.

Special thanks go to Stockholm University for giving Dr. Khan the leave of absence necessary to successfully accomplish writing this book. Some parts of the manuscript were discussed at Dr. Khan's graduate course on Global Competitive Strategy, which was attended by Japanese and foreign students at Kobe University. We want to thank all these students for their comments and suggestions. We also wish to express our deep appreciation to those who assisted us in preparing the manuscript: Debra Inazu, Kaori Kamata, Yoko Miyao, Peter Ohman, and Rie Takenouchi.

We are indebted to Elisabeth Berg Khan for her excellent work in arranging the voluminous data and preparing the graphs and tables. We would also like to thank our families, who have encouraged us in so many ways thus facilitating the preparation and completion of this book. Finally, we acknowledge complete responsibility for this study, its conclusions, and its weaknesses.

Sikander Khan and Hideki Yoshihara

EXPLANATORY NOTES

Dollars ($) refer to United States dollars.
Yens refer to Japanese yens.
A comma (,) is used to distinguish thousands and millions.
A full stop (.) is used to indicate decimals.
Throughout this book, the word billion = 1,000,000,000.
Throughout this book, the word trillion = 1,000,000,000,000.
Kanji refers to Chinese characters.
Korea refers to Republic of Korea.
NIEs refers only to the Asian NIEs, i.e., Hong Kong, Korea,
Singapore, and Taiwan.
PRC refers to the People's Republic of China.
East and Southeast Asia refer to developing East and
Southeast Asia, i.e., ASEAN, the NIEs, and the PRC.
Europe refers to Western Europe.
Sogo Shosha refers to Japanese general trading companies.
Figures have been rounded off, and therefore percentage figures
may not always add up to 100%.
The following abbreviations and contractions have been used in this book:

ECONOMIC AND TECHNICAL ABBREVIATIONS

Alt.   alternative
App.   appendix

CAD   computer-aided design

CAE	computer-aided engineering
CAM	computer-aided manufacturing
cc.	cylinder capacity
CD	compact disc
CE	concurrent engineering
CEO	chief executive officer
CI	corporate image
C.i.f.	cost, insurance, and freight
CKD	complete knock-down
CNC	computer numerically controlled
CY	calendar year
EC	European Community or EU (European Union)
FA	factory automation
FAZ	foreign access zones
FDI	foreign direct investment
FMS	flexible manufacturing system
FY	fiscal year
GNP	gross national product
HRM	human resource management
ICs	integrated circuits
IR	industrial robots
JIT	just in time
JV	joint venture
KD	knock-down
M & A	mergers and acquisitions
MNCs	multinational corporations
MNEs	multinational enterprises
MT	machine tools
NC	numeric control
NIEs	newly industrializing economies
NTBs	non-tariff barriers
OA	office automation
ODA	official development assistance

OEM	original equipment manufacturer
OJT	on-the-job training
ORAD	operational results after depreciation
OTC	over-the-counter
PCM	product cycle model
PLC	product life cycle
PRC	People's Republic of China
Q	question
QC	quality circles
R & D	research and development
RAM	random access memory
ROCE	return on capital employed
ROE	return on equity
ROI	return on investment
ROTC	return on total capital
SMEs	small and medium-sized enterprises
TNCs	transnational corporations
TQC	total quality control
TSE	Tokyo Stock Exchange
UK	United Kingdom
US	United States of America
US$	United States dollars
VA	value added
VCRs	videocassette recorders
VER	voluntary export restraints
VLSIs	very large-scale integrated circuits
Yens	Japanese yens

ORGANIZATIONAL ABBREVIATIONS

ABB	Asea Brown Boveri
ACCJ	American Chamber of Commerce in Japan
ASEAN	Association of Southeast Asian Nations

| BIS | Bank for International Settlements |
| BOJ | Bank of Japan |

EBC	European Business Community
EC	European Communities
EFTA	European Free Trade Association
EIAJ	Electronic Industries Association of Japan
EPA	Economic Planning Agency
EXIM Bank	Export-Import Bank of Japan

| FAMA | Foreign Affiliated Companies Management Association |
| FIND | Foreign Investment in Japan Development, Inc. |

| IBM | International Business Machines |
| IMF | International Monetary Fund |

JAIA	Japan Automobile Importer's Association
JAMA	Japan Automobile Manufacturers Association, Inc.
JCIA	Japan Chemical Industry Association
JDB	Japan Development Bank
JETRO	Japan External Trade Organization
JFBA	Japan Federation of Bar Associations
JPMA	Japan Pharmaceutical Manufacturers Association
JPO	Japanese Patent Office

| KEIDANREN | Japan Federation of Economic Organizations |

| MITI | Ministry of International Trade and Industry |
| MOF | Ministry of Finance |

NEC	Nippon Electric Company
NIKKEIREN	Japan Federation of Employers' Associations
NTT	Nippon Telegraph and Telephone Corporation

| OECD | Organization for Economic Cooperation and Development |

| PFC | People's Finance Corporation |

| RENGO | Japanese Trade Union Confederation |
| RIEB | Research Institute for Economics & Business Administration, Kobe University |

| SBFC | Small Business Finance Corporation |

UNIDO   United Nations Industrial Development Organization

VW   Volkswagen

EXECUTIVE SUMMARY

This book shows that the majority of foreign companies in Japan are successful and that they are making profits despite the problems they face in the Japanese market.

The book deals with the strategy and performance of foreign companies in Japan. At present, foreign companies are concentrating their efforts on increasing their FDI in Japan. Yet investment by EC and EFTA companies compared to the US in Japan have remained modest in comparison with Japanese FDI in Europe or the United States.

Japan's massive trade surplus and an FDI ratio of one to ten to twenty in favor of Japan has become the source of a trade war and fueled a growing call for protectionism from the major trading partners of Japan. The United States and Western European countries criticize Japan for unfair trade practices, for having tremendous FDI barriers in Japan for foreign companies, and for being a closed market; they believe that it is impossible for foreign companies to succeed in Japan. Market access is debated heatedly in the mass media every time Japan's trade surplus soars. The business climate in Japan is considered by many to be not as favorable as it is in Europe or the United States. Japan is also accused of unique and exclusionary business practices. The conclusion drawn by many governments is that the possibility of obtaining real, equal access to the Japanese market is remote.

Frequent obstacles for foreign companies making FDI in Japan are (1) the high cost of doing business in Japan, for example, exorbitant land prices; (2) high taxation levels on corporate profits; (3) difficulties in hiring qualified Japanese personnel; (4) extreme difficulties in acquiring Japanese companies (M & A), due to cultural aspects, high land prices, high stock prices (despite the fall of the Nikkei Stock average), and the strength of the yen; (5) complicated and multitiered distribution systems; (6) government guidelines, policies, and regulations that lack clarity; (7) Keiretsu (corporate groups with extensive cross-shareholdings) that favor doing business within the Keiretsu group rather than with domestic outsiders or foreign companies in Japan; (8) "old-boy/old-girl" networks, which also hinder foreign access to Japanese markets; (9) weaknesses in the intellectual property system; (10) lengthy testing and approval periods for new foreign products; and (11) practice restrictions for law companies.

According to the Japanese government, the tariffs are some of the lowest in the world, and with few exceptions, practically all the formal legal and regulatory barriers have been abolished. In order to slash the snowballing Japanese global trade surplus, the Japanese government is further easing various domestic regulations and standards that hamper FDI and import promotion, and has also established import incentive programs to provide assistance to foreign companies. However, the pace of liberalization is rather slow, since some protective policies still exist.

We argue that all the blame cannot be put on specific Japanese entry barriers, but that foreign companies must share some of the blame. Many foreign companies in Japan (1) pay strict attention to financial targets, with a short-term management perspective; (2) are unable or unwilling to modify products to suit the Japanese market; (3) have low-quality products; (4) lack market research; (5) lack proper pre- and post-sale services; (6) lack an understanding of Japanese customs, language, and business policies and practices; and (7) lack an understanding of the intensity of competition in the Japanese market.

There are several strategic reasons for making FDI in the Japanese market: (1) since Japan is the second largest single market in the world, ignoring this market's competition will reduce the overall ability to compete globally; (2) to obtain global dominance, companies competing in the global arena must become "insiders" in the Europe, Japan, and United States triad; (3) FDI capitalizes on technical leads companies from the United States and Europe have in several key industrial sectors or segments; (4) FDI generates reverse technology transfer and helps obtain global synergy in terms of production, R & D and marketing.

It is well known that Japanese consumers are sensitive to product quality and require a short delivery time and excellent service. The number of new products launched in the Japanese market is tremendous. The Japanese market is considered to be one of the most competitive in the world, and at the same time, it is both dynamic and rewarding.

There were three research purposes. First, we aimed to conduct fact finding based on empirical investigations of foreign companies in Japan. Second, we wished to form theoretical propositions that would reveal limitations of existing theories of multinational enterprises. We envisaged that the results and findings of this research would lead to new factors for development of MNE theories. Third, we hoped that practical propositions consisting of key success and failure factors in the Japanese market would be made to foreign companies that are already in Japan or are planning to invest in Japan. Furthermore, propositions would also be made to foreign and Japanese policymakers for their actions in order to boost FDI in Japan.

Research for this book focused on five basic questions:

1. What types of investment strategies were employed by foreign companies in Japan, and how did these strategies affect the performance of their business ventures in Japan? The purpose was to present the features of successful foreign companies in Japan, identifying which factors were critical for their success in Japan.

2. What problems did foreign companies face in the Japanese market, and how were these problems solved?

3. How were the foreign companies' communication networks functioning with headquarters outside Japan? Concerns included the headquarters-subsidiary relationship, the localization of top management, and information and the decision-making process within Japanese subsidiaries.

4. To what extent had foreign companies in Japan transferred their production technology, R & D results, patents, and marketing know-how, to their parent companies outside of Japan and/or to other subsidiaries outside of Japan?

5. What practical implications could be drawn regarding the features of successful foreign companies in Japan for foreign companies as well as Japanese and foreign policymakers? Finally, the study is expected to make further contributions toward developments in the theory of MNEs.

Field research in Japan was carried out by designing a comprehensive survey questionnaire. A total of 1,491 foreign companies were identified from a business directory showing detailed data available on their activities in Japan. They were all selected for inclusion in the sample survey. However, a minimum of 25% foreign capital was chosen as a benchmark for this survey. The survey questionnaire was supplemented by several case studies.

Responses were received from 436 foreign companies for a return ratio of 29.2%. A large number of respondents occupied top managerial positions. About 53% of the companies were 100% foreign-owned subsidiaries in Japan, 43% of the companies had less than 51 employees, about 26% of the companies employed over 200 persons, 62% of the companies were established before 1981, and another 19% were established after 1985 in Japan.

Sixty-seven percent of the companies on a list of the top 100 foreign companies in Japan took part in our present survey. Thus, a large number of parent companies of foreign companies in Japan taking part in the survey were MNCs or TNCs. Regarding distribution of business lines, the number of manufacturers was higher (69%) compared to the non-manufacturers (services and financial institutions). About 46 percent of the participating foreign companies were from the United States and a similar number of foreign companies were from the EC and EFTA.

In order to measure performance, we employed two criteria: (1) We requested foreign companies to evaluate their own performance based on financial criteria (i.e., sales growth, profitability, and ROI), and on non-financial criteria (i.e., market share, brand image, customer satisfaction, and reverse technology transfer). (2) We ourselves evaluated the performance of foreign companies based on their performance data, such as ordinary profits, annual sales, dividends paid, and accumulated profits.

Regarding financial criteria, the majority of foreign companies classified themselves as being "Successful" or "Very successful" in Japan (72%). "Failures" amounted to only 6%, whereas the "As expected" group consisted of 22% of the companies. If we took into consideration the non-financial criterion, then the "Successful/Very successful group" was even larger, at 75%, and the Failure group was even smaller, with about 4% of the foreign companies classifying themselves as "Failures."

Generally speaking, it is very difficult to make huge profits on the Japanese market, particularly in a short time period. In many cases it takes a longer time to reach satisfactory profit levels than it does with a similar level of investment outlay in the United States and Europe. The main reason for the longer time period necessary to reach a satisfactory level of ROI is the high cost of doing business in Japan. However, it is quite encouraging for us to see such a large number of foreign companies classifying themselves as financially successful or very successful in the presumably difficult Japanese market. Therefore, it is an unfounded myth that the Japanese market is unprofitable.

A wide number of success and failure factors were mentioned by the respondents. Foreign companies often referred to the following success factors: excellent products/services, highly qualified and talented Japanese personnel, excellent technology and know-how, parent company's total support, well-known company and brand name, proper timing for investment in Japan, an excellent Japanese joint venture partner, overall commitment toward the Japanese market, and excellent marketing capabilities.

The failure factors mentioned were too many competitors, difficulties in reaching satisfactory corporate profit levels in a short time period, lack of well-known company and brand name, inferior marketing capabilities, lack of highly qualified and talented Japanese personnel, and lack of overall commitment toward the Japanese market.

Eighty-three percent of the foreign companies have future plans to expand their activities in Japan. Surprisingly, 68% of the "Failure" companies indicated having expansion plans in Japan. Less than 2% of the companies mentioned that they have plans for decreasing their activities in Japan. This again gives strong indications that Japan is an important market for foreign companies that cannot be neglected and also that business in Japan is profitable, even if there is a recession here for the time being.

The purpose for making FDI in Japan for the majority of foreign companies was the size and growth of the Japanese market and the importance of Japan in global business. Few respondents mentioned that their purpose for doing business in Japan was to overcome protectionism in Japan or that Japanese government restrictive policies were causing them major problems. This indicates that overcoming protectionism in Japan is not an important issue considered by foreign companies when entering the Japanese market. In the eyes of many participating foreign companies, it is a myth that the Japanese market is closed.

Regarding investment strategies, it was observed that generally foreign companies entered Japan by building up their presence step-by-step over a period of several years. The first step has usually been to enter Japan through an intermediary; the second stage has been to form either a marketing/sales joint venture or a joint venture for manufacturing, establish a joint R & D laboratory, or acquire a Japanese company; and the third step has been to establish a 100% owned subsidiary.

Moreover, use of multiple channels in Japan is quite common. Foreign companies that have established a joint venture or a 100% owned subsidiary have at the same time a licensing agreement, an agent, a trading company, or another type of channel. Successful foreign companies were found to be flexible while deciding which channels to use for penetrating the Japanese market. They adapted to the conditions prevailing in the Japanese market and invested heavily in the distribution channels. This kind of investment by foreign companies enhanced their credibility and commitment to the Japanese market in the eyes of local customers and their own personnel.

We argue that the old strategy of always having a 100% owned subsidiary in every country of the world is outdated, at least for Japan. In order to be successful in the Japanese market, foreign companies may, depending on product and services, need a joint venture, a 100% owned subsidiary, technical tie-ups with competitors, or alliances with foreign and Japanese companies.

The trend for foreign companies has been toward 100% subsidiaries; however, JVs (joint ventures) are an important form of FDI in Japan, particularly for foreign SMEs (small and medium-sized enterprises), which generally lack resources. It is recommended that the foreign company play an active role in the management of a joint venture. We argue that foreign companies have to spend a considerable amount of time in developing a coherent and concise entry strategy for the Japanese market.

In our opinion, strategic alliances among foreign and Japanese companies are of mutual benefit to all the parties involved, and this option should not be overlooked by foreign companies. Alliances are particularly attractive for SMEs lacking knowledge about Japanese markets and contacts.

It was observed that the majority of foreign companies, in particular joint ventures, were using Japanese-style management, whereas wholly owned foreign subsidiaries were employing a mixture of Western and Japanese-style management. Over 63% of the CEOs and more than 80% of the departmental heads were Japanese. This way of operating a company removed the language and cultural obstacles that may be present in a company run by expatriates in Japan. Moreover, adaptation to the conditions prevailing in the Japanese market regarding management helped companies to compete effectively with their Japanese competitors.

For over two-thirds of the companies, parent companies were providing overall corporate policies and strategy but leaving the concrete operations to their local subsidiary. The headquarters were generally involved in the financial matters of the local subsidiary. It seems that to a large extent foreign companies were managed with autonomy, within limits.

We found that in the "Successful" group it was the US companies that had more Japanese CEOs, more often using Japanese management style. On the other hand, the European companies had more expatriates and were more often using Western management style. That is, it was the US companies that more often conformed to the local conditions prevailing in Japan.

Large numbers of foreign companies in Japan faced communication problems with their headquarters, but these problems did not necessarily affect the performance of the companies directly. However, they did affect the morale of the local and expatriate employees of the subsidiary. One reason for this problem, in our view, was the lack of knowledge at the headquarters of the unique characteristics of Japan: its language, norms and customs, work ethics, significant differences in business practices, and so on.

The issue of human resource management was of paramount importance for foreign companies operating in Japan. Their recruitment policy was built upon an extensive network of contacts with universities and by the development of an "old boy/old girl" network.

Generally, few foreign companies could expect to recruit students graduating from Japan's elite universities. Therefore, in order to recruit good personnel, foreign companies offered an attractive employment package. Foreign companies also banded together in order to improve their recruitment. Furthermore, foreign companies were also recruiting employees from their customers, since this type of hiring assisted in cementing relations between businesses. Foreign companies were spending a large amount of time and money in making their brand name or corporate image well known among their staff, customers, distributors, and suppliers, thus showing their long-term commitment in Japan. That is, recruiting activities were an integral part of their marketing strategy.

The intense recruitment of Japanese personnel by foreign companies in Japan has eased somewhat, mainly due to the ongoing recession in Japan and the difficulties faced by large Japanese companies in absorbing most of the new university graduates. Moreover, the pool of mid-career Japanese managers (both male and female) willing to switch from their present employers has increased dramatically, and most foreign companies rely more heavily on mid-career managers than on recent university and college graduates.

We personally recommend that short-term objectives such as sales or profitability per employee be disregarded by foreign companies in Japan if they sincerely desire to secure high-caliber Japanese personnel while giving a solid impression that they intend to firmly follow a policy of job security and stability.

In many ways the Japanese market is unique, particularly due to differences in culture, taste, and habits, and therefore it is not easy to standardize a product or service or a marketing strategy. Successful foreign companies have adapted to the peculiarities of the Japanese market. We argue that although some of these peculiarities are perhaps overtly discriminatory impediments for foreign companies in Japan, most of them are built upon deficiencies in the foreign companies themselves: ignorance, lack of patience, and short-term profit maximization and objectives.

Generally, successful foreign companies in our study were highly competitive in the Japanese market in terms of CI or brand name, sales and service network, exploiting market niches, being a market leader in product quality or service development, price, delivery time, and paying great attention to the demands and sensitivities of Japanese buyers towards product quality. Whenever possible, the joint venture partner's distribution channels were used effectively. Moreover, foreign companies provided repair and after-sales services (spare part centers and service stations), since these, among other factors, were found to be indispensable for protecting the brand image of a company.

Foreign companies were innovative in the Japanese market because of the fact that Japanese customers are the most demanding and quality sensitive in the world. Standardization (globalization) of marketing programs and strategies is difficult in the Japanese market, but marketing innovation done in Japan and the transfer of marketing know-how from Japan to the headquarters and to other subsidiaries outside Japan was rewarding for many foreign companies operating in Japan. These factors also gave a competitive edge to foreign companies in Japan.

European companies appeared to follow more often a global standardization of products and service compared to US companies in Japan. European companies appeared to transfer more often a successful marketing program or strategy outside Japan compared to the American companies.

Many foreign companies viewed Japan as an essential international center for R & D because Japan is the second-largest market in the world with very high-quality R & D and standards of production.

We found that investment in production facilities and R & D units was extremely costly (including high land prices and wages), and that this made it financially risky to pursue such a policy in Japan. In addition, there were difficulties in attracting qualified personnel. However, more and more foreign companies were realizing that it is strategically necessary to carry out production and R & D locally and were either opening or expanding units in Japan that resulted from joint ventures or strategic alliances or were 100% foreign-owned companies.

One of the main reasons for foreign companies to conduct R & D and carry out production in Japan was to come up with new products and processes in order to improve the competitive advantages of the parent company globally, both in production and R & D. Not only was Japan seen as a technology leader in production and R & D by foreign companies, but Japanese production and R & D personnel were seen as providing excellent guidance in and outside Japan.

This book shows that many foreign companies in Japan have been making innovations and in fact have obtained a large number of patents and a high degree of autonomy from their headquarters. Moreover, they used their own resources for creating new technology and know-how, which were then transferred to the parent company. In addition, there were several examples of horizontal technology transfer to other foreign subsidiaries, demonstrations of support for the parent company by in terms of the global synergy effects of R & D and production.

We have been able to show overwhelmingly that a number of inadequacies and shortcomings are associated with the existing theories of MNEs and international trade theories, including the Vernon and Wells (1991) product cycle model, since they fail to take into account entrepreneurship and innovation at foreign subsidiaries, the ability to develop products that meet the needs not only of the Japanese market but also of the parent company's global market. The subsidiaries can reverse the flow of technology and other managerial resources from Japan to the parent company and other foreign subsidiaries, thus showing that technology and managerial resource transfer is not a one-way but a two-way transfer. Since the existing MNE theories have reached their limits, we suggest that MNE and FDI theories be improved and reinforced by taking into consideration new dimensions that have been identified in this book.

Our findings also suggest some potential implications for Japanese and foreign policymakers. It is quite clear to us that at present the foreign investment climate is very favorable for foreign companies in Japan; however, there is still much in Japan's investment climate that needs to be improved so that there is freer competition in the market. This can be achieved by accelerating the opening of the Japanese market by deregulation, increased transparency of administrative policy, elimination of remaining tariffs and quotas, liberalizing and abolishing the oligopoly in certain sectors (for example, the distribution system), and harmonization of product testing procedures.

The Japanese government should intensify its efforts to remove the image of Japan as a closed market in the eyes of foreign investors overseas by offering more opportunities for foreign companies to come to Japan. This can be further achieved by closely scrutinizing the present situation in the following areas and taking actions to ease the hardships of foreign companies: (1) Japanese business practices, (2) FDI restrictions, (3) recruitment of Japanese personnel, (4) land prices, (5) tax incentives, (6) loan programs, and (7) various restrictions in the financial and capital markets, insurance and securities, and legal services.

Regarding implications for foreign policymakers, we recommend that contract research among Japanese and foreign businesses, universities, and research institutes be intensified. The results of this study indicate that successful penetration of the Japanese market can be gradual, occurring in a stepwise fashion. Foreign companies have to be advised to disregard the short-term objective of profit maximization; they should pay attention to using multiple entry channels; they have to invest heavily in the distribution channels; patience is required for building a positive image; and foreign companies have to adapt to the peculiarities of the Japanese market. The foreign chambers of commerce should advise their business communities on how to effectively penetrate the Japanese market based on the results of our study.

We recommend that there be increased public relations about successful foreign companies in Japan that have made profits, developed new products in Japan, reversed the flow of technology, and thus strengthened the competitiveness of their parent companies, despite various problems existing in the Japanese market. In other words, foreign companies should not be scared away from Japan.

Without a doubt, Japan is the costliest market in the world. It is therefore important that foreign governments, through their chambers of commerce, trade and technical commissioners, or representatives in Japan intensify their efforts in identifying business opportunities, in particular for their SMEs. They should furnish at preferential rates market and feasibility studies and provide other assistance (e.g., preferential loan schemes and insurance against currency fluctuation losses) in conjunction with Japanese governmental and semi-governmental organizations, as mentioned earlier. We believe that this type of assistance will boost FDI and imports into Japan.

Finally, we argue that any strategy for Asia by foreign companies must be based on a strategy for Japan, since Japan comprises over 80% of Asia's GNP and expects to hold this position for many years to come. This strategic fact cannot be ignored by foreign companies.

1 STUDYING FOREIGN COMPANIES IN JAPAN

This book deals with the business strategies and performance of foreign companies in Japan. Where possible, the study compares European and American companies' performances and strategies. Before proceeding further, it should be noted that this research focuses entirely on micro-level management problems of foreign companies in Japan.

One of the important reasons for carrying out this research is that we have limited knowledge and little relevant empirical data on foreign companies in Japan. Most of the knowledge of foreign companies in Japan is confined to journalistic accounts. It is also important to remember that, at present, foreign companies are putting efforts in increasing their foreign direct investments (FDI) in Japan. Therefore, it is strategically important to know more about them.

This chapter describes the background of the study and the importance of studying foreign companies in Japan. The research questions to be answered by the investigation, the study's theoretical framework, field research, and foreign companies' responses are also presented.

1.1 RESEARCH NEEDS

Figure 1.1 clearly shows that European countries are heavily dependent on international trade. The economic welfare of these countries depends to a large extent on the success of their exporting companies. Failure to generate a sufficient volume of exported goods and services can lead to recurring economic crises in these countries. Several of the European countries' domestic markets are extremely limited in size, and therefore exports are essential for their economies.

Figure 1.1 Dependency on international trade

Exports as % of GNP

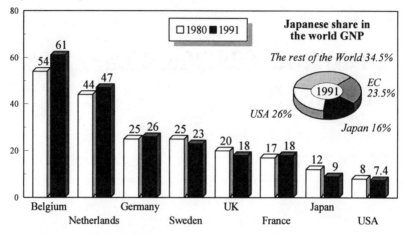

Source: Figure based on statistical data collected from IMF, International financial statistics yearbook. Washington: 1992.

It is interesting to note that the importance of exports both for the United States and Japan has rapidly increased during the period 1980 to 1991, but mainly in terms of dollars, whereas the share of exports in terms of total gross national product (GNP) has declined for both countries, that is, in 1980, it was 12% and 8% for Japan and the United States respectively, and in 1991 it had decreased to 9% and 7.4% respectively.

Motives or objectives behind FDI in Japan

What could be the motives or objectives for making an FDI in Japan? In our opinion, some of the motives and objectives could be:

1. The size and growth of the Japanese market; in other words, the Japanese market is too important to be overlooked.
2. To reduce R & D (research and development) and production costs; reverse technology transfer and obtain global synergy in terms of production, R & D, and marketing; and obtain access to many excellent staff members and facilities.
3. To meet Japanese competitors on their home market and test one's own strengths and weaknesses, and to keep an eye on Japanese competitors through surveillance.

4. To keep a close watch on technical developments and obtain new ideas from Japan. This may also lead to increased opportunities for collaboration and joint development of new technologies.
5. To increase internationalization. If a company is successful in a difficult foreign market such as Japan, then it may be successful in other markets.
6. Foreign companies from the United States and Europe have technical leads in several key industrial sectors and segments, such as aerospace, chemicals, pharmaceuticals, nuclear technology, environmental control, and telecommunications, as well as a wide variety of consumer goods and services.
7. Japan is also considered to be a key to penetrating other Asian markets.
8. To obtain global dominance; companies hoping to compete in the global arena must become "insiders" in the triad of Europe, Japan and the United States.[1]

It is well known that Japanese consumers are sensitive to product quality and require short delivery time and excellent service. The number of new products launched in the Japanese market is tremendous. Japan is sometimes used as a test market for the rest of the world. All of this makes the Japanese market highly competitive. The competition in Japan is very intense, not only among Japanese companies but also among Japanese, American, and European companies.

In industrialized countries, and in particular in high-tech ones such as Japan where technical advances are rapid and the diffusion and acceptance of new technologies is fast, companies export not only due to short product life cycle (PLC) and high R & D expenditures, but also to keep an eye on their competitors, to watch for technical developments, and to obtain profits in order to re-deploy some portion thereof in developing new products that require exorbitant R & D expenditures. The Japanese market provides all of the needed characteristics.

Moreover, Japan is known for its cultural differences, which in business have yielded Kanban (the Japanese way of organizing production) or the just-in-time (JIT) delivery system, the practice of total quality control (TQC), quality circles (QC), on-the-job training (OJT), company long-term perspective, patience, consensus management, lifetime employment, the role of Keiretsu (business groups and corporate groupings, which can be vertical [both in manufacturing and distribution] or horizontal [cross-holding]); and Sogo Shosha (trading companies).

Japanese workers, compared to those of most of the other OECD countries, have higher labor productivity combined with highly automated production facilities, a disciplined and skilled labor force, harmonious labor-management relations, and capital sources that accept a lower rate of return and a considerably longer payout horizon. All these factors make the FDI climate very conducive for foreign companies in Japan.

Japan is the second-largest market in the world after the United States. Its share in world GNP for FY 1991 (fiscal year, April 1, 1991, to March 31, 1992) was 16%, or $3.4 trillion[2] (the United States represented nearly 26% and the European Community [EC] represented about 23.5% of world GNP). Moreover, Japan has overtaken its competitors in many product fields, notably in the high-tech industrial manufacturing sector.

The Japanese are admired for their successful market penetration strategies in the United States and Europe, where they are asserting their economic and financial strength. However, at the same time, American and European companies claim to face difficulties in cracking the Japanese market.

American companies, and even more so European companies, have underrated the Japanese market. This can be seen clearly from their low trade figures with Japan. Both American and European companies have generally been following a two-legged strategy (Europe and the United States). It is only recently that a more appropriate and realistic three-legged strategy is being followed (Europe, Japan, and the United States).

Moreover, it is only during the last few years that American and European companies have started taking the competition from Japan seriously. It will take some time before foreign companies can take over substantial market shares in the Japanese market. The rivalry among Japanese and foreign companies is intense; however, we expect to see increasing cooperation and collaboration between Japanese and foreign companies. Alliances in the form of joint ventures, joint licensing, mergers and acquisitions (M & A) will considerably increase foreign companies' presence in Japan.

In the past, Japan was considered to have low labor costs and an undervalued currency. However, since the Plaza Accord of September 1985, this Japanese advantage has been nearly wiped out; by end of 1993 the Japanese yen had appreciated nearly 60% against the US Dollar and other major currencies. The sharp appreciation of the yen has presented both advantages and disadvantages to foreign companies' entry and FDI in the Japanese market.

Many foreign companies use Japan as a key to penetrate other Asian markets. Furthermore, for many foreign companies, their presence in Japan is for the purpose of acquiring technology and know-how. According to our prior research,[3] successful foreign companies in Japan generally are managed with autonomy, and top executives of foreign companies in Japan are in many cases Japanese nationals.

On the other hand, we still know little about the successes and, even more interesting, about the failures of foreign companies in Japan. Our knowledge is limited to the factors that contribute to foreign companies' success and failure. Concerning this subject, literature is sparse.

1.2 INVESTMENT FRICTION

Japan has been sharply criticized, in particular by the United States and the EC, for unfair trade practices.[4] This criticism stems from several factors, such as Japan's continuously large trade surpluses with most of the countries in the world and the low level of imports into Japan (see Figure 1.2). Moreover, although Japan has 2% of the world's population, its share of international trade was 7.7% in 1992. (The US and EC ratios were even higher, at 13.5% and 40% of world trade, respectively, in 1992.)[5]

Japan's trade surplus is massive, especially so in light of the severe recession in almost all of the Organization for Economic Cooperation and Development (OECD) countries and the appreciation of the yen against all other major currencies. The Finance Ministry statistics reveal that exports exceeded imports by about $111 billion in FY 1992, for with the highest surplus ever. According to the forecasts made by the Japan Research Institute, an affiliate of Sumitomo Bank, the surplus may amount to about $150 billion in FY 1993.

According to the European Business Community (EBC)[6] there is a substantial imbalance in investment between Japan and Europe. Over the last eight years, the flow of Japanese investment into Europe has exceeded the flow of European investment into Japan by 20-30:1. As a result, while investment by EC companies in Japan represents only approximately 0.1% of total direct

Figure 1.2   Japan's foreign trade and trade balance
(FY 1988 - 1992)

Billion US$

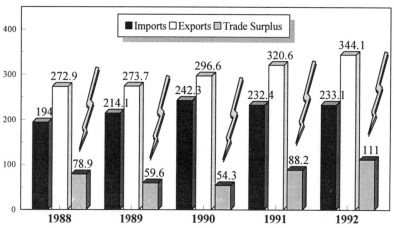

Source: Figure is based on statistical data collected from Japan Tariff Association, The summary report on trade of Japan. *Tokyo: September 1993.*
Note: Japanese fiscal year starts on April 1 and ends on March 31 the next year.

investment, Japan's share in Europe is approximately 5%. EC observers insist that it is essential that similar opportunities be created for European companies in Japan so that they can compete on an equal footing with Japanese companies in the global marketplace. According to the EBC, the present commercial and economic dimensions among Japan and the EC may develop into increasingly political dimensions.

The perceptions outside Japan, especially in the US Congress and at the EC headquarters in Brussels, are that there are tremendous barriers in Japan for foreign companies making FDI. A frequently cited example is that the Keiretsu (corporate groups) are impeding FDI in Japan or serving as an invisible trade barrier since they exclude foreign companies. The conclusions drawn by many governments due to Japan's persisting trade surplus with most of the countries in the world is that the possibility of obtaining real and equal access to the Japanese market is remote.

On the other hand, according to the Japanese government, practically all the formal legal and regulatory barriers have been abolished. The few exceptions are that prior FDI notice is required in agriculture, forestry, and fisheries; oil; mining; leather and leather products; and defense- or national security-related industries. FDI is also restricted on the basis of specific industry laws, for example, in communication and broadcasting, marine and air transport.

The custom duties in Japan are among the lowest in the OECD countries. Further, Japan is continuously harmonizing domestic business practices with international norms. Moreover, the Japanese government considers that it is grossly oversimplistic to believe that Japan's huge trade surplus is connected to its lack of market access.

Despite the comments mentioned above, there are considerable restrictions, in particular in the non-manufacturing industries. Moreover, certain laws dealing with land ownership, and immigration controls are also considered excessive by foreign companies. Foreign companies feel that all these regulations are discriminatory and that they close the Japanese market by limiting competition. These beliefs lead to low confidence on the side of foreign companies in the wisdom of making investments in Japan.

Problems in the Japanese market

According to some observers, it is impossible for foreign companies to succeed in Japan. The business climate in Japan is considered by many to be not as favorable as it is in Europe or the United States. Japan is also accused of unique and exclusionary business practices. A long list of impediments for foreign companies seeking greater access to the Japanese market is circulated by the EC Commission, mass media, and various chambers of commerce of foreign countries in and outside Japan.

The obstacles for foreign companies making FDI in Japan mentioned by many writers are:

1. The high cost of doing business in Japan, for example, exorbitant land prices (rents, housing, industrial real estate, and factories).
2. High taxation levels on corporate profits.
3. Difficulties in hiring qualified Japanese personnel (which is in short supply and, at the same time, more expensive).
4. Extreme difficulties in acquiring Japanese companies.
5. Multitiered and complex distribution and retail systems.
6. Government guidelines, policies, and regulations that lack clarity (including oral directions) and often consist of administrative guidance to Japanese companies, thus discriminating against foreign companies in Japan.
7. Keiretsu, which favor doing business within the Keiretsu group rather than with domestic outsiders or foreign companies in Japan. This makes it difficult to sell to companies belonging to Keiretsu groups. Further, the procurement methods of Keiretsu groups are not transparent or open, and they are accused of exclusionary business practices such as not letting foreign goods enter the Japanese distribution system. It is also difficult for foreign companies to acquire the stock of companies belonging to these groups (M & A). Keiretsu also have tremendous competitive advantages over foreign companies in Japan, especially in terms of R & D, marketing, production, cross-subsidization, and close contacts with governmental institutions.
8. "Old boy/old girl" networks hindering foreign access to Japanese markets.
9. Weaknesses in the intellectual property system.
10. Lengthy testing and approval periods for new foreign products.
11. Practice restrictions for law companies.

The Japanese distribution and retail system is known to be complex for both domestic and foreign companies, and it remains unclear whether foreign companies are making wholehearted efforts and showing real commitments to the Japanese market.

According to the National Tax Administration Agency, the price of land dropped by an average of 18.1% during FY 1992. The price of land in Japan is on the average yen 299,000 per square meter ($2,850; 1$ = yen 105 in October 1993), and in Tokyo it is around yen 1.3 million per square meter ($12,380), increasing to yen 29 million per square meter ($276,190) in the fashionable Ginza commercial district of Tokyo.

The exorbitant land prices produce an exceptionally high cost of doing business in Japan compared to other OECD countries, lower rates of return (ROI--return on investment), and a longer period of time to break even.

The United States, which has a massive trade deficit with Japan, together with its European allies, is driving up the value of the yen to curb Japan's growing trade surplus. However, this policy, in effect since 1985, has only worsened the United States' and most of the other countries' trade deficit with Japan.

On the other hand, a number of researchers and our previous studies have shown that the entire blame cannot be put on specific Japanese entry barriers but that the foreign companies must take their own share of the blame. Many foreign companies in Japan pay strict attention to financial targets, with a short-term management perspective; are unable or unwilling to modify products to suit the Japanese market; have low-quality products; lack market research; lack proper pre- and post-sale services; lack an understanding of Japanese customs, language, and business policies and practices; and lack an understanding of the intensity of competition in the Japanese market.

The feeling is that many foreign companies underestimate the competitiveness of Japanese industry. The Japanese market is one of the most challenging in the world, and at the same time it is both dynamic and rewarding. Moreover, according to many foreign companies, the profit margins in Japan are some of the highest in the world.[7]

1.3 RESEARCH DESIGN

We have combined our own experience in the field of international business with the theories and empirical observations made in a large number of areas, such as export performance, innovation, organization, international marketing, international trade theory, theory of the firm, and product life cycle, to name a few. Our empirical and theoretical knowledge about foreign companies in Japan is limited, and what little has emerged is anecdotal rather than analytical.

We find a tremendous amount of literature dealing with the success of Japanese companies (as success models), in particular in the United States, in what can be called success literature. Three studies in this area are by Abegglen and Stalk,[8] Kotler,[9] and Ohmae.[10]

Theoretically, it can be hypothesized that foreign companies with vast international experience, multinational companies (MNCs), and transnational companies (TNCs) will have a higher degree of success in the Japanese market, that is, the higher the degree of success for a company in Japan, the more it is globalized, compared to those companies with little or no experience operating in foreign markets.

Foreign companies with vast international experience and possessing brand name image, advanced technology, and innovative products and services can strategically adjust their ROI, sustain longer payback periods, and easily obtain financing and other services in Japan. Moreover, global companies have to create a presence in all the major markets even if their presence cannot be justified on financial criteria.

Several authors, in particular Porter,[11] have emphasized that competition is at the core of the success or failure of companies. Competition in Japan is considered to be among the most formidable in the world. Japanese companies are known to keep competitors continuously in their sights and to work closely with banks and shareholders in order to achieve competitive advantage. In many instances, the marketing costs in Japan exceed the manufacturing costs. Many foreign companies with innovative or unique products expend considerable amounts of effort educating Japanese customers, and after a certain period of time may find Japanese competitors introducing similar types of products and taking advantage of the already educated customers by expending less (or no) effort on customers' education.

In our view, the parent companies of many foreign companies in Japan maintain worldwide technological leadership or superior technological capabilities in numerous products and services with very high quality and standards. Despite these competitive advantages, however, foreign companies have disadvantages in competing with Japanese companies in Japan.

Foreign companies in Japan generally do not know well the Japanese users' needs. It is likely that they have to create new sales networks and procurement systems for their parts and components as well as raw materials. It is also likely that they are at a disadvantage when dealing with industrial associations and governmental agencies. The Japanese language might also be a barrier. Communication between the parent company and the subsidiary in Japan is costly, and there are efficiency problems due to the distances involved. Foreign companies also have disadvantages when trying to employ high-potential Japanese human resources.

In order to overcome these unfavorable conditions and succeed in Japan, foreign companies must have, as a basic condition, excellent products and technology with which to compete with Japanese companies. However, foreign companies have to take into consideration the innovation capabilities of Japanese companies, which can easily imitate and launch substitute products.

Generally speaking, foreign companies have to make product modifications for the Japanese market in order to be competitive. It has also been observed that, due to fierce competition, foreign companies in Japan sometimes surpass the technological levels of the parent company, that is innovation in production technology and R & D shifts in favor of the subsidiary in Japan. The reasons could be many, among others, the entrepreneurial spirit and autonomous management in the subsidiary in Japan. However, it has also been noted that many foreign companies face problems regarding their autonomy from headquarters. These problems or frictions between headquarters and subsidiaries may lead to, for example, low motivation in the subsidiary, for both the Japanese staff and the expatriates.

Theoretical framework

In this section we will discuss three conventional theories of MNEs: (1) the control model (industrial organization approach), (2) the product cycle model (PCM), and (3) technology transfer.

Theory of multinational enterprises

An analysis of multinational enterprises based on industrial organization theory is one of the approaches that has contributed to the development of the theory of the multinational firm.

A representative figure in this field is Hymer,[12] who claimed that control is one of the essential characteristics of FDI. Control means not only whole or majority ownership of the subsidiary by the parent company but is a broader concept that includes the utilization of technology and other managerial resources at the foreign subsidiary.

Hymer's theory of multinational enterprises does not allow for autonomous management of the foreign subsidiary. The foreign subsidiary is regarded as an entity to be controlled by the parent company. The organization is such that the parent company exercises control and the subsidiary is subordinated to the parent. However, this book will show the flaws in that type of relationship. We argue that a number of inadequacies are associated with existing theories of multinational enterprises, and call for new theoretical developments.

The product cycle model and technology transfer concept

Large-scale research on American multinationals has been conducted at the Harvard Business School under Professor Raymond Vernon's leadership.[13] The product cycle model was a common theoretical basis in this research.

According to the product cycle model, the process of multinationalization of American companies is explained as follows. American companies develop products that meet the needs of the American market and sell them in the domestic market. In due time, demand for the products appears in Europe, Japan, and other advanced countries. At first, the American firm responds to this foreign demand by exporting its products. Later, competing companies appear in advanced countries. Frequently, protective actions are taken, such as import restrictions. The American firm meets this situation by starting production in Europe, Japan, and other advanced countries. Again, with time, the firm starts exporting to developing countries in Central and South America, Asia, and so on, and then it moves production activities to these areas.

Moreover, according to the product cycle model, the American parent firm's managerial resources (such as technology and know-how) are first transferred to foreign subsidiaries in Europe, Japan, and other foreign countries. Later, they are transferred to foreign subsidiaries in developing countries in Central and South America, Asia, and so on. It is hypothesized that, just as water flows from upper to lower levels, the parent company's technology and other managerial resources flow in a hierarchy from the subsidiaries in advanced countries to those in developing countries. Furthermore, it is hypothesized that new products, technology, and know-how are developed at the American parent company and that technology transfer from the United States to other countries is more or less a one-way transfer.

Recently, the United States has been losing its position as the country where a large proportion of the world's new products are first produced on a commercial basis. The main argument in Vernon's PCM is that new products are generally introduced in the United States, and once the products reach the maturity stage, the developing countries, with their comparative advantage in terms of cheap labor, start to export these products back to the United States. No particular consideration is given to changing the parent company-subsidiary relationship to the point where the subsidiary could be the source of new product development and innovation, with the parent company receiving the new product or innovation. Vernon and Wells (1991) do mention, however, that considerable innovative activity has recently been taking place outside the United States.

Our previous studies and the study presented in this book show that many successful foreign companies in Japan create new products, technology, and systems. In addition, a number of innovations made by Japanese subsidiaries flow back to the parent company. The product cycle model cannot explain this feature of foreign companies in Japan. We suggest that the existing literature on international trade theory does not treat this kind of technology transfer satisfactorily.

We have examined three approaches to the study of multinational companies: research based on the industrial organization theory, on the product cycle model, and on technology transfer. It has become clear that a number of features of successful foreign companies in Japan cannot be dealt with successfully using existing theories of multinational enterprises. According to existing theories of multinational enterprises, foreign companies with these features are just deviations or abnormal cases.

This book aims to show that there are new factors to be accounted for in theories of multinational enterprises, factors such as entrepreneurship and innovation at foreign subsidiaries, reverse technology transfer, and global synergy. The objective of the study is to consider new developments in the theory of MNEs based on the features of successful companies in Japan we have mentioned. In general, new theories are born when existing theories reach their limits. When phenomena appear that cannot be successfully explained by existing theories, efforts are made to explain the new phenomena. Out of those efforts, new theories are born. We should make an effort to explain the features of successful foreign companies in Japan rather than simply disposing of them as deviations or abnormal cases. Out of that effort, it is expected that new developments in the theory of multinational companies will emerge.

Purpose of the research

There are three research purposes, namely, fact finding, theoretical propositions, and practical propositions. Fact finding deals with the empirical facts about foreign companies in Japan with respect to their past (history), present, and future.

Theoretical propositions are based on the theoretical implications of facts that are derived through limitations of existing theories of multinational enterprises. It is envisaged that the results and findings of this research will lead to new factors for development of MNE theories.

Finally, practical propositions consisting of key success and failure factors in the Japanese market are made to foreign companies that are already in Japan or are planning to invest in Japan. Furthermore, propositions are also made to foreign and Japanese policymakers for their actions.

Research questions

The aim of this research is to describe the strategy and performance of foreign companies in the Japanese market. The research focuses on five basic questions:

1. What types of investment strategies are employed by foreign companies in Japan, and how do these strategies affect the performance of their business ventures in Japan? The purpose is to present the features of successful foreign companies in Japan, identifying which factors are critical for their success in Japan. How can we compare the performance and strategy in Japan of foreign companies with each other and, especially, of European companies with American ones? Are there differences? If they do exist, what do they mean?
2. What problems do foreign companies face in the Japanese market and how are these problems solved?
3. How are the foreign companies' communication networks with headquarters outside of Japan functioning? Concerns include the headquarters-subsidiary relationship, the localization of top management, and the informing and decision-making processes within Japanese subsidiaries. Moreover, how do foreign companies finance their business ventures in Japan?

4. To what extent have foreign companies in Japan transferred their production technology, R & D results, patents, and marketing know-how to their parent companies outside of Japan or/and to other subsidiaries outside of Japan? This book attempts to make further contributions toward developments in the theory of multinational enterprises based on the features of successful foreign companies in Japan.

5. What implications can be drawn regarding the features of successful foreign companies in Japan for foreign companies and for Japanese and foreign policymakers? Finally, the book is expected to guide new entrants into the Japanese market.

The results of the study are expected to contribute to the understanding of foreign companies' performance, methods of marketing, and investment strategies in Japan. Moreover, this study attempts to provide a greater understanding of foreign companies in Japan, not only as competitors but also as potential partners in joint ventures and various other forms of technical and marketing collaborations, as customers, and as suppliers to Japanese companies.

The key variables

Based on our discussion so far, we find that there are five key variables that may explain the features of foreign companies in Japan (see Figure 1.3). The parent company is not the direct focus of this study; however, its influence on the local subsidiary cannot be excluded from our investigation. The parent company may decentralize decision making by giving autonomy to its subsidiary, for example, regarding human resource management, marketing, production, and R & D.

The parent company is expected to formulate overall strategies, such as market penetration and entry channels, budgeting, and finance, for its subsidiary, based on the environment (the Japanese market, rules and regulations, competition, and so on).

Based on our theoretical and prior field research in Japan and the Figure 1.3, a model for carrying out the field study was constructed (see Figure 1.4). It lists the independent and dependent variables. The study postulates 10 variables that are expected to affect the strategy and performance of foreign companies in Japan.

This approach enables us to explain a very complex phenomenon. However, it has the drawback of over-simplification. Moreover, no single variable can predict a foreign company's success or failure in the Japanese market. A whole set of variables is involved.[14]

Figure 1.3   Conceptual relationship among the five key variables of foreign companies in Japan

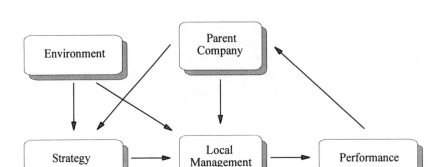

In order to measure the performance of foreign companies in Japan, that is, the dependent variables of success and failure, two classifying criteria were used: financial criteria (sales growth, profitability, and ROI) and non-financial criteria (market share, local entrepreneurship and innovation, reverse technology transfer, and various other internal assessments).[15] Data were collected from individual companies regarding their ordinary profits, accumulated profits, and dividend payments.

Regarding independent variables affecting the success and failure of foreign companies in Japan, we decided to study only the following nine variables.

Investment and business strategies.   Whether foreign companies will make investments in Japan depends on the degree of importance given to the Japanese market. Investment and business strategies refer to channels of distribution and the physical flow of goods and services. Foreign companies make known their presence in Japan via (1) an agent, wholesaler, or distributor, (2) a Japanese trading company, (3) the company's own branch office, (4) joint ventures for marketing and sales purposes, (5) joint ventures for production purposes, (6) the acquisition of a Japanese company, 7) wholly owned sales subsidiaries, 8) wholly owned manufacturing subsidiaries, (9) R & D laboratories, and (10) licensing and franchising rights, technology agreements, and the like.

Foreign companies that choose to export to Japan via an agent, wholesaler, distributor, trading company (Sogo Shosha), or through licensing and various other forms of technology collaboration recognize that the intermediaries assume an important role in the marketing and sales process in Japan. The export risks are also minimized or shared with the intermediaries.

Figure 1.4 Model: Nine independent variables and one dependent variable

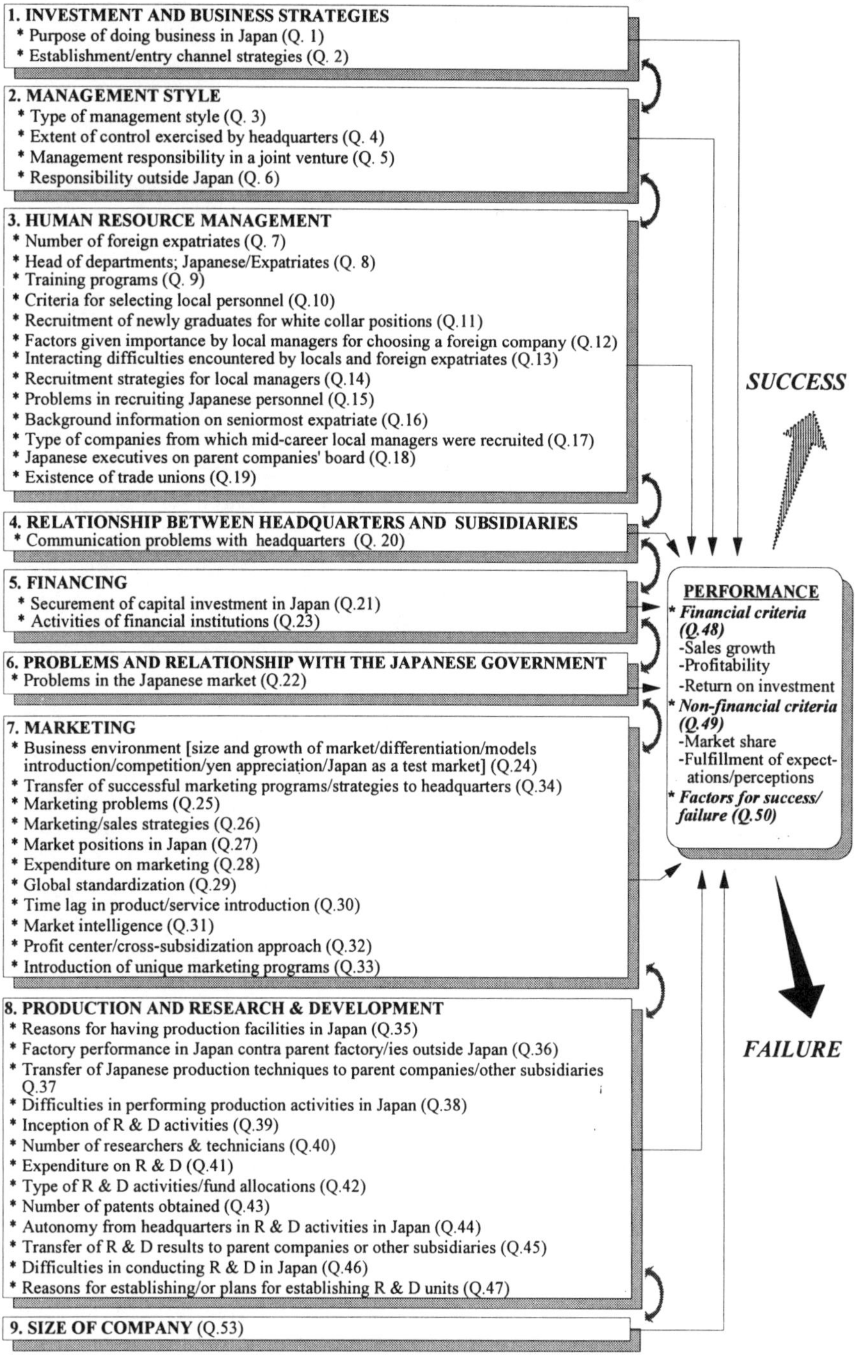

1. INVESTMENT AND BUSINESS STRATEGIES
* Purpose of doing business in Japan (Q. 1)
* Establishment/entry channel strategies (Q. 2)

2. MANAGEMENT STYLE
* Type of management style (Q. 3)
* Extent of control exercised by headquarters (Q. 4)
* Management responsibility in a joint venture (Q. 5)
* Responsibility outside Japan (Q. 6)

3. HUMAN RESOURCE MANAGEMENT
* Number of foreign expatriates (Q. 7)
* Head of departments; Japanese/Expatriates (Q. 8)
* Training programs (Q. 9)
* Criteria for selecting local personnel (Q.10)
* Recruitment of newly graduates for white collar positions (Q.11)
* Factors given importance by local managers for choosing a foreign company (Q.12)
* Interacting difficulties encountered by locals and foreign expatriates (Q.13)
* Recruitment strategies for local managers (Q.14)
* Problems in recruiting Japanese personnel (Q.15)
* Background information on seniormost expatriate (Q.16)
* Type of companies from which mid-career local managers were recruited (Q.17)
* Japanese executives on parent companies' board (Q.18)
* Existence of trade unions (Q.19)

4. RELATIONSHIP BETWEEN HEADQUARTERS AND SUBSIDIARIES
* Communication problems with headquarters (Q. 20)

5. FINANCING
* Securement of capital investment in Japan (Q.21)
* Activities of financial institutions (Q.23)

6. PROBLEMS AND RELATIONSHIP WITH THE JAPANESE GOVERNMENT
* Problems in the Japanese market (Q.22)

7. MARKETING
* Business environment [size and growth of market/differentiation/models
  introduction/competition/yen appreciation/Japan as a test market] (Q.24)
* Transfer of successful marketing programs/strategies to headquarters (Q.34)
* Marketing problems (Q.25)
* Marketing/sales strategies (Q.26)
* Market positions in Japan (Q.27)
* Expenditure on marketing (Q.28)
* Global standardization (Q.29)
* Time lag in product/service introduction (Q.30)
* Market intelligence (Q.31)
* Profit center/cross-subsidization approach (Q.32)
* Introduction of unique marketing programs (Q.33)

8. PRODUCTION AND RESEARCH & DEVELOPMENT
* Reasons for having production facilities in Japan (Q.35)
* Factory performance in Japan contra parent factory/ies outside Japan (Q.36)
* Transfer of Japanese production techniques to parent companies/other subsidiaries
  Q.37
* Difficulties in performing production activities in Japan (Q.38)
* Inception of R & D activities (Q.39)
* Number of researchers & technicians (Q.40)
* Expenditure on R & D (Q.41)
* Type of R & D activities/fund allocations (Q.42)
* Number of patents obtained (Q.43)
* Autonomy from headquarters in R & D activities in Japan (Q.44)
* Transfer of R & D results to parent companies or other subsidiaries (Q.45)
* Difficulties in conducting R & D in Japan (Q.46)
* Reasons for establishing/or plans for establishing R & D units (Q.47)

9. SIZE OF COMPANY (Q.53)

SUCCESS

PERFORMANCE
* *Financial criteria
  (Q.48)*
-Sales growth
-Profitability
-Return on investment
* *Non-financial criteria
  (Q.49)*
-Market share
-Fulfillment of expect-
  ations/perceptions
* *Factors for success/
  failure (Q.50)*

FAILURE

It is safe to assume that the burdens associated with selling directly to the final user are heavier than those associated with selling to or through the intermediaries (due to foreign companies' lack of Japanese language skills, communication problems, financing problems, etc.). The risks are substantially higher in establishing one's own subsidiary, acquiring a Japanese company, or establishing a joint venture in Japan. Generally speaking, prior to the establishment of a subsidiary, acquisition of a Japanese company, or establishment of an R & D laboratory, the company has achieved a certain level of sales volume to cover the costs or has found a good joint venture (JV) partner.

A joint venture (including strategic alliances) is usually formed between a foreign and one or more Japanese partners to attain better economies of scale in the areas of operation and risk spreading through sharing of technological, commercial, or financial risk. Foreign companies will generally form a joint venture that is a forward integration or market-seeking type. A JV with a Japanese company that has good access to the market can bring the product closer to the final user. In this way, commercial risk is shared with the partner, who in turn reduces risk by providing market knowledge.

In order to make this variable operational, we asked foreign companies their purpose for doing business in Japan and the types of market entry channels used in Japan.

Management style. The Japanese management style,[16] which includes lifetime employment, seniority-based pay and promotion, and the enterprise union--the three pillars of the corporate system--is known all over the world. Japanese companies are also known for making decisions by consensus.

Several studies have shown that there are wide business and cultural differences between Japan and Western countries. An interesting example worth mentioning here is Ouchi's (1982) study of American and Japanese organizations. The author highlights the differences between these two types of organization. This contrast also holds true for Japanese and European organizations.

Japanese organization	American organization
Lifetime employment	Short-term employment
Slow evaluation and promotion	Rapid evaluation and promotion
Non-specialized career paths	Specialized career paths
Implicit control mechanisms	Explicit control mechanisms
Collective decision making	Individual decision making
Collective responsibility	Individual responsibility
Wholistic concern	Segmented concern[17]

The concepts of the Ringi system and the practice of Nemawashi by Japanese managers (informal discussions behind the scenes before making decisions),[18] are also well known. This practice is usually contrasted with pyramid or Top-down decision making in Western companies.

The following aspects of the foreign companies' management style were studied: Type of management style used; extent of control exercised by headquarters in the affairs of the Japanese subsidiary; in case of a joint venture, which partner had the management responsibility; and whether headquarters had given any special responsibility to subsidiaries outside of Japan. One of our main interests was to discover whether foreign companies in Japan are managed with autonomy (within limits).[19]

Human resource management. We should note here that according to a large number of studies, it is rather difficult for foreign companies to recruit Japanese personnel, especially new graduates from well-known universities. In order to make this variable operational we studied the following factors: the number of foreign expatriates in a company and their positions, whether the head of a department was Japanese or an expatriate; training programs offered, criteria for selecting local personnel, recruitment of new graduates for white-collar positions, factors given importance by local managers for choosing employment with a foreign company, difficulties in interacting encountered between locals and foreign expatriates, recruitment strategies for local personnel, problems in recruiting Japanese personnel, background information on the seniormost expatriates (function and status, working experience, years stationed in Japan, knowledge of the Japanese language, and planned period of stay in Japan), type of companies from which mid-career local managers were recruited, Japanese executives on parent company's board, and the existence of trade unions.

Relationship between headquarters and subsidiary. For foreign companies, especially non-Asian companies, the distance to Japan is considerable, both physically and psychically. In terms of communication efficiency between the headquarters and the subsidiary in Japan, the time and cost will be considerably higher, especially the travel time and cost. "Headquarters" in our study refers to the parent company of a Japanese subsidiary located outside of Japan.

It is expected that there will be some problems with headquarters understanding the unique characteristics of the Japanese market. There may be difficulties for the local subsidiary staff in communicating with headquarters, or headquarters may overly emphasize short-term profit goals. Moreover, difficulties may arise for the subsidiary in Japan when the parent company exercises very detailed and strict control so that only narrow discretionary power is left to the subsidiary, leading to very low motivation among local employees.[20] All of these aspects were investigated in this study.

Financing. The Japanese yen has sharply increased against major currencies. At the same time, the rate of inflation and the interest rate are low among several of the OECD countries. For foreign companies there are both advantages and disadvantages in borrowing funds in the Japanese market. Due to a skyrocketing Japanese trade surplus and trade frictions, the Japanese government is offering foreign companies loans at preferential rates. In this study our interest was to find out how foreign companies were obtaining their capital investment in Japan.

Relationship with the Japanese government. Generally, foreign companies in an export market encounter various formalities in the form of trade barriers. When tariffs or import duties are reduced to the point of playing a minor role in international trade, then non-tariff barriers (NTBs) usually take on major importance.[21] At present, tariffs on most products have been removed or drastically reduced in Japan. However, some NTBs still exist, and foreign companies may face problems due to customs administration, government procurement from mainly Japanese suppliers, taxation, import permits, and various other restrictive business practices that may hurt foreign companies in Japan. All of these aspects were investigated in this study.

Marketing. For most foreign companies, their competitors are very often the Japanese. We will therefore explore indepth the role of marketing in the Japanese market; we argue that foreign companies have difficulties in understanding this phenomenon.

Japanese companies dominate most of the market segments very efficiently in terms of a large variety of products, service, distribution networks (despite several intermediaries), to name a few advantages in the domestic market. Moreover, Japanese companies in many sectors have global brand dominance, worldwide distribution networks, and large market shares.[22]

In the context of global marketing, Japanese companies are using two strategies, namely, standardized global products and homogeneous markets, and greater product variation for all segments. Japanese companies--especially the larger ones--generally aim to dominate all market segments irrespective of size and potential, achieving global brand dominance. For most foreign companies this may not be easy to imitate, at least not through operations in Japan.

The competition is also global, with cross-subsidization of product segments through worldwide distribution networks. Moreover, Japanese companies efficiently link various variables, such as product, price, quality, promotion, distribution, and service, in order to achieve success in the Japanese market.

Japan is one of the world's most competitive markets, with a number of competitors, including foreign global competitors and imitators, for virtually every product from the moment it is introduced on the market. The Japanese market is flooded with new products, making the life span of existing products shorter, irrespective of whether it is a consumer good or an industrial good.

Moreover, Japanese companies are known to develop new products several times faster than companies from other OECD countries in most product segments, by using concurrent engineering (CE), flexible manufacturing system (FMS), factory automation (FA), mechatronics, robotics, computer-aided design

(CAD), computer-aided manufacturing (CAM), and computer-aided engineering (CAE). These products are of high quality, with a huge product differentiation, and low production cost.[23] All these factors provide Japanese companies with a competitive advantage over foreign companies in Japan.

Foreign companies generally have to adapt to Japanese market requirements, not only to variations in standards (calibration, voltage and so on) but also to the sensitive and unique character of Japanese consumers and corporate customers. Moreover, delivery punctuality and proper packaging of the product is a must. Foreign companies are generally forced to charge a higher price for their product in Japan, mainly due to special packaging and handling, translation costs, travel costs, and so on.

In many cases, the price level of similar types of products is higher in Japan than in the rest of the world, and on the other hand, the market and product segments that are less brand oriented are also very price sensitive. Moreover, global competitors (both Japanese and foreign) supposedly can dictate a lower price by cross-subsidizing product segments, that is, providing wide varieties of products and services at low cost. Moreover, Japanese companies are known to follow a market-share pricing strategy, using a low entry price to build up market share (pricing lower than the competitors) and thus establishing a dominant market position in the long run.

According to many writers, Japanese companies' strategy is to manufacture high-quality products and sell them, if required, at a low price even if they incur a loss. The greater the market share, the higher the chances for increasing volume and the profit margins. Although this strategy requires patience and a long-term perspective of the market, Japanese companies are known to possess both these qualities.

It has been generally assumed that global companies will achieve economies of scale (at least to some extent) through sales promotion of global brands or globally standardized products, in contrast to small and medium-sized companies. Japanese companies are known for their exhaustive market intelligence, which helps them identify market opportunities, confront opponents and capture a large market share. They also give special importance to face-to-face contact with their buyers. Moreover, face-to-face communication is indispensable in industrial markets, since personal relations between the buyer and the manufacturer are an important element in the purchasing decisions of the former.[24]

Foreign companies are expected to pay special attention to this part of the marketing strategy, though carrying it out is very expensive in Japan. Furthermore, for industrial goods, where the buyer and seller interact intensively, the cultural closeness or psychic distance is considered to be extremely important for success in the Japanese market. Japanese companies have the obvious advantage here; however, if foreign companies can recruit high-caliber Japanese personnel, then their chances for success are considerably higher in the Japanese market. Successful foreign companies will also be able to make marketing innovations and some of these may flow back to their parent companies.

The role of Keiretsu is also important. The Japanese defend the Keiretsu relationship by arguing, among other points, that joint product development and long-term projects are carried out fruitfully among the manufacturers, suppliers and buyers in the Keiretsu relationship.

In order to make this important variable operational, we studied the following aspects: the business environment in Japan, marketing and sales strategies, market position, marketing problems, expenditure on marketing, global standardization, time lag in product and service introduction, market intelligence, the profit center or cross-subsidization approach, the introduction of unique marketing programs, and the transfer of successful marketing programs or strategies to headquarters or to subsidiaries outside Japan.

Production and research and development. Recently Japanese companies have introduced technologically oriented new products based on entirely new inventions and innovations. Japan is known for its production efficiency. In the automobile, iron and steel, and electronics sectors, for example, Japanese production efficiency in most cases exceeds that of other similar types of plants around the world. The Japanese market is also characterized by rapid cross-licensing and, in particular, by large Japanese companies (including Keiretsu), that provide easy access to licenses to their subcontractors and maintain close cooperation over production quality and R & D.

Foreign companies having a production base in Japan--especially the manufacturers of industrial goods--will also be able to learn the Japanese production system and acquire know-how. This will make it easier both to recruit Japanese personnel and to show a commitment to Japanese clients. Moreover, delivery security will increase considerably, thus strengthening the competitive edge in Japan.

Regarding production in Japan, our main goal was to observe the factory performance of foreign companies compared to parent factories outside Japan and the transfer of Japanese production techniques to the parent company or to its subsidiaries outside Japan.

A brief discussion regarding technology transfer is appropriate since this concept is related to both production and R & D. It is important to note two features of the conventional view on technology transfer in the field of multinational business.[25] The first is that technology is regarded as flowing from the parent company to the foreign subsidiary. The foreign subsidiary uses it as a weapon to compete against local companies. The case in which technology and know-how are born at the foreign subsidiary and then transferred to the parent company--reverse technology transfer--is ignored. Horizontal transfer from a particular subsidiary to other foreign subsidiaries is also not taken into consideration. The second feature of the conventional view is that technology transfer is realized under the parent company's technological leadership or guidance. Engineers and managers at the parent company play a central role in the technology transfer. They provide guidance and advice to the foreign subsidiary's local engineers and managers.

This study will eventually show that some characteristics of successful foreign companies in Japan contradict these two features of the usual view of technology transfer. Sometimes the Japanese subsidiary, using its own resources, creates new technology and know-how, which are then transferred to the parent company. In addition, there are examples of horizontal technology transfer to other foreign subsidiaries. These reverse and horizontal technology transfers seem to be active in Japanese subsidiaries; however, they are not satisfactorily treated by existing literature on technology transfer.

Japanese companies are known to have a strong commitment to R & D and to the most advanced and sophisticated manufacturing processes, as already mentioned. Joint R & D between the Japanese manufacturer and its customers is very common in Japan. Furthermore, the development of new products through collaboration strengthens the ties between the manufacturers and buyers, and this factor may indirectly serve as a market entry barrier to foreign companies seeking to enter a particular segment.

At a certain stage of presence in Japan, foreign manufacturers have to establish an R & D base there. This decision will depend on the type of product sold in the Japanese market and the technological level of its competitors. In order to succeed in Japan, foreign companies need to have the technological capabilities required to develop new products, technologies, software, and systems with their own means. By establishing an R & D base in Japan, foreign companies are able to participate in a market where new technologies and know-how are continuously being developed. R & D refers to innovative activities undertaken by a company, the share of employees engaged in R & D, the expenditure on R & D, the number of patents obtained in Japan, and the transfer of R & D results to the parent company. All of these aspects were investigated in this study.

The size of the foreign company in Japan.   Size is measured on the basis of number of full-time employees, sales, assets, and paid capital. This study adopted the OECD's common way of grouping companies by size:

Small   < 51 employees
Medium   > 50 and < 201 employees
Large   > 200 employees

We should note that we are studying the size only of the foreign company in Japan, not the parent company of a foreign partner outside Japan or a Japanese joint venture partner's parent company in Japan. We should be careful in comparing one branch with another branch since the degree of capital and labor intensity is not always equal, especially when comparing manufacturing with non-manufacturing sectors.

In general, large companies find it easier to obtain economies of scale in production, management, finance, and marketing, especially if they are following a global market strategy.

Large foreign companies in Japan can raise capital easily. This factor also increases their risk-taking capacity in the Japanese market. Additionally, a longer time perspective, a lower ROI requirement, and a more global perspective means that these foreign companies can, if required, afford to have longer runs of unsuccessful ventures than can small companies in Japan (cross-subsidization was discussed earlier). However, not too much should be made of the difficulties of SMEs (small and medium-sized enterprises), since there are also examples of successful SMEs in Japan. In this study we have collected some background information, such as the foreign company's year of establishment in Japan, total number of employees, sales, and levels of imports, exports, and exports to the parent company.

1.4 FIELD RESEARCH IN JAPAN

Our earlier studies in and outside of Japan provide an important framework for this investigation.[26] A comprehensive survey questionnaire (see Appendix A) was designed to study the strategy and performance of foreign companies in Japan.[27] The questionnaire for the most part is structured, and most of the questions are combined with a set of possible answers. The number of alternatives varies from question to question. Moreover, we thought that the adoption of a two-, three-, or five-point scale was necessary, since for some variables we felt that no finer distinction could be made. Prior to mailing the questionnaire, we tested it on a number of foreign companies in Japan.

The questionnaire consists of several types of scales: nominal, ordinal, and interval. Statistical techniques generally require that the variables be measured on an interval or ratio scale and that the relationship between the variables be linear and additive. Since the questionnaire is, to a large extent, based on ordinal scales, we decided not to use statistical tools such as regression, discriminant, and factor analysis, which as a rule require interval or ratio scales. Furthermore, several factors are operational on a two-point scale. A two-point scale is not considered statistically suitable. Therefore, the entire analysis is based on qualitative methods, including cross-tabulations among various variables.

In order to select foreign companies for the survey, contact was made with various institutions, such as MITI, JETRO, and foreign chambers of commerce. Numerous corporate directories were also consulted. Depending on which source is used and the definition of foreign ownership employed, the number of foreign companies in Japan varies from approximately 1,500 to a little over 3,000. Finally, we decided to select Toyo Keizai's *Directory of Foreign Affiliated Companies in Japan.*

The Toyo Keizai "A" list consists of 1,487 foreign companies with foreign equity (minimum 20%).[28] This listing includes manufacturing (consumer and industrial goods with or without local production in Japan), service, and financial companies, with rather comprehensive background data regarding their operations in Japan, including information about any Japanese subsidiaries they may have.

All the foreign companies on this list were selected for inclusion in the survey sample. However, the requirement of a minimum of 25% foreign capital was chosen as a benchmark for this survey, that is the minimum foreign equity had to be 25% for companies to take part in the survey. Additionally, four foreign companies from the "B" list (which contains limited information on the companies) having more then 25% foreign equity were also selected, mainly due to our prior knowledge about these particular companies.

The survey was sent in both English and Japanese to 1,491 foreign companies. Accompanied by letters of recommendation from the ACCJ, EBC, and the Commercial Office of the Embassy of Sweden, surveys were directed to CEOs or senior level managers during November 1991. MITI carries out an industrial survey of foreign companies in Japan every year. The major differences between the MITI annual survey and our study are that MITI's foreign equity benchmark is 51% (i.e., the foreign company has to be a majority equity holder to be included),[29] and the MITI survey concentrates mainly on various financial ratios.

The investigation time period was both the calendar and fiscal year 1990 (January 1 to December 31, 1990 and April 1, 1990 to March 31, 1991). The deadline for filling in the questionnaire was extended two times, and two reminders were sent to all the foreign companies that did not return the completed questionnaire during December 1991 and January 1992. Responses were received from 436 foreign companies for a return ratio of 29.2%. However, contacts with most of these foreign companies were maintained throughout 1992.

The questionnaire with aggregated responses is attached as Appendix A, which also includes detailed information on internal non-responses. Appendix C provides the names of the participating companies in our survey. Table 1.1 provides detailed information regarding the response and non-response rate in terms of nationality. The majority (80%) of the participating companies' headquarters are located in the Tokyo metropolis (for details, see Table B1.1 in Appendix B).

The lowest non-response rate (regionwise) was received from Asia, and particularly from Hong Kong. One of the reasons could be that these companies are more involved in trading than in making FDIs.

Table 1.1 Response and non-response rate by nationality

Region/country	Number of companies	Number of responses	% responses
North America	(744)	(208)	(28)
U.S.A	718	201	28
Canada	26	7	27
Europe	(622)	(201)	(32)
EC	(479)	(149)	(31)
Germany	149	47	32
U.K.	112	35	31
Netherlands	84	28	33
France	84	25	30
Italy	19	6	32
Belgium	7	2	29
Denmark	18	4	22
Spain	4	2	50
Ireland	1	-	-
Other EC countries	1	-	-
EFTA	(141)	(51)	(36)
Switzerland	102	25	24
Sweden	30	20	67
Liechtenstein	4	3	75
Finland	5	3	60
OTHERS	(2)	(1)	(50)
Poland	1	1	100
USSR (Russia)	1	-	-
Australia	10	3	30
New Zealand	3	2	67
Asia	(95)	(16)	(17)
S. Korea	20	6	30
Hong Kong	43	4	9
Taiwan	4	2	50
P. R. of China	12	2	17
India	2	1	50
Singapore	5	1	20
Pakistan	1	-	-
Malaysia	2	-	-
Thailand	1	-	-
Indonesia	5	-	-
Middle East	(2)	-	-
Saudi Arabia	1	-	-
Israel	1	-	-
Caribbean and South America	(14)	(5)	(36)
Panama	8	3	38
Bermuda	1	1	100
Brazil	2	1	50
Bahamas	2	-	-
Others	1	-	-
Unknown	1	1	100
Total	1,491	436	29

The participating companies were given full freedom to choose one or all the products or services as examples in answering specific questions especially related to performance and marketing.

All 436 of the companies were contacted either by telephone, mail, or fax to provide further details regarding their operations in Japan during the period March to September 1992. Two seminars were also organized during March and May 1992 in Osaka and Tokyo, respectively. Among other people, officials from ministries, banks, chambers of commerce, and participating foreign companies attended. Comments were solicited on the tentative results during these seminars.

All the data collected were input into the database program PARADOX4.0 for further analysis. Out of all 436 questionnaires received, only 17% (74 expatriates) were returned in English; the remaining 83% (362 Japanese) were returned in Japanese. A large number of respondents occupied top managerial positions (see Appendix A).

Finally, in order to supplement the survey results, several case studies on foreign companies in Japan were also completed during 1992 and 1993. The case studies are expected to be published separately, in book form, during 1994. However, in the following chapters, wherever it seemed necessary, results obtained through the case studies are also presented.

Reasons for external non-responses

Sixty companies informed us that they were not able to take part in the survey due to various reasons. Due to time constraints and limited resources, only a random check was done (during the spring of 1992) to determine the reasons for non-responses by the remaining 995 foreign companies that did not respond to our questionnaire. One hundred of these companies were randomly selected and contacted, primarily by telephone. The following reasons for non-responses were given by 160 companies (including the 60 companies that declined to take part in the survey):

- Company policy not to take part in surveys
- Lack of time or very busy
- Questionnaire is too long or is not suitable for their business
- Acquired by a Japanese company, foreign capital ratio is less than 25%, or company has been dissolved
- Not too active in the Japanese market, business level has been drastically reduced, or they have only a representative office in Japan

Foreign companies' responses

A brief presentation of the background variables of the 436 participating companies was constructed (see Figures 1.5 and 1.6 and Appendix A). Regarding distribution of business lines, the number of manufacturers is higher as compared to the non-manufacturers (services and financial institutions).[30] Some other important features are:

- About 53% of the companies are 100% owned foreign subsidiaries in Japan.
- 43% of the companies have less than 51 employees, and about 26% of the companies employ over 200 persons.
- 62% of the companies were established in Japan before 1981, and another 19% were established after 1985.

Figure 1.5 Nationality of parent company
n = 435

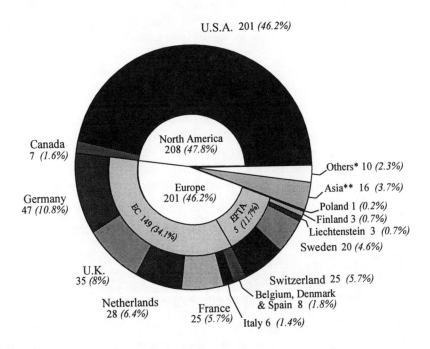

Number of Companies

Note: *Others = Caribbean & South America: Panama, Bermuda & Brazil 5 (1%) and Australia & New Zealand 5 (1%). **Asia = S.Korea, Hong Kong, Taiwan,P.R.China, India & Singapore.

Figure 1.6 Distribution of companies according to branches

n = 436

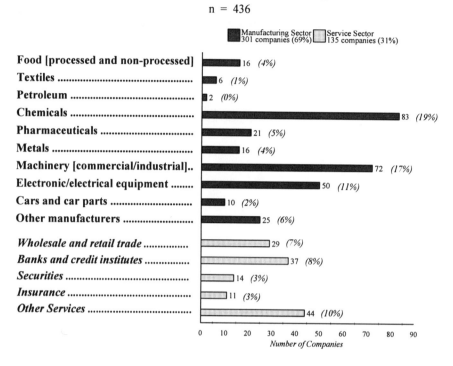

Manufacturing Sector
301 companies (69%)

Service Sector
135 companies (31%)

Food [processed and non-processed]   16 *(4%)*
Textiles   6 *(1%)*
Petroleum   2 *(0%)*
Chemicals   83 *(19%)*
Pharmaceuticals   21 *(5%)*
Metals   16 *(4%)*
Machinery [commercial/industrial]   72 *(17%)*
Electronic/electrical equipment   50 *(11%)*
Cars and car parts   10 *(2%)*
Other manufacturers   25 *(6%)*

Wholesale and retail trade   29 *(7%)*
Banks and credit institutes   37 *(8%)*
Securities   14 *(3%)*
Insurance   11 *(3%)*
Other Services   44 *(10%)*

0   10   20   30   40   50   60   70   80   90

Number of Companies

Questionnaire survey results confirm that the United States has by far the largest representation of affiliates in Japan. It has representation in almost all industrial sectors. The 53% of the foreign companies that reported 100% foreign holdings of their Japanese operations turned out in many cases to be the older, larger, more established companies, many of them MNEs and TNCs. Companies that chose less than 100% holdings (47%) cite cooperative arrangements with their Japanese partners, which allow them to "buy into" an already existing Japan presence. Detailed discussions regarding this point are presented in Chapters 3 and 4.

Table 1.2 presents a brief summary concerning the financial data on the participating companies (see Q 53 in Appendix A).

The data for sales indicate that out of the 293 companies responding to this question (see Appendix A), 69 indicate sales of up to one billion yen ($7.5 million), while 129 respondents reported over one billion yen and up to 10 billion yen ($75 million) in sales for CY/FY 1990. The remaining 95 companies had sales of over 10 billion yen. Gemini Consulting Company in Japan has published a list of the top 100 foreign firms in Japan during 1989-1990.[31] Sixty-seven percent of the companies on this list took part in our survey.

It is interesting to note that foreign companies' imports (5.8% of Japan's total imports) exceeded six times in value their exports from Japan (0.8% of Japan's total exports). For more details concerning the location of headquarters of parent companies,[32] basic data, and background information on the participating companies, consult Appendix A.

Table 1.2   Financial data on the participating foreign companies

(Fiscal year/calendar year 1990)

	Yen million	$ Billion	n =
Total assets	18,032,978	171.743	259
Paid capital	1,097,127	10.449	322
Sales	7,892,125	75.163	293
Ordinary profits	466,132	4.439	263
Imports	1,963,254	18.698	216
Exports	325,429	3.099	211
Total number of employees		147,023	435

Note: Exchange rate: 1 $ = Average Yen 105 in November, 1993
n = Number of responses (out of 436 companies)

NOTES

1.   See Ohmae, K., 1985b.
2.   Source: Economic Planning Agency, 1993.
3.   See Yoshihara, H., 1990, 1991, pp. 17-24, and 1992.
4.   See ACCJ (American Chamber of Commerce in Japan) and A. T. Kearney, Inc., 1991.
5.   Source: IMF, 1993.
6.   See, among others, EBC, 1992.
7.   See "Does Japan play fair?" 1992, pp. 22-31.
8.   See Abegglen, J. C., and Stalk, G., 1985.
9.   See Kotler, P., et al., 1985.
10. See Ohmae, K., 1985b.
11. Regarding competition, Porter has written several books. See Porter, M. E., 1980 and 1985.
12. See Hymer, S. H., 1976.
13. Vernon, R., and Wells, L. T., Jr., 1991, pp. 82-86; Vernon, R., 1971, pp. 65-77; Vernon, R., 1966, pp. 190-207.

14. For more details, see Khan, S., 1978, 1988, 1990 (Japanese edition), and 1994.
15. In our previous studies for measuring performance, we used three classifying criteria, namely, (1) objective, (2) semi-objective, and (3) subjective. For more details see Khan, S., 1988.
16. See Abegglen, J. C., and Stalk, G., 1985, pp. 181-213; and Yoshihara, H., 1985, pp. 179-189.
17. Ouchi, W., 1982, p. 58.
18. See Ballon, R. J., 1992.
19. An interesting discussion regarding autonomy can be found in Takeuchi, H., and Nonaka, I., 1986, pp. 137-146.
20. An interesting discussion regarding headquarters and foreign subsidiary relationships can be found in Bartlett, C. A., and Ghoshal, S., 1986, pp. 87-94.
21. See Oppenheimer, M. F., and Tuths, D. M., 1987.
22. See Czinkota, M. R., and Woronoff, J., 1986.
23. See Hamel, G., and Prahalad, C. K., 1988, p. 38.
24. See Johansson, J. K., and Nonaka, I., 1987, pp. 16-32.
25. See Saito, M., 1979.
26. For details, see Khan, S., 1978, 1988, 1990; Yoshihara, H., 1985, 1990, 1991, 1992.
27. A Study Group on Foreign Companies in Japan was formed in June 1991 at the Kobe University, Research Institute for Economics & Business Administration (RIEB). The survey questionnaire for this study was prepared within this group. The other research group members are expected to publish their research results separately.
28. Toyo Keizai, 1991.
29. Note: MITI has recently changed its benchmark for the manufacturing sector to one-third foreign equity.
30. "Manufacturer" refers to the parent company (of a foreign partner) who manufactures and exports goods to its subsidiary for sales in Japan. In addition, the subsidiary may also manufacture goods in Japan.
31. See Gemini Consulting (Japan), 1991.
32. Throughout the questionnaire, parent company of a Japanese subsidiary (including those in joint ventures) and "headquarters" refer only to the foreign partner's parent company outside Japan.

2 THE JAPANESE ECONOMY

In this chapter a brief description of the Japanese economy is given. We present the historical perspective regarding FDI in Japan, Japanese foreign trade; Japanese and foreign companies' FDI in and outside Japan, incentives offered to foreign companies, problems faced by foreign companies in Japan, and an overview of the Japanese manufacturing and non-manufacturing industries.

2.1 INTRODUCTION

The total population of Japan at the end of 1992 was 124.6 million, and the GNP per capita was over US$30,000, one of the highest among the OECD countries. In FY 1991, Japan's GNP amounted to yen 458.6 trillion ($3.4 trillion, up nearly 5% from the previous year), in nominal terms.[1] This constituted 16% of the total global GNP, making Japan the second largest market in the world (after the United States). Japan's GNP in FY 1992 was twice as large as that of France and the UK combined. Despite the recent world recession and consequent bursting of the bubble economy, the GNP growth rate has been more or less healthy, and Japan boasts one of the lowest unemployment rates, one of the lowest interest rates, the lowest inflation rate, moderate wage increases, and the lowest rate of industrial conflicts in the entire OECD.[2] All of these factors have increased the international competitive advantage of Japanese products despite the appreciation of the yen.

The yen--formerly considered to be an undervalued currency ($1 = yen 360 in the 1960s)--has, since September 1985 (when $1 = yen 250) and the G-5 Plaza Accord,[3] rapidly appreciated in value. Thus, by the end of 1992 one dollar was equivalent to yen 123, over 50% appreciation since 1985. This rapid rise has had very few negative effects (despite the previous two oil crises) on the Japanese economy.

During the period January to October 1993, the yen has further appreciated by 15% ($1 = 105 yen in October 1993). However, it is too early to see if this trend will harm the Japanese economy or exports, or will lead to increased imports into Japan.

Historical perspective

In the past (the 1950s and 1960s), the Japanese government followed a policy of import substitution and provided trade protection and even some export subsidies to domestic industries. Such policy gave Japanese companies the opportunity to charge a higher price on the domestic market and invest the profits in product development, to expand plants, and to sell products on the export market for a lower price than on the domestic market--in some cases even below fixed costs (so-called dumping). Further, the undervalued yen and a supply of cheap labor gave an additional competitive edge to Japanese export manufacturers.

The history of Japanese government regulations and restrictions on foreign investment can be divided into three phases. First, between 1952 and 1964, only yen companies were allowed to be established in Japan, with no ownership or sectoral ownership, that is, if capital was transferred into Japan without government approval, capital and earnings could not be repatriated unless or until the yen became convertible.

Very few companies at that time found Japan to be worth making FDIs. The Japanese government did give approval to some foreign investors to repatriate their capital and earnings in foreign currency if they had unique technologies or a proposed venture in Japan's national interest. In the main, joint ventures (new companies) were permitted with preferably minority foreign equity participation (less than 50%). Most of the foreign companies that did decide to make FDI in Japan chose this way of penetrating the Japanese market--forming a joint venture after obtaining Japanese government approvals and guarantees.[4]

The second phase of FDI lasted from 1964 to 1973. In 1964 yen became convertible, and the yen company route for FDI was closed. All FDI now required specific government screening and approval. Foreign companies still were not able to establish 100% owned subsidiaries and could not easily transfer profits in hard currency to their parent companies outside Japan. For these reasons, joint ventures became the most common pattern for FDI. Moreover, Japanese government policy made it virtually impossible for outsiders to buy control of a Japanese company.

The third phase started on May 1, 1973, when the Japanese law, which in principle allowed 100% direct foreign investment in new or existing Japanese companies, was changed, making Japan as open to FDI as was any other OECD country. In the early 1980s most of the formal capital controls were also abolished, beginning a new period for foreign companies in Japan. The last decade has been a period of construction and expansion of production facilities, R & D laboratories, and M & A (to some extent). Together with sales operations, this activity has made the corporate presence of many foreign companies very well integrated in the Japanese market.

Today, we also know that the yen has greatly appreciated in value, that Japanese labor costs have risen substantially, and that land prices are also very high in Japan.

2.2 JAPANESE FOREIGN TRADE

For the past several years, Japan has been running a remarkable surplus in its external accounts, mainly due to soaring trade surpluses with most of the countries in the world. In fiscal year 1992, Japan's trade surplus reached a record high of $111 billion. Japan's exports during this fiscal year were $344.1 billion (a 7.3% increase from the previous year, or a 1% increase in yen value), and imports during the same period were $233.1 billion (a 0.3% increase from the previous year, or a 5.6% decline in yen value). In the first half of FY 1993 (April 1 to September 30, 1993) Japan's trade surplus hit a record $60 billion (up 15.2% from the same period in FY 1992).

Japan's surplus with the EC in FY 1992 rose to a record $31 billion (28% of Japan's total trade surplus). More than half the EC's 1992 trade deficit was due to imports of Japanese cars, computers, telecommunications equipment, and electronics. The surplus with Southeast Asian countries including newly industrializing economies (NIEs) also hit a record in FY 1992, at $49.6 billion (44.7% of Japan's total trade surplus), outstripping the surplus with the United States. Japan's surplus with the United States accounted for $45.8 billion (41.3% of the total surplus in FY 1992; see Figures 2.1 and 2.2). The trade surplus has been the major cause of exacerbated trade friction and the rising protectionist wall between Japan and the rest of the world.

The decline in value of the dollar and the simultaneous (and not unconnected) appreciation of the yen suggest a continuous increase in exports, at least for some time in the future. In terms of total world exports and imports, Japan ranked third, with about 9.4% and 6.2%, respectively, in 1992.

Figures 2.1 and 2.2 show that Japan's exports and imports with the OECD countries were 54% and 48% respectively in FY 1992. Practically all exports were manufactured goods, among which machinery and equipment, metal products, and chemicals represented nearly 90% of the total. It is worth noting that exports from various industries are very unevenly distributed. The exports are mainly concentrated in certain industrial sectors and on particular products,

Figure 2.1   Japan's exports by area
(FY 1992 - Billion US$)

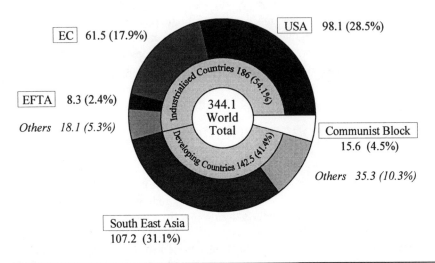

Source: *Figure is based on statistical data obtained from Japan Tariff Association, The summary report on trade of Japan. Tokyo: October 1993.*

such as automobiles, motorcycles, cameras, videocassette recorders (VCRs), office machinery, watches, and semiconductors.[5] For all these products, the export to production ratio ranges from 30% to over 94%. Regarding the United States, cars and car parts made up 72% of 1991's $43.4 billion trade deficit with Japan.

Japan, like the NIEs, depends heavily on the importation of raw materials for its industries and for food needed for its population. Japan's dependence ratio for most natural resources and several food items is extremely high, i.e. ranging from 50% to nearly 100%.

The appreciation of the yen has had one positive effect on the Japanese economy: the imported raw material prices, which are quoted in dollars, have become cheaper for industries. The ratio of imports of manufactured goods to total imports is rising (about 52% in FY 1992); however, it is still low compared with those of other OECD countries (over 70%).

Figure 2.2   Japan's imports by area
(FY 1992 - Billion US$)

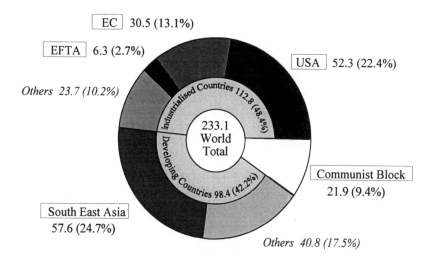

EC   30.5 (13.1%)

EFTA   6.3 (2.7%)

Others 23.7 (10.2%)

USA   52.3 (22.4%)

Industrialised Countries 112.8 (48.4%)

233.1
World
Total

Developing Countries 98.4 (42.2%)

Communist Block
21.9 (9.4%)

South East Asia
57.6 (24.7%)

Others 40.8 (17.5%)

Source: Figure is based on statistical data obtained from Japan Tariff Association, The summary
report on trade of Japan. Tokyo: October 1993.

Japanese foreign direct investment

Japan's FDI abroad during fiscal year 1991 was nearly 10 times greater than FDI made by foreign companies in Japan. In terms of global direct investment, Japan was the world's leading direct investor, with outflow reaching $41.6 billion in FY 1991.[6] According to the Ministry of Finance, Japanese FDI in fiscal year 1992 fell 18% from the previous year, to $31.2 billion--a large drop-- but Japan maintained its position as number one in the world in terms of outflow of FDI. A large portion of Japan's FDI has been in the United States (40.5% of the total share), and most of it in the non-manufacturing sectors (69.5% of the total Japanese FDI; see Figure 2.3).

The decline in Japanese FDI (and the fall in global FDI) is attributed mainly to the recession in and outside Japan, falling stock prices, lower corporate earnings in Japan, and the fact that Japanese companies have already established a sufficient production base outside of Japan. On the other hand, Japan remained the world's largest net creditor at the end of 1992, with its net external assets ballooning by 34.1% from a year earlier to a record $513.6 billion.

Figure 2.3   Japanese foreign direct investment abroad
by region and industry
(FY 1988 - 1992)

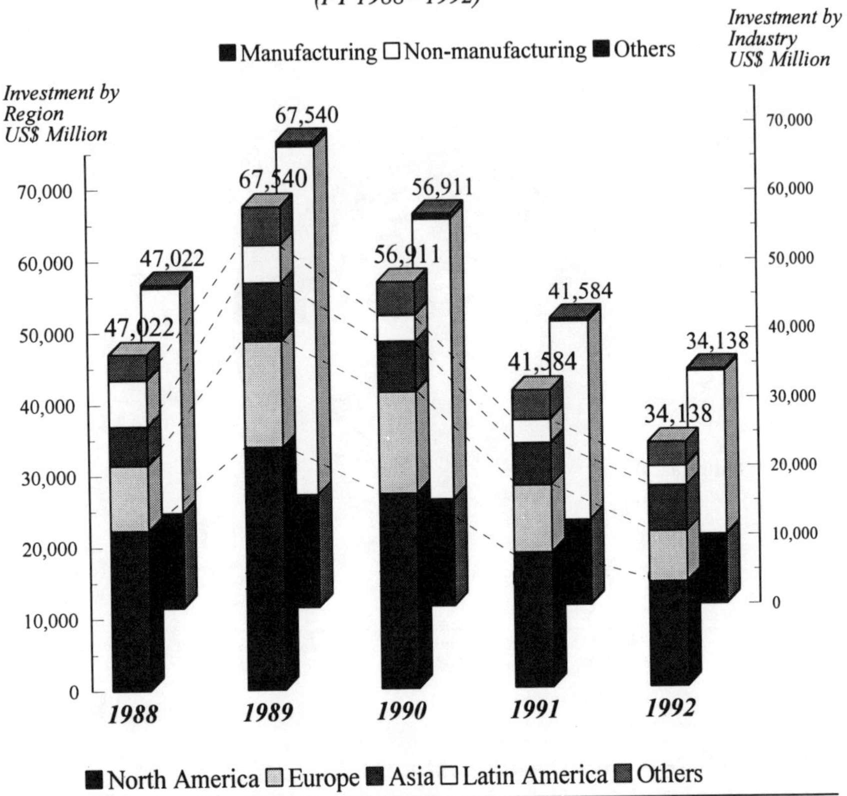

Source: Figure is based on statistical data compiled from MITI's various publications including MITI, the 22nd survey on Japanese business activities abroad. Tokyo: NR-406 (93-4), June 1993.

During the 1980s, Japan invested abroad $280 billion in FDI. There are 9,560 Japanese-affiliated companies in the United States and Canada, 2,298 in the EC, and 3,191 in ASEAN (Association of Southeast Asian Nations), employing a total of 28 million people worldwide.[7]

Foreign direct investment in Japan

For some time, FDI into Japan has been increasing steadily, but it is still at a low level compared with Japan's GNP, Japan's FDI overseas, and foreign companies' FDI into other countries. Furthermore, FDI in Japan remains low relative to aggregate exports to Japan. We should note that FDI refers not only to capital flow but also to management resources that are used to acquire a lasting interest in a company operating in Japan.[8]

In FY 1992, FDI made by foreign companies in Japan reached $4.1 billion (a fall of 6% from the previous year; see Figure 2.4). By country, the United States led the way by accounting for 32.7% of the total, followed by Switzerland (12.6%), and the UK (6.2%). By industry, non-manufacturing industries (such as commerce and trade, services, banking, and insurance) absorbed 61% of the total FDI, and the remaining 39% went to the manufacturing industries.

Total sales of foreign companies in Japan during FY 1991 reached yen 17.8 trillion ($144.6 billion), whereas the total sales of Japanese companies' overseas subsidiaries during the same period was yen 88.7 trillion ($721.1 billion).

Figure 2.4 Foreign direct investment in Japan by country/region and industry *(FY 1988 - 1992)*

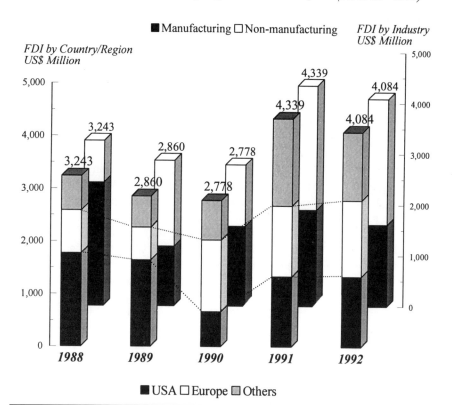

Source: Figure is based on statistical data compiled from MITI's various publications including MITI, the 26th survey on business activities of foreign affiliates in Japan. Tokyo: NR-407 (93-5), June 1993.

According to JETRO, the following trends have been seen during 1991-1992 regarding foreign companies' FDI in Japan: rapidly increasing foreign investment in the processing and assembly as well as the service industries, a growing number of 100% foreign-owned companies (and also an increase in joint ventures, joint R & D, and joint technical centers), and higher ordinary profit/sales ratios than those for Japanese firms in Japan (discussed in detail in Chapter 3).

Moreover, a shift in location of foreign companies' factories was noted during the period 1985-1992, a shift toward locating factories in the inland areas of the Kanto region, the southern part of the Tohoku region, and the southern Kyushu region and a sharp plunge in investing in factories in the coastal area of the Kanto region.

Regarding M & A, during 1991 Japanese companies made 294 M & A abroad, while only 18 foreign company-initiated M & A transactions took place in Japan. The main reason, according to many foreign observers, for the low M & A in Japan was that the environment does not seem to be conducive to foreign investments.

The reasons for low-level FDI in the second largest market in the world are considered by the Japanese government to be: (1) the high cost of investment, mainly due to soaring real estate prices, (2) difficulty in securing necessary manpower, (3) lack of information about investing in Japan, and (4) social and cultural differences, particularly in business practices. However, the collapse of the "bubble economy" is expected to work as a plus factor for future FDI in Japan. On the other hand, the on-going recession in and outside Japan and the sudden rapid appreciation of the yen, if the yen continues to surge in value against other currencies, may lead to even lower FDI in Japan.

According to MITI,[9] the share of foreign companies in Japan's economy is minimal compared to that in the United States or EC, where foreign companies (including Japanese ones) play a substantial role. For example, outsiders own 20% of US assets.

The foreign companies' share in terms of total employees, total assets, and total sales in Japan during FY 1991 was merely 0.5%, 0.9%, and 1.2%, respectively. On the other hand, the foreign companies' share in Japan's total exports was 4.5%, and their share in total imports was an impressive 17.4%. This indicates that foreign companies in Japan are greatly contributing to the expansion of Japanese imports, particularly of manufactured goods. We mentioned in Chapter 1 that participating foreign companies in this study imported six times more than they exported from Japan (see Table 1.2). Moreover, if imports into Japan continue to rise, this will lead to reducing the massive trade surplus of Japan and at the same time decrease investment frictions with Japan's major trading partners, since Japan's massive trade surplus is increasingly becoming a political issue.

The Japanese government, realizing the difficulties faced by foreign companies and under heavy pressure to facilitate easy access to the Japanese market, has adopted several measures to facilitate the activities of foreign companies operating in Japan. These measures are designed to reduce initial costs, facilitate raising funds, and facilitate the employment of qualified Japanese personnel by foreign companies.

Incentives offered for promoting FDI into Japan

In order to slash the snowballing Japanese global trade surplus, the Japanese government is further easing various domestic regulations and standards that hamper import promotion.

Japan has one of the highest corporate taxes in the OECD countries, over 50% on profits.[10] At present some tax incentives are offered to importers or manufacturers using imported items, for example, manufacturers can obtain tax credits amounting to 5% of the increase in the value of product imports (10% to 15% of corporate tax), and 10% to 20% accelerated depreciation on purchased equipment and machinery, and wholesalers and retailers can obtain extra provisions for reserve funds if they increase their value of imports on eligible products by 10% compared with their most recent high year.

Other tax incentives are the deficit carry-over period for foreign companies making new investments, which has been extended to seven years; accelerated depreciation by 20% of annual depreciating amount of assets (buildings and equipment); and exemption from special landholding taxes.

At present, low-interest financing (to promote FDI) to foreign companies is provided by the Japan Development Bank (JDB) and the Hokkaido-Tohoku Development Finance Corporation. However, the funds made available for the promotion of FDI to these financial institutions by the government are very limited.

Moreover, the Japanese government--through MITI (Ministry of International Trade and Industry), JETRO (Japan External Trade Organization), EXIM Bank (Export-Import Bank of Japan) and various other governmental and prefectural entities--is financially assisting foreign companies in Japan. This assistance occurs through various means: (1) investment subsidies in target areas or industries; (2) a government fund guaranteeing obligations of foreign companies that lack the collateral security needed to borrow from private banks; (3) liberal governmental procurement of foreign-made goods; (4) the amendment of the foreign exchange and foreign trade control law in order to make the relevant procedures more open and transparent; and (5) the provision of investment-related information, establishment of a semi-government-financed business-supporting company for foreign investors (e.g., JETRO's Business Support Center), and numerous import expansion programs.[11]

In October 1992, MITI designated seven areas as Foreign Access Zones (FAZ) [12] and made them eligible for government funding to set up facilities to promote imports (examples are warehouses, plants, exhibition halls, and distribution facilities to receive imports). The areas are the prefectures of Hokkaido, Osaka, Ehime, Nagasaki and the cities of Osaka, Kobe, and Kitakyushu. These projects commenced during the 1992 fiscal year. This scheme is funded with 1.2 billion yen (about $10 million) from 1992 budget already allocated to MITI. It is important to note that the budget for import promotion for fiscal year 1992 was yen 10 billion (over $81 million).

Additional funds for this scheme were obtained from the supplementary budget (in a yen 10.7 trillion [about $87 billion] fiscal stimulus package announced in August 1992) to stimulate the domestic economy.

MITI, together with JETRO, provides support activities through a support agency called FIND (Foreign Investment in Japan Development, Inc.) established in June 1993, with half of the capitalization coming from the government's Industrial Structure Improvement Fund and the other from about 100 private corporations. FIND, among other organizations, is expected to publish an employment information magazine for foreign companies in Japan and to assist foreign companies in hiring qualified personnel in the Japanese labor market. Since March 1993, JETRO has provided an office in central Tokyo at a reduced rate to some new foreign companies for a limited time period so that these companies can rapidly develop contacts with potential Japanese companies.

All of these measures and programs are expected to stimulate domestic demand and boost efforts to promote imports and FDI, and at the same time further accelerate and improve the access of foreign companies to the Japanese market. At present the climate for trade and investment in Japan is more favorable than it was five or ten years ago.

2.3   PROBLEMS AND RELATIONSHIPS WITH THE JAPANESE GOVERNMENT

In this section we will present briefly our questionnaire results regarding the participating companies' perceptions on problems and relationships with the Japanese government. More detailed discussions are presented in the later chapters.

Problems that foreign companies are encountering with respect to the Japanese government's behavior (Q 22, see Figure 2.5) include: too many regulations and/or administrative guidelines (more emphasis placed by financial and various other service sectors, mainly due to oral directives), the taxation system (more emphasis placed by service and financial sectors), and cumbersome customs clearance procedures. Non-tariff barriers, foreign exchange and foreign trade control laws, and difficulties in obtaining loans and credits were more often mentioned by financial and various other service sectors.

Regarding many regulations, a close examination reveals that a large number of companies citing this problem are in the service sector (banking, securities, insurance, etc.) and that the majority of these companies were established after 1980 with a foreign capital ratio of over 50%. In the manufacturing sector, mainly companies producing chemicals, pharmaceuticals, machinery mentioned that they were facing the problems with too many regulations. Concerning lack of intellectual property protection, only a few companies mentioned this problem, with a majority of the companies active in the manufacturing sector. Very few companies criticized the Japanese government procurement policy.

It appears that generally a large number of foreign companies are facing problems due to too many regulations and/or administrative guidelines (including oral directives); the taxation system; and cumbersome customs

Figure 2.5 Problems encountered with respect to the Japanese government

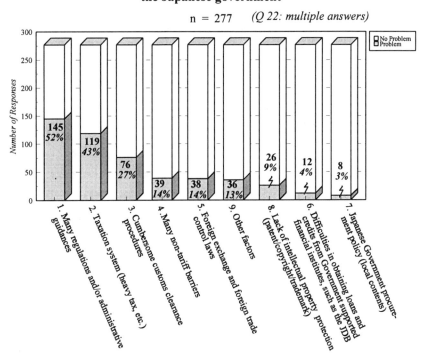

clearance procedures in Japan. On the other hand several impediments to FDI in Japan mentioned in the mass media did not receive any support from the 436 foreign companies in our survey (e.g. lack of intellectual property protection; Japanese Government procurement policy; difficulties in obtaining loans and credits; etc.). In Section 2.5 of this Chapter and in Chapter 6 more details regarding the problems faced by foreign companies in the financial and service sectors are discussed.

2.4   THE JAPANESE MANUFACTURING INDUSTRY

The Japanese manufacturing industry is characterized by capital-intensive, sophisticated manufacturing technologies and products requiring high R & D expenditures. The manufacturing sector in Japan is considerably large, varying from semiconductors, computers, telecommunications equipment, office automation equipment, robots, optics, aerospace, new materials, and biotechnology to machine tools, chemicals, iron and steel, transport equipment, and other products.

In this book, only a few crucial industrial sectors are highlighted due to space limitations, namely, the chemical industry, the pharmaceutical industry, the machinery industry, the electronic industry, and the transport equipment industry. In each industry, one or two selected subsectors are briefly described.[13]

The chemical industry

In the chemical industry,[14] in which foreign companies are very active, Western companies enjoy strong international competitiveness and have aggressively developed their businesses in Japan from an early stage. The Japanese chemical industry (especially large-scale petrochemical plants and oil refineries) uses capital-intensive, advanced, sophisticated technologies. Compared to that of several other OECD manufacturers, the quality of Japanese chemical products is considered superior, and deliveries are punctual (pharmaceuticals are discussed in detail in the next section).

Total production of chemicals during FY 1991 in Japan was worth yen 24.3 trillion ($189.4 billion).[15] When viewed by country classification, the Japanese chemical industry is ranked second in the world after the United States in terms of sales. The share of the chemical industry output within the total manufacturing industry in Japan was 7.1% in 1991. The number of companies in the chemical industry was 5,390 (establishments employing more than four people), and the number of employees was 406,000 (see Table 2.1).

Table 2.1 Basic data on the Japanese manufacturing industry (1991)

	Number of establishment	In %	Number of employees (Thousand)	In %	Value added (yen billion)	Production (yen billion)	In %
Food	44,068	10.3	1,104	9.7	8,672	24,089	7.1
Textile	29,773	7.0	520	4.6	3,201	7,975	2.3
Pulp & Paper	11,186	2.6	283	2.5	3,117	8,969	2.6
Petroleum & Coal	1,093	0.2	34	0.3	1,138	8,885	2.6
Chemical Industry	5,390	1.3	406	3.6	11,595	24,253	7.1
Plastic Products	20,266	4.7	456	4.0	4,374	11,568	3.4
Iron & Steel	6,406	1.5	340	3.0	6,501	18,629	5.5
Non-ferrous Metals	4,170	1.0	174	1.5	2,159	7,697	2.2
Fabricated Metal Products	51,049	11.9	866	7.6	8,878	20,240	5.9
Industrial Machinery	46,264	10.7	1,233	10.9	14,740	36,174	10.6
Electric Machinery	36,976	8.5	1,987	17.5	21,378	58,607	17.2
Transportation Machinery	15,483	3.6	983	8.7	12,628	48,902	14.6
Other industries	158,269	36.7	2,968	26.1	27,226	64,621	18.9
Total manufacturing	430,393	100	11,354	100	125,607	340,609	100

Source: The above data has been compiled from the Ministry of International Trade and Industry (MITI), Census of manufacturers 1991 - Report by industries. Tokyo: 1993.

Notes: MITI's survey was conducted based on the establishments employing more than 4 people.

In FY 1992, exports of chemicals amounted to yen 2.4 trillion ($19.7 billion). The chemical industry's share of Japan's total exports that year was 6%. Three high value added (VA) products--organic and inorganic chemicals and plastics-- accounted for over 70% of all chemical exports. The most important regional export markets for chemicals were Southeast Asia (49%), western Europe (21%), and North America (18%). Japan has a trade deficit in the chemical industry with most of the industrialized countries, the Middle and Near East, and Latin America.

Chemical imports in FY 1992 amounted to yen 2.2 trillion ($17.7 billion). The chemical industry's share of Japan's total imports that year was 7%. Of the chemical imports, about 79% originated in industrialized countries, mostly coming from western Europe (43% of total chemical imports) and North America (35%).

The chemical industry is characterized by a large number of sellers of plants and equipment, and can be described as a buyer's market. The Japanese market is highly competitive, with fierce price wars, particularly in basic petrochemicals, fertilizers, and pesticides. Specific products such as soda ash and fertilizers have restricted market access as well. Moreover, ethylene and first-line derivatives of ethylene such as polyethylene and polypropylene are subject to protective tariffs, mainly due to excessive production capacity in Japan.

Most of the foreign companies in Japan in this sector are active within the high value added specialty chemical segments, and several companies have their own R & D in Japan in order to demonstrate commitment. They also provide top quality after-sales service, timely delivery, and so forth.

The expenditures for R & D by the Japanese chemical industry amounted to yen 1.5 trillion ($12.1 billion) in 1991, accounting for 15.9% of the R & D expenditures of all industries (see Figure 2.6).[16] The ratio of R & D expenditures to sales (to manufacturing industries) for the chemical industry in 1991 was 5.24%. This ratio is the second highest following the electric machinery industry (see Figure 2.7).

The pharmaceutical industry

The Japanese pharmaceutical market is the second largest in the world (over 20% of the world production),[17] just after the United States. MITI has targeted this industry--which also includes some areas of biotechnology--as a priority sector and is facilitating joint research among various Japanese manufacturers. At present Japanese companies are, along with companies from other countries, world leaders in the field of antibiotics. Large Japanese pharmaceutical companies have R & D expenditures similar to those of their European and American competitors, in other words, usually exceeding 10% of total sales.

Figure 2.6   R & D expenditure in Japanese industry
(FY 1991)

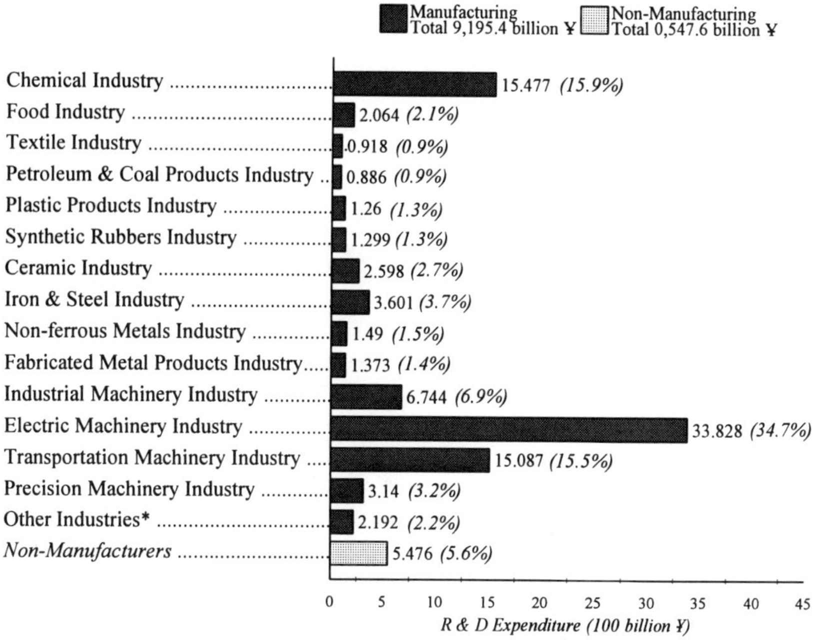

| ■ Manufacturing Total 9,195.4 billion ¥ | □ Non-Manufacturing Total 0,547.6 billion ¥ |

Chemical Industry .... 15.477 *(15.9%)*
Food Industry .... 2.064 *(2.1%)*
Textile Industry .... .0.918 *(0.9%)*
Petroleum & Coal Products Industry .. 0.886 *(0.9%)*
Plastic Products Industry .... 1.26 *(1.3%)*
Synthetic Rubbers Industry .... 1.299 *(1.3%)*
Ceramic Industry .... 2.598 *(2.7%)*
Iron & Steel Industry .... 3.601 *(3.7%)*
Non-ferrous Metals Industry .... 1.49 *(1.5%)*
Fabricated Metal Products Industry..... 1.373 *(1.4%)*
Industrial Machinery Industry .... 6.744 *(6.9%)*
Electric Machinery Industry .... 33.828 *(34.7%)*
Transportation Machinery Industry .... 15.087 *(15.5%)*
Precision Machinery Industry .... 3.14 *(3.2%)*
Other Industries* .... 2.192 *(2.2%)*
Non-Manufacturers .... 5.476 *(5.6%)*

0   5   10   15   20   25   30   35   40   45
R & D Expenditure (100 billion ¥)

Source: Figures based on statistical data compiled from Management and Coordination Agency,
Report on the survey of research and development - 1992. Tokyo: Statistics Bureau, April 1993.
*Note: * including: Pulp & Paper, and Publishing & Printing Industries*

The number of pharmaceutical manufacturers (ethical and over-the-counter [OTC] drug makers) in Japan is estimated to be over 1,500, with a finished product production of yen 5.6 trillion ($45.6 billion) in 1992. The number of employees in this industry is about 195,000. However, the majority of manufacturers are small. Only 12.4% of the companies have more than 100 employees (192 companies) and can be considered major manufacturers, and 20 of these companies were responsible for over 50% of the total production in 1992.

The demand for pharmaceuticals is expected to continue rising in Japan, due to such factors as:

- A rapidly aging population, in which the number of persons 65 years old and over is estimated to reach about 20% of the total population by the year 2000.
- Prescription drugs covered by the national health insurance system.
- A positive attitude toward drug consumption.

**Figure 2.7   R & D expenditure as percentage of total sales in various
Japanese manufacturing industries** *(FY 1988 - 1991)*

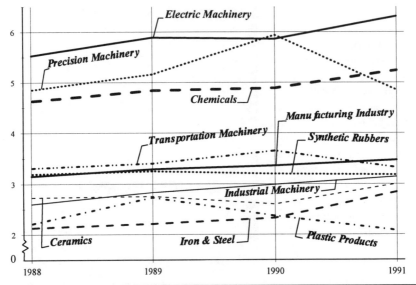

R & D expenditure as percentage of sales

*Source: Figures based on statistical data compiled from Management and Co-ordination Agency,
Report on the survey of research and development - 1992. Tokyo: Statistics Bureau, April 1993.*

Japanese firms in the pharmaceutical sector do not have the global influence that their counterparts in the electronics and automobile sectors do. At present, several of the leading manufacturers in Japan are from the United States and Europe. However, Japanese companies are catching up with their foreign competitors by developing new drugs, and are gradually increasing their direct export activities globally.

The number of new drugs being developed in Japan is still low (21 in FY 1991). Few Japanese companies are in a position at present to compete on the world market with products that they have developed themselves. Furthermore, there was only one Japanese pharmaceutical manufacturer on the list of the world's 20 leading pharmaceutical companies in 1991 (Takeda Chemical Industries Ltd., number 16). Several of the large Japanese companies derive a large portion of their domestic sales from products introduced to the market from outside Japan.

The Japanese market for pharmaceuticals is one of the most competitive in the world and differs widely in some respects from those of other OECD countries. This can easily be illustrated with the following example. Physicians in Japan at present number around 200,000, of which drug companies consider

85,000 worth visiting, since they prescribe a high proportion of drugs. Drug manufacturers are estimated to have over 35,000 salesmen (medical representatives) and a wholesale sales force of around 40,000. Allowing for some over-simplifications, the total estimated number of more than 75,000 medical representatives for 85,000 physicians means nearly one full-time salesman per physician!

The salesman generally keeps contact with a physician if not on a daily basis, then at least on a weekly basis. This kind of attention given to the physician is practically impossible to achieve in other OECD countries, where one visit by a salesman every third month per physician is considered normal. This fact makes it rather difficult for a new manufacturer to enter the Japanese market, at least from the point of view of cost and recruitment.

Unlike other industries, pharmaceuticals have not been severely affected by the appreciation of the yen, since this industry is oriented to the domestic market, and both domestic and foreign manufacturers and wholesalers were showing high profit levels up to 1990-1991. However, during 1992/1993 the profit levels have gone down for most of the manufacturer, due to the recession prevailing in Japan.

On the other hand, some observers claim that with large profits made in the domestic market, the Japanese manufacturers cross-subsidize their unprofitable ventures outside Japan, sustaining short-term losses in those ventures for long-term market share gains.

In the field of pharmaceutical machinery and medical devices (e.g., x-ray diagnostic equipment and ultrasonographic equipment), some of the Japanese manufacturers are already ahead of their foreign competitors. Their plants are not only large in scale, but they are also multifunctional (using FMS and the like) and equipped with sophisticated production technologies. A large amount of pharmaceutical machinery and numerous medical devices are also exported by these manufacturers.

Foreign manufacturers' presence in Japan. Compared to other highly competitive high-tech industries such as semiconductors, machine tools, and robots, the Japanese pharmaceuticals sector is the least internationally competitive. This is mainly due to the technological gap between Japan and other major OECD countries.

All the leading American and European pharmaceutical manufacturers have either their own 100% owned subsidiaries or have joint ventures, licensing agreements, or some other form of technical collaboration with a Japanese manufacturer. The number of foreign-affiliated companies in Japan in 1992 was less than 200, with most of them based in the United States, Germany, Switzerland, France, and the UK. About 90 foreign companies have manufacturing facilities in Japan (with foreign equity ownership of more than 50%).

The pharmaceutical market was largely liberalized by a new patent law that went into effect in January 1976. Previously, unlike the system in most OECD countries, only the process patent was granted, which gave increasing opportunities for copying. However, with the product patent system, copying was made difficult in Japan, if not impossible.

Despite some of the problems faced by foreign manufacturers in the Japanese market, most of these companies are expanding their activities in Japan by such activities as the following:

- Establishing 100% owned subsidiaries and manufacturing plants, in many cases on a joint venture basis.
- Establishing their own marketing and sales channels.
- Establishing R & D laboratories, either on their own or in collaboration with a Japanese partner.
- Carrying out M & A or purchasing smaller pharmaceutical manufacturers or wholesalers in order to obtain full control of the distribution channels.

The aim of foreign companies is to become firmly rooted in Japan by establishing their own integrated production, marketing, and R & D.

Imports and exports. The pharmaceutical industry is one of the very few industrial sectors in which Japan has a trade deficit; Japan imports more than two times what it exports. Therefore, in terms of exports, pharmaceuticals are one of the weakest Japanese industries. Successful companies in Japan are expected to be able to respond to the demands of physicians and tailor their product to meet specific end-use applications.

In 1992 Japan imported pharmaceuticals worth yen 430.1 billion ($3.5 billion), and at the same time exports barely reached yen 183.3 billion ($1.5 billion). The ratio of exports to production is 3.3%, while the ratio of imports to production was remarkably 7.7%. Over 90% of these imports were from the OECD countries, whereas about 50% of pharmaceutical exports went to OECD. Royalty payments by the Japanese companies to foreign pharmaceutical manufacturers are also considered very high. The United States alone had a surplus in trade of health care equipment and drugs amounting to $11 billion, $3.5 billion more than it imported in 1991.

The technology gap is getting narrower between Japanese and other OECD pharmaceutical manufacturers. The domestic market is highly competitive. Moreover, Japanese manufacturers have recently increased their exports, not only by selling licenses (passive strategy), but also by establishing joint ventures (active strategy). One important strategic reason for choosing joint ventures is that the pharmaceutical industry is one of the most competitive in the world, restricted by severe governmental regulations. The local joint venture partner is expected to make market entry easier. Recently, there has been an increase in the number of wholly owned Japanese subsidiaries in the export market (aggressive strategy).

The machinery industry

Japan is at present a world leader in several subsectors of this industry. The machinery industry in Japan is primarily export oriented and very large, amounting to 42.4% of Japan's total industrial production in 1991 (see Table 2.1). There are practically no barriers to entry into this industry by foreign companies. However, a large capital investment is required for after-sales service facilities (personnel, repair services, and spare parts inventories) and for tailoring products to customer specifications. Two important sectors, namely machine tools (MT) and industrial robots (IR) are briefly presented here.

The machine tool industry. Like other OECD countries, the quantitative position of the MT (consisting of metal-cutting units) industry in Japan as a whole was less than 1% (yen 1.1 trillion, or $9.2 billion) of the total production of the machinery and equipment industry in 1991. However, machines for making other machinery or equipment occupy an important position in the Japanese industry.[18] The number of employees in the MT industry in 1992 was 37,776.

Japan's output of MT is the highest in the world. The production of MT in FY 1992 was yen 761.3 billion ($6.2 billion, a 35% decrease over the preceding year due to the recession) and the consumption was yen 784.2 billion ($6.4 billion, a 34% decrease over the preceding year). On the world market, the Japanese are competitive not only in price, but also in product quality and service. The MT industry uses advanced technology, resulting in a high degree of precision and reliability. The Japanese manufacturers' global market share in this high-tech sector is increasing, and manufacturers are quickly upscaling their products.

Japanese manufacturers emphasize the production of numeric control (NC) MT, in particular computer numerically controlled (CNC) units. Most of the demand for MT comes from OECD countries.

In value terms, Japan's MT exports were yen 313 billion ($2.5 billion), of which NC types accounted for about 70% of total exports in FY 1992.[19] OECD countries absorbed over 70% of Japan's MT exports. The US government has reacted to Japan's massive exports of MT by imposing voluntary export restraints (VER) on Japanese MT.[20] On the other hand, Japan imports barely 5% (yen 36.1 billion or $294 million)[21] of its total consumption (yen 784.2 billion in FY 1992), mostly from other OECD countries. Three countries account for 70% of the total imports, namely, Germany, Switzerland, and the United States.

Industrial robots (IR). Japan has the largest number of IR in the world.[22] Approximately 62% of IR in use in the world is concentrated in Japan (see

Figure 2.8). Under MITI supervision, joint R & D among various companies within the MT and IR sectors is being promoted.

In 1992, IR worth yen 427.5 billion ($3.5 billion, a 29% decrease over the preceding year) were manufactured and the consumption during the same year was yen 428.6 billion ($3.5 billion, a 28% decrease over the preceding year). Over 40% of the IR are used in the electric machinery and automobile

Figure 2.8   Number of industrial robots in operation worldwide

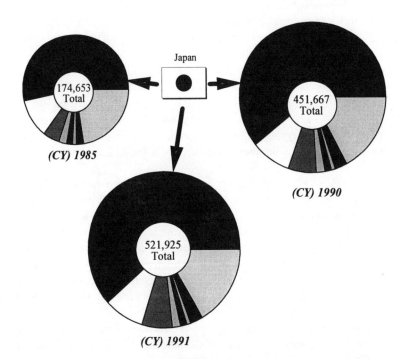

	(CY) 1985	(CY) 1990	(CY) 1991
Japan	93,000	274,210	321,895
USA	20,000	40,000	44,000
Germany	8,800	28,210	34,140
France	4,150	8,551	9,000
UK	3,208	6,410	7,165
Sweden	2,046	3,711	4,099
Italy	4,000	12,500	14,100
Rest of the World	39,449	78,075	87,526
Total	174,653	451,667	521,925

Source: Figure is based on statistical data obtained from Japan Industrial Robot Association. Tokyo: 1993.
Note: Excluding manual manipulators and fixed sequence robots.

industries. The IR have been largely responsible for FMSs, improved product quality and variety, and high productivity. At the same time, IR have decreased production costs, defect rates, and industrial accidents.

There is keen competition in the world market. In 1992, nearly 30% of total IR production was exported, mainly to other OECD countries (total exports = yen 126.6 billion or $1 billion). Direct imports of IR into Japan are rather limited, since the 200 domestic manufacturers of IR already create keen competition. Most of the well-known foreign companies already have some form of collaboration with the major Japanese manufacturers (licensing or joint ventures). One of the reasons for low Japanese imports is that the buyer requirements are based on tailor-made specifications requiring close contacts with the buyer, sophisticated systems engineering, and excellent service and maintenance. In 1992, IR imports amounted to yen 1.7 billion, or $13.7 million, mainly from OECD countries.

The electronics industry

Japan is the second largest computer market and the second largest computer producer in the world after the United States.[23] Japan's share of the world market for computers is estimated to be around 25%. The Japanese computer industry is highly concentrated, with less than 2% of more than 1,500 manufacturers controlling more than 70% of production and almost half of total industry employment. Fujitsu, Hitachi, NEC, Toshiba, Matsushita, and Mitsubishi are dominant suppliers to the industry in Japan.

The Japanese manufacturers have at present world leadership in consumer electronics and also, to a large extent, in industrial electronics, such as VCRs, video cameras, integrated circuits (ICs), semiconductors, very large-scale integrated circuits (VLSIs), optic fibers, lasers, carbon fibers, and CDs.

Japanese manufacturers hold substantial world market shares in this industry and have become global. Several Japanese companies are world known, such as Sony, Toshiba, Matsushita (Panasonic), Fujitsu, and NEC. They have succeeded in establishing product differentiation through creative marketing, and each has developed a strong brand name and image and customer loyalty. The Japanese manufacturers' world market share is over 95% in VCRs, 70% in 64K random access memory (RAM), 70% in IR, 85% in copiers, and 95% in CDs. Moreover, Japanese semiconductor manufacturers combined represented over 47% of the world's semiconductor market share in 1990 (the US world market share was less than 40%).

The large Japanese manufacturers (including in-house operations) are also more diversified than their competitors from other OECD countries. They manufacture everything from computers and telecommunications equipment to home appliances, in highly automated plants using IR and unmanned carriers.

The distribution strategy of Japanese manufacturers is also sophisticated; they generally use multiple distribution channels, such as the use of several distributors for selling some products, with the rest sold directly to original equipment manufacturer (OEM) businesses. In the domestic market, the chain of vertical linkages, stretching from the manufacturers to retail outlets (i.e., the Keiretsu system), has greatly benefited the industry, maximizing its sales.

According to world standards, R & D expenditures in the Japanese electronics industry are extremely high. Moreover, joint cooperation in R & D between Japanese and foreign companies is on the increase. The triad power concept is more prevalent in this industry, that is, the development of highly advanced technologies through close cooperation among European, Japanese, and American manufacturers, examples of which are found in the development of fifth-generation computers, integrated supercomputers, and supermicrocomputer systems.

It is estimated by the EIAJ (Electronic Industries Association of Japan) that the electronics industry's R & D expenditures in 1991 amounted to 21% of Japanese industry's total expenditures. This was a larger figure than for any other industry. In FY 1992, electronics industry R & D expenditures were yen 2.4 trillion ($19.3 billion).

Many well-known American and European companies seem not to want the competition from Japan to completely take their already dwindling market share, so they have chosen to position themselves on their Japanese competitors' home ground. Excellence in Japanese electronics and materials is pulling foreign R & D to Japan (for more details, see Chapter 7).

Production, exports and imports. Total electronics production in FY 1992 was yen 22.12 trillion ($179.8 billion).[24] It is estimated that Japan is the second largest producer of electronics in the world (after the United States). The electronics industry is the most export-oriented industry in Japan, and in FY 1992 combined exports accounted for yen 11.31 trillion ($92 billion), or over 26% of Japan's total exports.[25] Fifty-one percent of total production was exported. Concerning industrial electronic equipment and electronic components and devices, OECD countries are the major export markets. The EC and the United States have imposed up to 100% anti-dumping duties on some kinds of imported Japanese electronic equipment.

Imports of electronic products into Japan during FY 1992 reached more than yen 2 trillion ($16.63 billion, or 7% of total imports).[26] Over 60% of total imports to Japan came from the United States, mostly consisting of advanced technological products such as computers and ICs.

Under the Japanese-US semiconductor agreement, foreign-made semiconductors took 20% of the Japanese market share for the first time in 1992. The reason for this success in the Japanese market, apart from quality, customer service, and the like, is the weakening of the dollar vis-à-vis the yen, which makes imported microchips more competitive. There is a growing number of "design-in" projects in which Japanese manufacturers of computers, telecommunications equipment, and electronic products work closely from the first stage of product development with American and European chip makers so that special semiconductors can be tailor-made to their requirements. Some of the recent cooperative arrangements have been among Matsushita Electric, Motorola, and LSI Logic; Hitachi and Intel; and Sony and Motorola.

Imports into Japan are expected to increase gradually due to the rising yen, government market-opening measures such as the withdrawal of import duties on computers and communications equipment, and the privatization of Nippon Telegraph and Telephone Corporation (NTT).

Many companies see the need to follow their Japanese rivals, competing to supply their products to the world's leading automobile, electronics, and electrical machinery industries. Practically all the formal barriers in the electronics, electrical equipment, and component industries have been abolished. However, foreign companies have to tailor their products to the local market (e.g., use Kanji characters for computers, catalogues, and manuals) and to provide, among other things, excellent service and complete support to local dealers. Moreover, proximity and close working relationships (in order to design and develop products) with the customer through local manufacturing and R & D is considered a must, so a physical presence in Japan is of the utmost importance.

The transportation equipment industry

This huge sector includes motorcycles, cars, trucks, tractors, trains, ships, helicopters, and other aircraft. Japanese manufacturers are highly competitive in most of these sectors and hold substantial world market shares. One subsector, the automobile manufacturing industry, is briefly described in the following section.

The automobile industry. Japan is the largest automobile-producing country in the world.[27] In CY 1992, 12.5 million vehicles (cars, trucks, and buses) were manufactured (a 6% decline from the previous year), out of which 9.4 million were cars (see Figure 2.9). Automobile and related industries employ about 10% of the total work force, and the value of output is over 12% of Japan's total manufacturing output.

There are 10 automobile manufacturers in Japan. The largest company is Toyota, followed by Nissan, Honda, Mazda, and Mitsubishi, each with a production of over 1 million automobiles.

Fierce competition in the automobile industry has led Japanese manufacturers to invest heavily in robots and automation by introducing office automation (OA), FMS, FA, CAD, and CAM with zero defects and error-free production. All this has enabled them to produce different models on a single line and carry

Figure 2.9 Japan's motor vehicle production and exports
and number of imported cars   *(CY 1990 - 1992)*

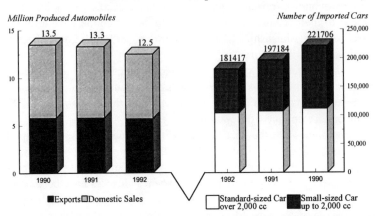

Source: Figure based on statistical data collected from Japan Automobile Importers' Association, Imported car market of Japan - 1993. Tokyo: 1993; and Japan Automobile Manufacturers Association Inc., Automobile statistics - Monthly Report, Vol. 27, No. 2. Tokyo: May 1993.

out model changeovers with minimum retooling, thus bringing substantial increases in production efficiency. The cars manufactured are of a high quality, reasonably priced, and of sufficient variety to meet most consumer demands. The companies supply a wide array of options as standard equipment and provide excellent service and maintenance.

R & D expenditures are high in this industry, with intensive cooperation among manufacturers and automobile parts and components suppliers.

In 1991, 5.8 million vehicles, 43% of total production, were exported (see Figure 2.9). Automobile exports of yen 7.4 trillion ($54.7 billion) accounted for 17% of total Japanese exports. Due to the recession and various other export restrictions, exports of automobiles in 1992 declined by about 1.5% from the previous year to 5.7 million vehicles, but only in quantities and not in values (1992 exports = $61.5 billion), due to the rise in the value of yen.

Nearly 70% of total exports are sold to Europe and the United States. In 1992, Japanese manufacturers exported over 1.773 million cars and trucks to the United States and 1.185 million vehicles to the EC. The largest Japanese exporter worldwide is Toyota, followed by Nissan, Mazda, Mitsubishi, and Honda.[28]

The Japanese car manufacturers have substantial world market shares in the small and medium-sized car segments (less than 2,000 cylinder capacity [cc.]), and they are rapidly moving into the "upper niche" (over 2,000 cc.), competing directly with such manufacturers as BMW, Mercedes, Saab, Volvo, and the three US giants (Chrysler, General Motors, and Ford). Japanese manufacturers have been so successful that they have been forced to accept VER or face quotas, high custom duties, or outright prohibition in several of the OECD countries.

For example, under a 1993 agreement, Japanese car exports to the EC from 1993 to 1999 are frozen at 1991 levels of about 1 million cars a year. Similar quotas have been set up for Japanese car exports to the United States (1.65 million vehicles for FY 1993).

The automobile industry in most OECD countries is considered to be the key industrial sector, and most of the major manufacturers in this industry are globalized. In order to avoid trade friction, VER, or quotas, Japanese auto manufacturers have started manufacturing operations overseas, through joint ventures, equity participation, technical tie-ups, business cooperation, or established "transplants," which manufacture Japanese cars in the United States and EC. The procurement of parts and components from overseas into Japan is also increasing.

Cars imported into Japan still account for less than 5% of the total car market, although Japan is the second largest car market in the world. In contrast, imported cars for most of the OECD countries account for 25% to 75% of their car market. With recent improvement in the market environment, partly due to the Japanese government's import promotion measures, the appreciation of yen, increases in the standard of living, and increased sales efforts by foreign car manufacturers, the sales of imported cars have noticeably grown.

In 1992, Japan imported a total of 181,417 cars (an 8% decline from the previous year). Fifty-eight percent of the cars had an engine displacement of over 2,000 cc. One country alone, Germany, holds about 58% of the imported car market in Japan. The three most successful foreign car exporters in Japan are Volkswagen (VW), BMW, and Mercedes. VW has an assembly plant with Nissan for its Santana model in Japan.

Generally, foreign carmakers are competing within the luxury market segment, with a large number of cars having an engine displacement of over 2,000 cc. (particularly US-made cars) and priced at over yen 3 million ($28,500). US automakers have not yet marketed right-hand-drive cars in Japan, with the exception of Chrysler's Jeep Cherokee. The Japanese cars in this segment are reasonably priced, more adapted to the Japanese consumer preferences, which include better after-sales service and higher fuel efficiency compared to foreign-made cars. All of these factors have retarded the sales growth of foreign-made cars in Japan, especially in the ongoing recession.

Recently, Japanese transplants have increased their exports to Japan (mainly Honda, Toyota, and Nissan in the United States and Europe). The foreign car manufacturers estimate that by decreasing market access problems and intensifying their own efforts (such as marketing), they will capture a market share of over 10% in Japan by the year 2000.

2.5 THE SERVICE SECTOR IN JAPAN

This is an extremely large sector that is rapidly expanding. For example, the air transport industry is showing phenomenal growth. Traffic routes to Japan are considered extremely lucrative, especially since the Japanese government inhibits price competition in Japan. Japan's software market in 1990 was estimated to be worth $18 billion, thus making it the second largest market after the United States. Japan's advertising industry is also the second largest in the world, with total estimated advertising revenues exceeding $38 billion in 1990. The following service sectors are briefly presented: banking, financial services, insurance, legal services, and retail trade.[29]

Banking

Japan dominates global banking in both domestic and international markets.[30] In 1991, Japan had 13 of the world's 20 largest banks, as ranked by size of assets and deposits. The world's eight largest banks were all Japanese. According to the Ministry of Finance (MOF), there are 89 foreign banks operating in Japan, with 143 branches (as of the end of March 1993). Most of the foreign banks and their branches are located in Tokyo; some are in Osaka.

The competition is intense in the banking sector in Japan, and most of the global banks maintain a presence there in order to follow their global strategy. Some banks have left the Japanese market because they were not able to show commitment to the Japanese market, and investing neither sufficient effort nor adequate funds to establish, among others things, a name.

The Japanese banking industry has been undergoing liberalization reforms since 1984. However, the banking environment is still considered to be restrictive in comparison with that of other OECD countries. Frequent examples given are the Keiretsu relationships (large banks are key members of industrial Keiretsu groups) and restrictions regarding the acquisition of Japanese banks by foreign banks. Moreover, foreign banks claim to face problems in introducing their sophisticated money management techniques in the Japanese market, mainly due to length of time (at least six months) needed to secure MOF's approval.

Financial services

There has been spectacular growth during the 1980s in Japan's financial services industry, although during 1992 (after the bubble economy burst), a slowdown has been felt in this industry. Many foreign financial service companies have entered the Japanese market. This sector is also gradually being opened to foreign companies, in particular with the start of the liberalization process in the mid-1980s. However, many foreign observers still consider Japan not yet fully liberalized in this market.

Japan is the world's largest securities market, offering equities, bonds, and derivative products. Over 2,000 companies are listed on five exchanges, with a market value of equity over $4 trillion in 1990. The trading volume of shares during the same year was over 260 billion, and registered over-the-counter trades reached 530 million shares of 280 companies. There are eight licensed securities exchanges, with the largest in Tokyo and others in Osaka and Nagoya.

Large foreign financial companies have entered the Japanese market. As of March 1993, there were 49 foreign securities companies with about 60 foreign branches operating in Japan. The majority of these foreign securities companies were given licenses to conduct a full range of securities business in Japan. Foreign companies compete with Japanese financial companies, which offer their sophisticated products and services. Some of the foreign companies complain that the Japanese government controls access in competitive areas, such as pension funds and investment trust management. They also complain about the lack of regulatory clarity and M & A restrictions, or legal restrictions and procedures that may make sales of Japanese companies to other Japanese companies more likely than sales to foreign companies. Other complaints refer to the tight foreign exchange controls that hamper the easy flow of money in international markets.

Insurance

Japan is the world's largest market for life insurance. Over 92% of all households are enrolled in an insurance plan of some sort. The Japanese insurance industry is tightly regulated by the MOF, which sets standards for forms and rates, and as a result there is virtually no price competition. Companies compete on the basis of established networks, products, and service and product innovation. The insurance industry is divided into two distinct segments: life and property/casualty. Companies can work in only one segment under the provisions of the Insurance Business Law or the laws concerning foreign insurers. Moreover, insurers are not allowed to operate freely in the third sector.

Life insurance companies have about $1 trillion in total assets, and the largest, Nihon Life, controls about one-fifth of those assets. Tokio Marine and Fire, the largest non-life insurer, controls assets of more than $15 billion. There are more than 400,000 agencies for sales operations.

Currently, 33 foreign insurance companies are operating, with over 40 branch offices. It is estimated that all the foreign insurance companies combined have less than a 2% share of Japan's life insurance segment, and only about 2.9% of the non-life-insurance segment. More than 80% of the market share is in the hands of seven American companies. Successful foreign companies are involved in various types of products, such as personal accident, travel accident, cancer, and variable life insurance. During the past several years, the Japanese government has liberalized its licensing policy for foreign insurers. However, some insurers claim that obstacles still exist in this industry, especially in Japan's non-life-insurance market for foreign firms, including the commercial sector, which insures corporate clients.

According to the ACCJ, 11 Keiretsu-member companies dominate over 80% of Japan's non-life-insurance market, with at least 92% of non-life business handled by financially related insurers.

Legal services

Japanese legal services and non-Japanese legal services are the two main segments of the Japanese legal services market. Since 1987, legal services have been partially liberalized. International law companies can operate only in the non-Japanese legal services segment. At present, restrictions still prevail in this sector. Foreign law companies are not allowed to hire Japanese lawyers, give advice on Japanese law, or use their company name. In addition, they are not allowed to enter into partnership or other formal associations with Japanese lawyers.

Foreign companies, particularly those from the United States and Europe, are known to rely on legal advisers when making FDI in a foreign country. Restrictions by the Japan Federation of Bar Associations (JFBA), which almost completely inhibit the activities of foreign lawyers in the Japanese market, prevent FDI in Japan from substantially increasing. Within OECD countries, Japan can be considered to have some of the toughest restrictions concerning legal services.

As of 1991, 96 foreign lawyers were qualified by the Ministry of Justice and registered by the JFBA. It is estimated that there are about 30 foreign law firms operating in Japan, with a majority from the United States.

Retail trade

Retail in Japan experienced unprecedented growth until the end of 1991. During 1993, sales and profit levels went down due to the ongoing recession in Japan. Foreign retailers are trying to enter this market. Japanese retailers, due to their success in the Japanese market, have been expanding their activities outside of Japan, particularly in East and Southeast Asia and the United States.

Japan has about 272 department stores operated by 118 companies, and a large number of small retail stores. This coexistence of very large and very small retailers is unique in the world. Combined sales from department stores and supermarkets reached a total of yen 22.2 trillion ($180.5 billion) in 1992.

The Large-Scale Retail Store Law, approvals and licenses, exclusive relationships among retailers, wholesalers, and manufacturers, and high land costs are some of the obstacles to the expansion of foreign retail companies in Japan. Toys R Us of the United States has entered the Japanese market with very aggressive plans. However, non-traditional retail methods (door-to-door sales and mail order) are growing in popularity in Japan, and several foreign companies have entered this market.

It is estimated that in FY 1992, sales through direct selling reached $34 billion, thus making Japan the largest market in the world. Amway Japan Ltd., the Japanese subsidiary of US-based Amway Corporation, saw sales in FY 1992 of over $1.2 billion.

NOTES

1. In FY 1992, Japan's GNP amounted to yen 470.7 trillion, or $3.8 trillion (source: Economic Planning Agency, 1993). Throughout this book, the yen to dollar conversion rate (average rate for December of each year), for the sake of simplicity, has been as follows: yen 133.72 = $1 for 1990; yen 128.07 = $1 for 1991; yen 123 = $1 for 1992; and yen 105 = $1 for 1993 (sources: Bank of Japan, 1993; IMF [International Monetary Fund], 1992).
2. The data sources for this section include IMF, 1993, 1992.
3. The Group of Five (Japan, Germany, France, the United Kingdom, and the United States), meeting at the Plaza Hotel in New York. Later G-5 expanded to G-7, with the addition of Canada and Italy.
4. For a detailed discussion regarding the historical perspective related to FDI in Japan, see Encarnation, D. J., 1992, pp. 36-96.
5. Sources: Japan Tariff Association, 1993; JETRO, 1993a, 1993b, 1992; Keizai Koho Center, 1993.
6. Source: JETRO, 1993b.
7. See Emmott, B., 1992.
8. For more discussion regarding the definition of FDI, see Sakurai, K., 1992.
9. Source: MITI, 1993b; and 1993d. MITI annually conducts a survey of business activities of foreign affiliates in Japan. This survey covers business enterprises that had a foreign capital ratio of 1/3 or more (previously over 50% foreign capital) in all industries except for financial and insurance institutions as of the end of March 1992 (FY 1991). Of the 2,586 foreign affiliates covered by the 1992 survey, 1,341 replied to the questionnaire, a

response ratio of 51.9%. We should note here that a large number of foreign affiliates in MITI's survey are small trading companies having, most probably, little to do with making FDI in Japan.

10. According to the calculations of KEIDANREN (Japan Federation of Economic Organizations), the real corporate tax rate in Japan is approximately 49%. However, several foreign companies do not agree, since the calculations are based on the general assumption that the companies will be able to utilize all the tax reductions available to them. For details, see KEIDANREN, 1993.

11. For more details, consult Delphos, W. A., 1993.

12. For more details, consult MITI, 1992.

13. For more details, consult, among others, ACCJ and A. T. Kearney, Inc., 1991.

14. Source: information provided by JCIA (Japan Chemical Industry Association), and MITI. See JCIA, 1993; MITI, 1993a (in Japanese).

15. JCIA estimates that the chemical production in FY 1992 was yen 23,300 trillion ($189.4 billion), a 4% decrease (in yen value) over the preceding year, due to the recession.

16. Source: Management and Coordination Agency, 1993.

17. Sources: based on interviews with Japanese and foreign pharmaceutical manufacturers and Yakugyo Jiho Co., Ltd., 1992. Information has been also provided by the Japan Pharmaceutical Association and JPMA (Japan Pharmaceutical Manufacturers Association), both based in Tokyo. See JPMA, 1992.

18. Source: based on interviews carried out during 1993 by the authors and data provided by the Japan Machine Tool Builders' Association, Tokyo.

19. In FY 1991 the exports of MT were higher, at yen 398.1 billion ($3.1 billion).

20. Other products covered by VER measures are steel and automobiles.

21. Imports in FY 1991 of MT were yen 57.1 billion, or $446 million.

22. Source: based on interviews carried out during 1993 by the authors and data provided by the Japan Industrial Robot Association, Tokyo.

23. Source: based on interviews carried out during 1993 by the authors and data provided by EIAJ (Electronic Industries Association of Japan) and the Japan Electronic Industrial Development Association, Tokyo. See EIAJ, 1993.

24. Electronics production in FY 1991 was much higher, at yen 24.98 trillion ($195 billion).

25. Exports in FY 1991 were yen 11.27 trillion ($88 billion).

26. Imports in FY 1991 were yen 2.11 trillion ($16.5 billion).

27. Source: based on interviews carried out during 1993 by the authors and data provided by JAIA (Japan Automobile Importer's Association), Tokyo, and

JAMA (Japan Automobile Manufacturers Association, Inc.,), Tokyo. See JAIA, 1993; JAMA, 1993.

28. Excluding CKD (complete knock-down) and KD (knock-down) sets. In 1992, about 4.7 million KD and CKD sets were exported.
29. For more details, consult ACCJ and A. T. Kearney, Inc., 1991.
30. Based on interviews carried out during 1993 by the authors and data provided by Zenginkyo (Federation of Bankers Associations of Japan), Tokyo. See Zenginkyo, 1993.

3 SUCCESSFUL FOREIGN COMPANIES IN JAPAN

In this chapter we investigate the performance of foreign companies in Japan in detail. We will employ several measures to check the extent of success of foreign companies in Japan. We will also attempt to determine which foreign companies have failed in Japan.

3.1 MEASUREMENT OF DEPENDENT VARIABLES-- SUCCESS AND FAILURE

The available research provides little help in establishing a universally accepted criterion for success and failure. We will not make any attempt in this book to present a detailed theoretical discussion regarding performance measurement, since this can be found in many other sources.[1]

In this study, we first asked foreign companies to evaluate their own performance in Japan based on strict financial criteria (objective criteria) and on non-financial criteria (subjective criteria). The objective criteria consist of measures of financial performance in terms of key financial ratios during past years, including sales growth, profitability (ordinary profits before corporate tax), and return on investment (ROI).

The subjective criteria take into account the non-financial factors (including the degree to which expectations are met compared to the actual outcome) that foreign companies in Japan use to measure their performance, such as market share, brand image, customer satisfaction, and reverse technology transfer. In Chapter 8, we present foreign companies' own views as to which factors they attribute to their success or failure in the Japanese market (See Q 50 in Appendix A).

Second, we ourselves evaluated the performance of foreign companies based on their performance data, such as ordinary profits, annual sales, dividends paid, and accumulated profits. Using this method, we were also able to compare performance data with the foreign companies' self-assessment of their performance (success or failure).

The individual company's financial and non-financial performance refers to calendar/fiscal year 1990 (see Q 48 and Q 49 in Appendix A).[2] During the calendar/fiscal year 1990, the business cycle in Japan was reasonably good and the recession prevailing in Europe and the United States had not affected business in Japan.

We should note here that there are certain pitfalls in using ordinary profits or ROI as performance criteria. For example, the TNCs and MNCs may use cash flow generated in one market to cross-subsidize their unprofitable business venture in Japan. These companies have a long-term perspective of the Japanese market, and therefore may consider short-term losses normal.

Moreover, in some cases it is very difficult to establish the actual profitability of foreign companies in Japan due to transfer pricing, especially since corporate taxes in Japan are some of the highest in the OECD countries (over 50%). It is possible that a foreign subsidiary in Japan running at a loss can in reality be providing profits to the parent company. This situation can occur if the parent company charges a very high transfer price from its subsidiary in Japan--one substantially higher than full cost or one that includes exceptionally higher overhead costs--thus retaining profits at home and at the same time squeezing the subsidiary's profit margin in Japan. Some companies did mention that they were using transfer pricing as an instrument to lower profits or to show no profits in their subsidiary in Japan.

During our interviews, several foreign companies mentioned that the Japanese yen has been strong compared to European currencies; in truth, some European currencies actually underwent devaluation during 1990-1992 by as much as 10% to 25% compared to the Japanese yen. However, in some cases while a parent company has been invoicing its subsidiary in Japan only in Japanese yen (especially the transfer price for raw materials, and so on), it has been able to maintain healthy profits and has not found any reason, despite the high cost of doing business in Japan, to reduce the price of goods purchased by the subsidiary in Japan. We think these factors make it difficult to say if a foreign company is really taking a loss or to determine what the actual profit levels in Japan may be. However, we believe that there is no reason to doubt the integrity of most of the foreign companies in Japan.

Finally, companies were requested to provide data concerning their owner-ship and various other financial data, such as sales, ordinary profits, accumu-lated profits, dividends paid, imports, exports, and number of employees. For-eign companies were also requested to provide annual reports and any other printed material that would be useful in judging their performance in Japan.

Participating foreign companies in some cases have been reluctant to disclose information such as sales and profit figures. The annual reports have not been of much help since in Japan, as compared to American and western European countries, governmental bodies and shareholders do not make it mandatory for companies to disclose detailed financial information about their operations.

3.2 PERFORMANCE EVALUATION BY FOREIGN COMPANIES

Classification of foreign companies into successes and failures

In order to analyze the performance data, we classified the foreign companies in Japan in three clear performance groups:

- "Successful/very successful" (Sample 1)
- "As expected" (Sample 2)
- "Unsuccessful/very unsuccessful" (Sample 3)

Companies that chose alternative 3 (see Q 48/Q 49) on a five-point performance scale were classified into the "As expected"/sample 2 group. The "Successful"/sample 1 group consists of those companies that chose alternatives 4, "Successful," and 5, "Very successful." Failures/sample 3 refers to those companies that chose the alternatives 1, "Very unsuccessful" and 2, "Unsuccessful."

Performance is a sensitive issue, and therefore it proved difficult to obtain this information from all 436 participating companies. However, 417 companies provided information on their financial performance, and 391 companies did this for non-financial criteria. For more details regarding the response rates, consult Appendix A.

Regarding financial criteria, the majority of foreign companies classified themselves as being "Successful" or "Very successful" in Japan (72%, according to Q 48/financial criteria). "Failures" were only 6%, whereas the "As expected" group consisted of 22% of the companies (see Figure 3.1). If we take into consideration the non-financial criteria, then the "Successful/Very successful group" is even larger, about 75%, and the "Failure" group is even smaller, about 4% of the companies (see Q 49, Appendix A). The "As expected" group consists of 21% of the companies.

In our present analysis we treat the "As expected" group as a separate entity. We consider the companies in the "As expected" group to be uncertain at the

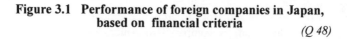

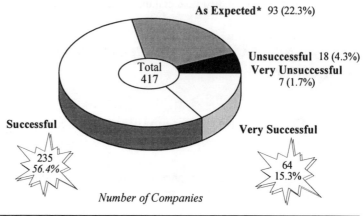

Figure 3.1 Performance of foreign companies in Japan, based on financial criteria *(Q 48)*

As Expected* 93 (22.3%)

Unsuccessful 18 (4.3%)
Very Unsuccessful
7 (1.7%)

Total
417

Successful

235
56.4%

Very Successful

64
15.3%

Number of Companies

Note: * As Expected = neither successful nor unsuccessful

moment regarding their performance, and due to their uncertainty they are unable to place themselves in the success or failure group. Our telephone conversations with representatives of these companies indicated that if we had not provided the "As expected" alternative, then a large number of these companies would have chosen the "Successful" alternative to "Failure" or to neglecting to answer the question at all (Q 48/Q 49).

The conclusion that can be drawn is that the majority of participating companies in the study were successful. Thus, our intentions of studying a large number of failures is not fully realized in this study. The research is biased toward successful foreign companies in Japan. It appears that successful foreign companies respond easily to a survey like ours, compared to the failures. However, it is quite encouraging for us to see such a large number of foreign companies classifying themselves as financially successful or very successful in the presumably difficult Japanese market.

Appendix A (Q 48) shows that foreign companies in Japan use profitability as one of the main financial criteria in judging their performance. Moreover, the participating foreign companies consider the Japanese market highly profitable, although it takes some time before a venture becomes profitable. This is somewhat contrary to emphasis in Japanese companies, which pay more attention to sales growth, market share, and various other non-financial criteria. Generally the profit objective is downplayed by Japanese companies, particularly short-run profits.[3]

Regarding non-financial criteria (see Appendix A, Q 49), we find a very long list of factors that are taken into consideration by foreign companies when judging their performance in the Japanese market. The three most important factors are market share, new product developments, customer satisfaction, and product adaptation to Japanese requirements or services.

Close scrutiny of the list of non-financial criteria shows that foreign companies to a large extent judge their performance using marketing variables, apart from market share and reverse flow of technology and know-how to the parent company. These factors are product development and quality (including product adaptation), service, brand name and image, quick delivery, and customer and employee satisfaction.

In the following sections we will focus mainly on the financial criteria for the analysis, since practically all the foreign companies have classified their companies into "Success" or "Failure" by using both the financial and non-financial criteria without any significant difference. However, where appropriate, we will also mention the non-financial criterion.

Success and failure groups according to nationality and region

Table 3.1 shows that a very high percentage of successful companies are from the United States, whereas within the "As expected" group a large number of companies are from Europe. In the "Failure" group European companies have a very slightly high percentage of failures. Moreover, the most failures are recorded by the Netherlands (four companies), France (three), and Sweden (three). Practically no other significant observations can be made from our study.

Success and failure groups according to ownership

Table 3.2 shows that out of 299 successful companies, 158 companies (53%) are 100% foreign owned. Similarly, in the "As expected" group, 45% of the companies are 100% foreign owned, and in the "Failure" group 56% of the companies are 100% foreign owned. One tentative conclusion that can be drawn here is that the number of failures in joint ventures--in particular in those with less than 50% foreign capital (minority share holding)--is exceptionally low, at 4% (e.g., there is only one failure from China). Among the 50% joint ventures, all five failures are from the United States.

Table 3.1 Region and nationality division according to performance

(Q 48.1)

	Nationality	Sample 1 Successful	Sample 2 As expected	Sample 3 Unsuccessful	Total number
I	North America				
	Canada	4	1	1	6
	USA	147	40	10	197
	Total	151	41	11	203
II	Europe				
	EC				
	Germany	30	14	1	45
	UK	24	10		34
	Netherlands	16	8	4	28
	France	14	5	3	22
	Italy	2	4		6
	Belgium	2			2
	Denmark	3	1		4
	Spain	2			2
	Total	93	42	8	143
	EFTA				
	Switzerland	19	4		23
	Sweden	14	2	3	19
	Liechtenstein	3			3
	Finland	1		1	2
	Total	37	6	4	47
	Others				
	Poland	1			1
	Total	131	48	12	191
III	Asia				
	S. Korea	4			4
	Hong Kong	1	2		3
	Taiwan	2			2
	China	1		1	2
	India	1			1
	Singapore	1			1
	Total	10	2	1	13
IV	Others				
	Australia	2			2
	New Zealand	2			2
	Panama	1	2		3
	Bermuda			1	1
	Brazil	1			1
	Total	6	2	1	9
	Grand Total	298	93	25	416

Legend: Sample 1 = "Successful " and "Very Successful" companies; Sample 2 = "As Expected"
companies; and Sample 3 = "Failure" companies.

Table 3.2 Performance according to ownership
distribution   (Q 48.1)

Range of ownership	Sample 1 Successful	Sample 2 As expected	Sample 3 Failed	Total
25-49%	39	11	1	51
50%	55	27	5	87
51-99%	47	13	5	65
100%	158	42	14	214
Total	299	93	25	417

Legend
Sample 1 = "Successful" and "Very successful"; Sample 2 = "As expected"
Sample 3 = "Unsuccessful" and "Very unsuccessful"

Success and failure groups according to year established

Table 3.3 shows that a large number of successful companies have been established in Japan for a long time. However, 11 out of 25 (44%) failures were also established before 1971.

On the other hand, if we take a look at recent comers, foreign companies that were established in Japan after 1985, we find that both the "As expected" group and the "Failure" group consist of relatively high percentages compared to companies that established themselves before 1986; there are 30 recent comers out of 93 "As expected" companies (32%), and 9 recent comers (includes 6 American companies) out of 25 failed companies (36%).

Moreover, 50% of the companies that were established in Japan after 1985 classified themselves as successful. A very tentative conclusion to be drawn is that in order to be successful in the Japanese market a presence of at least some years is required; companies should have a long-term perspective of the Japanese market.

During our interviews and in the questionnaire, foreign companies did mention that the start-up costs are substantial and also that the payback period is generally longer in Japan than that for similar investments made in the United States or Europe (see Q 52). The acceptable profit levels in Japan also take a longer time to reach compared to those in other OECD countries.

However, several responding companies mentioned that their operations in Japan were highly profitable and that the profit levels in many cases were far higher in Japan than elsewhere (the appreciation of the yen also boosted their profits). For many of them, the Japanese market was the most lucrative. For some products the sales in Japan represented 5% to 10% of worldwide sales of

**Table 3.3 Performance of foreign companies according to
year established in Japan**   (Q 48.1)

Year established	Sample 1 Successful	Sample 2 As expected	Sample 3 Failed	Total %
< 1971	28	5	3	35
1971 - 1980	23	6	-	29
1981 - 1985	12	4	1	18
1986 -	9	7	2	18
Total	72	22	6	100

Legend: Successful = Includes "Very successful" and "Successful" companies;
Failed = Includes "Very unsuccessful" and "Unsuccessful" companies;
see Appendix A for more details.

the parent company, but the contribution to the parent company's net profit from the Japanese operation was 20% or 30%. The profitability levels, however, vary from branch to branch.

We also carried out cross-tabulation on the year of establishment of foreign companies in Japan and the type of ownership with the performance variable based on the financial criteria. Table 3.4 shows that among the successful groups, in all the time periods, the 100% owned companies occupy a larger share.

In the "As expected" group we find the number of companies that established themselves in Japan after 1985 to be slightly higher among all types of ownership compared to companies that established themselves earlier. This may indicate that it takes several years before a company can, with certainty, classify its operation as a success or a failure. Finally, in the "Failure" group no special tendencies are seen.

Success and failure groups according to the size of company

A considerable number of successful companies, and a majority of the companies in the "As expected" and "Failure" groups, have less than 51 employees, or are small companies. The cross-tabulation on the number of employees (size of company) of the foreign companies in Japan and on the type of ownership with the performance variable based on the financial criteria shows that in the successful group, among all types of ownership, a large number of companies are of small size, with less than 51 employees (38%). Similar tendencies are seen in the other two performance groups (see Table 3.5).

Table 3.4 Performance of foreign companies according to year of establishment and ownership (Q 48)

Year of establishment	Ownership % (foreign capital)	Performance (financial criteria)			Total (%)
		Successful	As expected	Failed	
< 1971	100	15	4	2	21
	51 - 99	4	1*	1*	5*
	50	4	-	-	4
	25 - 49	5	-	-	5
	(Total)	(28)	(5)	(3)	(35)
1971 - 1980	100	11	3	-	14
	51 - 99	4	1	-	5
	50	6*	2*	-	7*
	25 - 49	2	1	-	3
	(Total)	(23)	(6)*	-	(29)
1981 - 1985	100	7	2	-	9
	51 - 99	2*	-	-	2
	50	2*	2	-	4
	25 - 49	2*	-	1	3
	(Total)	(12)*	(4)	(1)	(18)*
1986 -	100	5	2	-	7
	51 - 99	1	1	1	3
	50	2	3	1	6
	25 - 49	1	1	-	2
	(Total)	(9)	(7)	(2)	(18)
TOTAL (%)		72	22	6	100

Legend: Successful = Includes "Very successful" and "Successful" companies; Failed = Includes "Very unsuccessful" and "Unsuccessful" companies; see Appendix A for more details.
n = 417 companies.
* Figures have been rounded up or downwards.

Finally, companies having more than 500 employees are most successful (82% of them are successful), with only one failure (from Sweden). On the other hand, nearly 50% of the failures in the small-sized group (companies with less than 51 employees), are from the United States. We are not in a position to say clearly that a certain type of ownership leads to success or failure.

Since the European FDI lags behind that of the United States in Japan (total FDI during the last decade), we find that the US companies are of a larger size and have been established longer in Japan than the European ones. Appendix B3.1 shows, though, that more European companies established themselves in Japan after 1985 compared to American companies. Similarly, more European companies than American companies have less than 51 employees.

Table 3.5 Performance of foreign companies according to number of employees and ownership   (Q 48)

Number of employees	Ownership % (foreign capital)	Performance (financial criteria) Successful	As expected	Failed	Total (%)
< 51	100	15	5	2	22
	51 - 99	4	2	1	7
	50	5	4	1	10
	25 - 49	3	2*	-	4*
	(Total)	(27)	(13)	(4)	(43)
> 50 - < 201	100	11	2*	1*	15*
	51 - 99	3*	1*	-	3*
	50	5	2	-	7
	25 - 49	4	1	-	5
	(Total)	(23)	(6)	(1)	(30)
>200 - < 501	100	5	1*	1*	7
	51 - 99	2	-	-	2
	50	2	-	-	2
	25 - 49	1	-	-	1
	(Total)	(10)	(1)	(1)	(12)
> 500	100	6	2	-	8
	51 - 99	3	-	-	3
	50	2	-	-	2
	25 - 49	1*	-	-	2
	(Total)	(12)*	(2)*	-	(15)*
TOTAL (%)		72	22	6	100

Legend: Successful = Includes "Very successful" and "Successful" companies; Failed = Includes "Very unsuccessful" and "Unsuccessful" companies; see Appendix A for more details.
n = 417 companies.
* Figures have been rounded up or downwards.

Success and failure groups according to industry and branch

Table 3.6 shows that non-manufacturing companies are a bit more successful than the manufacturers, 76% are successful as compared to 70% for the manufacturers. Similarly, the number of failures is much higher in the manufacturing sector compared to the non-manufacturing sector; 88% of failures (or 22 out of 25) are manufacturers. The "As expected" group among manufacturing and non-manufacturing companies is nearly the same, 22%.

If we take a look at consumer and producer goods within the manufacturing sector, then the success ratio is slightly higher for producer goods (71% as

Table 3.6 Performance according to line of business
(financial criteria, Q 48)

Business line	Performance %			Total %
	Successful	As expected	Failed	
Manufacturing (consumer goods)	17	5	2	24
Manufacturing (producer goods)	32	10	3	45
Non-manufacturing (services)	13	4	1	18
Non-manufacturing (financial institutions)	10	3	-	13
Total	72	22	6	100

Legend: Successful = Includes "Very successful" and "Successful" companies;
Failed = Includes "Very unsuccessful" and "Unsuccessful" companies; for details
see Appendix A. n = 417 companies.

compared to 68% for consumer goods), whereas the failure ratio is slightly higher for consumer goods (9% as compared to 7% for producer goods).

Within the non-manufacturing sector, the success ratio is slightly higher for financial institutions compared to service providers. On the other hand, the failure ratio is slightly higher for these companies. The "As expected" group's percentage does not show any major variation in any of the four sectors.

Regarding performance of foreign companies in individual branches within the manufacturing and service sectors, we are again not in a position to draw any major conclusions (see Table 3.7). The larger sectors within the manufacturing sector are chemicals, machinery, electronics and pharmaceuticals. The companies in the pharmaceutical sector are highly successful (80%), with no failures.

In the electronics sector, the failure ratio is slightly higher (12%, with a majority established after 1985 in Japan). In the services sector, bank and credit institutions are highly successful (84%) within their group, followed by wholesale and retail trade (82%). There are no failures in the securities and insurance sectors.

Table 3.7 Performance according to branch distribution

(Q 48)

Branch	Successful	Performance As expected	Failed	Total (number)
Manufacturing sectors				
1. Food (processed & non-processed)	10	4	1	15
2. Textiles	3	3		6
3. Petroleum	2			2
4. Chemicals	55	18	6	79
5. Pharmaceuticals	16	4		20
6. Metals	9	3	2	14
7. Machinery (commercial/industrial)	51	14	5	70
8. Electronic/electrical equipment	34	9	6	49
9. Cars & car parts	5	3	1	9
10. Other manufacturing	17	7	1	25
Sub-total	(202)	(65)	(22)	(289)
Service sectors				
11. Wholesale & retail trade	23	3	2	28
12. Banks & credit institutes	27	4	1	32
13. Securities	7	6		13
14. Insurance	9	2		11
15. Other services	31	13		44
Sub-total	(97)	(28)	(3)	(128)
TOTAL	299	93	25	417

Legend: Successful = Includes "Very successful" and "Successful" companies; Failed = Includes "Very unsuccessful" and "Unsuccessful" companies; for details see Appendix A.

3.3 EVALUATION BASED ON PERFORMANCE DATA

Success and failure groups based on profitability

In this section we will be making a final attempt to pinpoint some of the characteristics of successful and failed foreign companies in Japan based on the actual profits shown. Actual profitability is calculated in the traditional way, that is, ordinary profits (pre-tax) divided by sales. Only 245 foreign companies provided both the ordinary profits and sales figures (for details see Appendix A).

Average profitability

From Table 3.8 it can be clearly seen that average profitability is higher in the non-manufacturing sector, in particular in the service sector. In the manufacturing sector, the producer goods sector has a higher average profitability, whereas the lowest average profitability is in the consumer goods sector.

The main reasons for low ordinary profits in the consumer goods sector are tough competition in broad market and product niches in which the foreign companies are operating, which leads to high marketing expenditures in Japan (for advertising and promotion, packaging, service, a large sales force for personal selling, product adoption, and so on).

If we compare our figures with MITI's annual survey during the same period (FY 1990), which covers quite a large number of foreign companies in Japan (about 1,300), we find that our average figures for both the manufacturing and non-manufacturing industries are higher than MITI's figures (see Table 3.9).[4]

Moreover, if we compare foreign companies' average profitability figures with all Japanese companies in the same industry in Japan (see Table 3.9), we find that foreign companies have a far higher average profitability ratio in both the manufacturing and non-manufacturing industries. The conclusion that can be drawn is that foreign companies that took part in our study have higher earning ratios than Japanese companies in Japan. In other words, the foreign companies in this study outperformed Japanese companies with respect to profitability.

Table 3.8 Average profitability of participating foreign companies   (CY/FY 1990)

Industry	Number of companies	Average profitability %
Manufacturing (total)	179	5.33
Consumer goods	58	3.87
Producer goods	121	6.03
Non-manufacturing (total)	55	6.53
Services	43	6.54
Financial institutions	12	6.50
Total: Average profitability	234*	5.62

Note: Profitability = Ordinary profits (pre-tax) divided by sales.
* 11 companies were excluded from the present calculations, since they had exceptionally high losses or profits, i.e. over + or - 50%.

**Table 3.9 Average ratio of ordinary profits to net sales for foreign
and Japanese companies**   (FY; %)

	1988	1989	1990	1991
All industries	6.8	5.7	3.9	3.8
	(2.8)	(3.0)	(2.7)	(2.3)
Manufacturing	8.1	6.7	4.4	4.6
	(4.5)	(4.7)	(4.3)	(3.4)
Manufacturing (excluding petroleum)	9.9	8.5	5.6	5.4
	(4.6)	(4.8)	(4.4)	(3.5)
Chemical, pharmaceutical	9.5	7.3	4.3	5.3
	(7.5)	(7.4)	(6.8)	(6.8)
Petroleum	4.2	2.4	2.2	3.0
	(2.8)	(1.6)	(1.8)	(2.1)
General machinery	4.9	4.7	4.9	3.8
	(4.8)	(5.2)	(5.6)	(4.8)
Electrical machinery	14.4	12.6	8.5	6.6
	(4.7)	(5.1)	(4.7)	(3.0)
Transport machinery	4.8	3.7	3.3	0.3
	(3.9)	(4.0)	(3.8)	(2.9)
Commerce and trade	4.2	3.6	3.0	2.7
	(1.4)	(1.3)	(1.2)	(1.3)

Sources: JETRO, Investment in Japan-fact and figures, Tokyo, 1992 and MITI, The 26th survey
         on business activities of foreign affiliates in Japan, Tokyo, 1993d.
Notes: (1) The Ministry of International Trade and Industry (MITI) surveyed foreign affiliated
           companies, with foreign capitalization ratios of 50% or greater.
       (2) Figures in parentheses are for all companies in Japan.

If we compare foreign companies' average profitability figures with those of
Japanese companies abroad, then we again find that foreign companies have a
much higher earning ratio in Japan compared to Japanese companies abroad.[5]
Several foreign companies, both large and small, told us that their return on
investment has been higher in Japan than elsewhere.

Comparison of ordinary profits with the companies' self assessment of their performance

From the 245 foreign companies' calculated profitability figures, 238
companies answered the performance question based on financial criteria (Q
48.1). We will make an attempt to compare the actual ordinary profits figures
with the companies' self-assessment of their performance based on financial
criteria.

The analysis indicates that 38 foreign companies showed a loss during the
calendar/fiscal year 1990; among these companies, nine classified themselves as

failures and 20 as "As expected," which is quite understandable since these companies were expecting to incur losses. However, nine foreign companies--despite their losses--classified themselves as successful based on financial criteria. The reasons, we believe are several. For example, due to the transfer pricing policy (headquarters policy of charging higher prices), the losses are far lower than were expected, particularly since the losses for seven out of nine companies are less than 5% of sales (see Appendix B3.2).

On the other hand, four companies that have a positive profitability classified themselves as failures. We again think that the reasons are that the actual profitability (despite being positive) happens to be lower than expected. This and the reason just mentioned were confirmed by the companies when we contacted them by telephone.

One conclusion that can be drawn is that if a strict actual profitability criterion had been used then the number of "failures" would have been a bit higher than the 25 companies that are classified as failures by this research methodology, since 9 companies that had losses in the "Successful" group and 20 in the "As expected" group would then have fallen into the "Failure" group. However, despite this drawback, a majority of the foreign companies in this study were "Successful" or "Very successful," after a thorough screening of the more than 300 companies that provided figures on dividend payments, accumulated profits or losses, and ordinary profits as well as annual reports and telephone conversations.

Ordinary profits and sales and nationality

The analyses regarding profitability shows that out of 38 foreign companies making losses, 24 (63%) are European, in particular from the United Kingdom, France, and Germany. Foreign companies showing very high profitability, over 10%, are more often from the United States (see Appendix B3.2).

Profitability and type of ownership

The analysis shows that 58% of the companies taking losses are 100% owned and that the majority of these companies are European (48%; see Appendix B3.3). A preliminary conclusion can be drawn that the American companies have a higher profitability ratio compared to the Europeans. All types of ownership groups (whether 100% owned or joint ventures) are profitable.

Profitability in various line of business

Industry-wise analyses do not show any significant tendencies except that 80% of the companies that had losses are manufacturers. Thirteen out of 32 companies in this category have production facilities in Japan, and 7 of these are American. The ownership structure of 13 is either 100% owned or joint venture with 50 % or more foreign equity.

One hundred and six manufacturing companies (43%) have profitability within the 10% range. In the manufacturing sector, some companies in pharmaceuticals, chemicals, machinery, and electronics have a rather high profitability of over 10%. In the non-manufacturing sector, we find similar high profitability levels for wholesale and retail trade, banks and credit institutions, and securities (see Appendix B3.4).

Profitability and year of establishment

The analysis shows that a large number of loss-making companies were established quite a long time ago in Japan, prior to 1971 (35%), or had established themselves in Japan recently, after 1985 (30%). Another weak conclusion that can be drawn is that the majority of the high-profit-making companies established themselves in Japan prior to 1981 and after 1971.

Profitability and size of companies

A large number of loss-making companies have less than 51 employees (58%), and out of these, 57% are European. The general tendency is that American companies are a bit larger in size and make slightly higher profits than European companies in Japan.

Accumulated profits and distribution of dividends

A large number of successful foreign companies have accumulated profits (86%), whereas in the "As expected" and "Failure" groups the number of companies showing accumulated losses is higher, at 64% and 76%, respectively (see Appendix B3.5).

Moreover, in the successful group, 62% of the companies have distributed dividends to their shareholders; however, in the "As expected" and "Failure" groups a majority of the companies (84% and 82%, respectively) have not made any dividend distribution (see Appendix B3.6).

3.4 FUTURE PLANS OF FOREIGN COMPANIES IN JAPAN

In overwhelming numbers (83%) the foreign companies' future plans are to expand their activities in Japan (Appendix A, Q 51, alt. 1, and Appendix B3.7). Over 68% of the failures indicated having expansion plans in Japan. Alternative 4 is given secondmost importance. In this group, foreign companies plan either to diversify or to start new businesses by themselves. This indicates that foreign companies have plans to change their ownership structure or form of presence in Japan. Thirteen percent of the companies expect to maintain the same levels (Q 51, alt. 2; more emphasis placed by non-manufacturers).

One group of firms also plans to start new businesses by forming alliances with Japanese companies (Q 51, alt. 5). Exceptionally few companies mentioned that they have plans for decreasing their activities in Japan (less than 2%). We carried out a large number of telephone conversations with the participating companies during 1992; these and our case studies indicate that foreign companies had not changed their minds regarding their investment plans despite the prevailing recession in Japan. This again gives a strong indication that Japan is an important market for foreign companies, one that cannot be neglected and is at the same time profitable, despite the recession.

3.5 CONCLUSIONS

Some important findings of this chapter regarding successful foreign companies in Japan are:

- 72% of the companies classified themselves as successful or very success-ful in Japan based on financial criteria.
- 70% of the successful companies were established in Japan before 1981, and 13% of the successful companies established themselves in Japan after 1985.
- 53% of the successful companies are 100% owned foreign subsidiaries.
- The majority (82%) of the large companies (those with over 500 employ-ees) are successful.
- American companies are a bit larger in size and make slightly higher profits than European companies.

It is interesting to observe that over half of the companies that started their activities in Japan after 1985 classified themselves as successful or even very successful. Within this success group, 50% of the companies are in the manufac-turing sector, and the other 50% are in the service sectors.

Our findings regarding foreign company failures in Japan include the following:

- Only 6% of the companies classified themselves as failures based on financial criteria.
- 56% of these companies are 100% foreign owned.
- There is only one failure with less than 50% foreign capital in a joint venture.
- About 52% of the failed companies have less than 51 employees.
- 56% of the failures were established after 1970, and 36% were established after 1985.
- 88% of the failures are in the manufacturing sector (mainly in metals, chemicals, machinery, and electronics).

Finally, a majority of foreign companies in this study are successful or very successful and are making profits in Japan. We believe, then, that it is an unfounded myth that the Japanese market is unprofitable.

In the following chapters we look in depth at foreign companies' strategies in terms of investments, management, entry channels, personnel, marketing, production, and R & D. We will list their key success factors in the Japanese market.

NOTES

1. See, for example, Khan, S., 1978, pp. 140-160, and Khan, S., 1988, pp. 206-218.
2. We are using "fiscal" and "calendar" year interchangeably in this book, since most of the foreign companies in Japan are either using a "calendar" year or the Japanese "fiscal year". MOF permits companies to choose either of the two alternatives. We are assuming in our book that using "calendar" or "fiscal" year interchangeably will not effect the result of this study.
3. See, for example, Kotler, P., et al., 1985.
4. See MITI, 1993d. (Note: the MITI study also covered over 8,500 Japanese companies in Japan, with a response rate of 78.5%.)
5. See: MITI, 1993c (note: the MITI survey covered about 3,400 Japanese companies with affiliates abroad in FY 1990 and FY 1991); JETRO, 1993b; Sakurai, K., 1992, pp. 32-34.

4 INVESTMENT AND MANAGEMENT STRATEGIES

In this chapter we will focus mainly on foreign companies' rationales for doing business in Japan, the type of entry channels used, the type of management style used and management responsibility in a joint venture, the extent of control exercised by headquarters in the affairs of the Japanese subsidiary, the particular responsibility given to the subsidiary outside of Japan, the relationship between headquarters and the subsidiary, and how foreign companies obtain capital in Japan. All of these factors shed light on foreign companies' business, investment, and management strategies in Japan.

4.1 PURPOSES OF DOING BUSINESS IN JAPAN

Foreign companies--in particular during the last decade, as they began to realize the economic power of Japan--started to emphasize vigorously the importance of the Japanese market. Thus foreign companies began to view Japan as one of the top three markets in their global strategies (along with the United States and European markets). Moreover, in the banking and financial sector, foreign companies were considered successful and global only if they had established themselves in Japan (Tokyo or Osaka), London, and New York. Succeeding in the Japanese market required a long-term commitment to Japan.

In our study, most of the foreign companies in Japan mentioned that they were attracted by the size and growth of the Japanese market (reported by 50% of the companies with 100% foreign capital), the importance of Japan in global business (reported by 60% of the companies with 100% foreign capital), and the need to establish a base in Asia (see App. A, Q 1, and alternatives [alt.] 1, 7, and 11 in Figure 4.1.).

Figure 4.1 Purpose of doing business in Japan

n = 422   *(Q 1: multiple answers)*

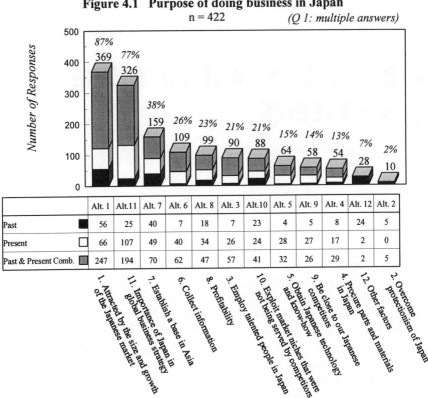

		Alt. 1	Alt.11	Alt. 7	Alt. 6	Alt. 8	Alt. 3	Alt.10	Alt. 5	Alt. 9	Alt. 4	Alt. 12	Alt. 2
Past	■	56	25	40	7	18	7	23	4	5	8	24	5
Present	□	66	107	49	40	34	26	24	28	27	17	2	0
Past & Present Comb.	▨	247	194	70	62	47	57	41	32	26	29	2	5

1. Attracted by the size and growth of the Japanese market
11. Importance of Japan in global business strategy
7. Establish a base in Asia
6. Collect information
8. Profitability
3. Employ talented people in Japan
10. Exploit market niches that were not being served by competitors
5. Obtain market niches and know-how
9. Be close to our Japanese competitors
4. Procure parts and materials
12. Other factors
2. Overcome protectionism of Japan

It is of interest to note that whereas the large number of foreign companies that established their businesses in Japan prior to 1981 (in particular from the United States) were attracted by the size and growth of the Japanese market, those companies (particularly US ones) that established their business after 1980 were more likely to be attracted also by the importance of Japan in global business. This is mainly due to the fact that during the last decade Japan has become an economic superpower (including the leading high-tech nation) and more active in global business.

Another important attraction for foreign companies is that they view Japan as a production and export base for Asian markets located close to Japan (in East and Southeast Asia). In other words, several foreign companies established themselves in Japan in order to secure a base for doing business in Asia. One rationale behind this strategy is the strong economic role played by Japan in this region in terms of FDI, foreign trade, capital, technology, and official development assistance (ODA).

As mentioned earlier, Japan comprises over 80% of Asia's GNP and expects to hold this position for many years to come.[1] This strategic fact cannot be ignored by foreign companies; thus any strategy for Asia must be based on a strategy for Japan.[2]

We find that it is more often American companies (and to some extent German companies) that gave more importance to doing business in Japan in order to establish a base in Asia (Q 1, alt. 7). This holds true particularly for companies in the chemical and financial sector. One reason could be that US companies see Japan as a gateway to other Asian countries, whereas European companies are already comparatively more established in Asian countries, and thus give slightly less importance to this factor. On the other hand, the rapid recent appreciation of the yen may cause foreign companies to alter this strategy and concentrate all their efforts in the Japanese market.

Regarding expectation of high profitability (Q 1, alt. 8), the service sectors (banks, financial institutions, etc.) gave a higher rating than the manufacturing sector. The same holds true for alternative 10 (exploiting market niches).

Regarding Q 1, alternative 9 (being close to Japanese competitors) we find that this factor is given more importance presently than in the past, in particular by European companies. The major branches that gave high importance to this factor were the chemical, machinery, and financial sectors. One reason for this could be that more and more companies (especially European) that initially neglected the competition from Japan have started to realize the importance of being close to their competitors in Japan, of competing on the home turf of their Japanese rivals.

Secondary reasons for doing business in Japan included: to collect information in Japan, to employ talented people in Japan, and to obtain Japanese technology and know-how. It is of interest to note that only 2% of the respondents mentioned that their purpose for doing business in Japan was to overcome protectionism in Japan (Q 1, alt. 2, in the past). This indicates that overcoming protectionism in Japan is not an important issue taken into consideration by foreign companies when entering the Japanese market. Therefore, we question the arguments presented in the mass media that the Japanese market is closed to foreign companies.

We carried out various types of cross-tabulations, such as nationality/region, year of establishment, and branches to find out whether differences existed regarding purposes for doing business in Japan. However, no significant conclusions could be drawn other than the ones already mentioned.

4.2 INVESTMENT STRATEGIES

Entry channels

It is well established through research that the types of distribution and sales channels used in Japan play a significant role in the success or failure of foreign companies in Japan. The main entry channels used in Japan by foreign companies (Q 2; see Figure 4.2) are establishing a joint venture for marketing and sales purposes, establishing the company's own branch office (more emphasis given by the service sectors), using a Japanese agent or distributor, establishing a joint venture for production purposes, and establishing a wholly owned sales subsidiary. Exceptionally few foreign companies had been able to acquire a Japanese company (Q 1, alt. 6).

A large number of companies entered Japan by establishing a joint venture with a Japanese company and gradually shifted their equity participation to 100%, one of the main reasons being that in the past, it had been difficult to establish a 100% foreign-owned subsidiary. Moreover, companies that entered Japan in the past through a Japanese agent or distributor or by giving licenses shifted later either to a joint venture or to being a 100% owned subsidiary.

Figure 4.2 Market entry channels used in Japan

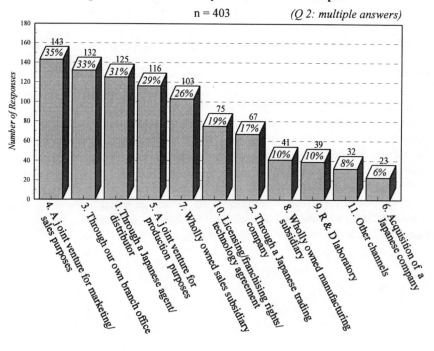

n = 403   *(Q 2: multiple answers)*

At present, a large number of companies with production and/or R & D in Japan are establishing themselves via joint ventures with a Japanese partner, for example, Yokogawa, with 25% equity, and Hewlett-Packard from the United States, with 75% equity, and Toshiba, with 40% equity, and L M Ericsson from Sweden , with 60% equity. In the case of production and R & D in Japan, about 38% of the companies are 100% foreign owned. The advantages and disadvantages of forming joint ventures and becoming a 100% owned foreign subsidiary are already well known, and have been mentioned in Chapter 1.

Change in ownership form from the initial entry stage to the present

When we analyze the entry channel data for the channels presently used by the foreign companies (see Table 4.1 and App. A, Q 2; ownership structure is 47% joint ventures and 53% wholly owned subsidiaries), we find the termination ratio being the highest when using a Japanese agent (46%) or a Japanese trading company (52%). A large number of companies shifted after a certain period of time from using an agent or trading company to establishing their own representative office, joint venture, or a 100% owned subsidiary.

Table 4.1 Foreign companies' initial entry channels and ongoing channels

(Q 2)

Type of channels*	Earliest starting year	Entry channels (Number of companies) A	Channels terminated B	Ratio B/A, %	On-going channels C	Ratio C/A %
Japanese agent/distributor	1870	125	58	46	67	54
Japanese trading company	1906	67	35	52	32	48
Own branch office	1859	132	38	29	94	71
Joint venture for marketing/ sales purposes	1923	143	34	24	109	76
Joint venture for production purposes	1923	116	23	20	93	80
Acquisition of a Japanese company	1952	23	6	26	17	74
Wholly owned sales subsidiary	1906	103	19	18	84	82
Wholly owned manufacturing subsidiary	1966	41	4	10	37	90
R & D laboratory	1929	39	4	10	35	90
Licensing/franchising rights/ technology agreement	1950	75	18	24	57	76

* Regarding other channels (alternative 11), 32 companies either provided an explanation of their rationale for choosing or terminating various channels, or gave some other explanation.

Use of multiple channels

It is quite clear that as the Japanese market has started to open in the 1980s, the trend has been a shift from using Japanese middlemen to establishing joint ventures and 100% owned subsidiaries. However, the use of multiple channels in Japan is quite common (see Table 4.2). Several companies are presently using two or more channels. Foreign companies that have established joint ventures or are 100% owned subsidiaries have at the same time a licensing agreement, an agent, trading company, or another type of channel. In an exceptional case, one company is presently using nine different types of channels.

A large number of foreign companies--mainly in the manufacturing sector--use multiple channels due to specific types of products and/or special buyers. Examples are Ciba-Geigy from Switzerland and Astra from Sweden.

Some buyers or final users want to deal only through Japanese middlemen. Moreover, several of the products are technically sophisticated and foreign companies have to deal directly with the Japanese buyer (including providing pre- and post-sales services), but payments (commercial transactions), for example, are in many cases made through a Japanese agent, Sogo Shosha (trading company), or some other type of middleman. This is one obvious reason for high cost of doing business in Japan.

Thus it is important (where required) to have one or more channels into the Japanese market, and at the same time this factor complicates selling in the Japanese market. Foreign companies have to spend considerable amounts of time in developing a coherent and concise entry strategy for the Japanese market.

Other important reasons for having multiple channels in Japan are the high native level of product quality (nearly zero defect rates), the need for product modification to meet Japanese customer requirements, and high local service levels. In order to meet the stringent demands of Japanese customers, a foreign company is required, for example, to have a marketing and sales group, a manufacturing subsidiary, and an R & D laboratory in Japan. This kind of investment by foreign companies enhances the credibility and commitment to the Japanese market in the eyes of local customers and local personnel.

In many cases in this study, foreign companies decided on a joint venture because the Japanese partner could provide easy market access, including a distribution network, personnel, and facilities. This alternative requires less financial commitment, but at the risk of losing one's technology or control of the venture, not having direct access to customers, and lacking loyalty from the transferred staff of the Japanese joint venture partner. On the other hand, the manufacturing facility of the Japanese partner can make it easier for the foreign partner to meet Japanese customer requirements.

Table 4.2 Number of entry channels used by foreign companies in Japan

Entry Channels (Q 2)

Number of channels	n=	Alt. 1		Alt. 2		Alt. 3		Alt. 4		Alt. 5		Alt. 6		Alt. 7		Alt. 8		Alt. 9		Alt. 10	
		G	T	G	T	G	T	G	T	G	T	G	T	G	T	G	T	G	T	G	T
1 Entry channel	142	7	4 Total 11	1	3 Total 4	42	14 Total 56	21	6 Total 27	22	3 Total 25	3	Total 3	17	2 Total 19				Total 1	2	2 Total 4
2 Entry channels	115	22	18 Total 40	6	12 Total 18	19	11 Total 30	37	11 Total 48	35	7 Total 42	3	Total 3	25	5 Total 30	9	Total 9	1	1 Total 2	17	7 Total 24
3 Entry channels	54	20	14 Total 34	10	6 Total 16	10	3 Total 13	22	9 Total 31	12	4 Total 16	4	3 Total 7	18	5 Total 23	5	1 Total 6	4	Total 4	12	3 Total 15
4 Entry channels	26	4	9 Total 13	6	8 Total 14	8	4 Total 12	10	4 Total 14	9	6 Total 15	1	Total 1	9	3 Total 12	9	2 Total 11	10	1 Total 11	11	2 Total 13
5 Entry channels	24	11	9 Total 20	6	4 Total 10	10	4 Total 14	13	2 Total 15	10	2 Total 12	4	Total 4	9	2 Total 11	7	Total 7	14	1 Total 15	10	2 Total 12
6 Entry channels	6	2	2 Total 4	1	1 Total 2	2	2 Total 4	2	2 Total 4	2	1 Total 3	1	2 Total 3	3	2 Total 5	3	1 Total 4	2	2 Total 4	3	2 Total 5
7 Entry channels	2			1	1 Total 2	1	Total 1	2	Total 2	1	Total 1			2	Total 2	2	Total 2	2	Total 2	1	Total 1
8 Entry channels	1	1	Total 1	1	Total 1	1	Total 1	1	Total 1	1	Total 1	1	Total 1			1	Total 1	1	Total 1		
9 Entry channels	1	1	Total 1	1	Total 1	1	Total 1	1	Total 1	1	Total 1	1	Total 1	1	Total 1	1	Total 1	1	Total 1		

Legend   G = On-going;   T = Terminated;   n = Number of companies;   Alt. = Alternative.

(continued)

Table 4.2 (continued)

Alt. 1 = Through a Japanese agent/distributor   Alt. 2 = Through a Japanese trading company
Alt. 3 = Through our own branch office   Alt. 4 = A joint venture for marketing/sales
                                                              purposes
Alt. 5 = A joint venture for production   Alt. 6 = Acquisition of a Japanese company
           purposes
Alt. 7 = Wholly owned sales subsidiary   Alt. 8 = Wholly owned manufacturing
                                                              subsidiary
Alt. 9 = R & D laboratory   Alt. 10 = Licensing/franchising rights/
                                                              technology agreement

In this study, there are many foreign companies of large size (their parent companies are MNCs or TNCs) that are financially strong. These have usually opted for a 100% owned subsidiary. Examples are Nihon Tetra Pak (the largest packaging company for liquid food in Japan) and Sandvik from Sweden (the third largest company in the carbide tools market in Japan), and Applied Materials from the United States (a market leader in semiconductor manufacturing equipment).

In some cases, such companies have initially staffed the subsidiary with management and technical staff from their headquarters. This alternative may require very high risks overall, and it may take considerable time before well-qualified Japanese personnel can be recruited and proper market access built. The main advantages of 100% owned subsidiaries for these companies are direct contact with customers and total control of marketing, production, loyalty of staff in Japan, product image, and corporate image (CI).

Table 4.3 shows that foreign companies that have joint ventures with less than a 50% equity have joint ventures either for marketing and sales or for production purposes. Similar observations are made for the 50%/50% joint venture. In the case of the joint venture with over 50% foreign equity, we find that many foreign companies had over time, terminated their contracts with their Japanese agent or trading company and increased their equity in the joint venture. In the case of 100% foreign-owned companies, we find that the termination ratio regarding Japanese agents and trading companies is the highest. Moreover, a large number of foreign companies also terminated their joint ventures in marketing and sales or converted branch offices into wholly owned sales and production subsidiaries.

American companies have more often used a Japanese agent or branch office, a joint venture (Q 2, alts. 4 and 5), or a 100% owned subsidiary for entering the Japanese market (see Appendix B4.1). European companies show similar tendencies, with slightly higher importance given to establishing 100% owned subsidiaries and less importance given to establishing joint ventures for production purposes. According to the ratios, it appears that Swiss and Swedish companies are more inclined toward establishing 100% owned subsidiaries and also to making licensing agreements. Branch offices are more common in the

Table 4.3 Cross-tabulation between ownership and entry channels

Ownership	n=	Alt. 1 G	T	Total	Alt. 2 G	T	Total	Alt. 3 G	T	Total	Alt. 4 G	T	Total	Alt. 5 G	T	Total	Alt. 6 G	T	Total	Alt. 7 G	T	Total	Alt. 8 G	T	Total	Alt. 9 G	T	Total	Alt. 10 G	T	Total	Responses received
< 50 %	53	6	3	9	8	2	10	3	2	5	18	4	22	15	5	20	2		2	1	1	2	1		1	1	1	2	10	5	15	46
50 %	88	14	5	19	7	7	14	5	4	9	36	4	40	45	5	50				4		4	1		1	3	1	4	16	6	22	80
>50% – <100%	66	9	13	22	4	6	10	6	3	9	34	4	38	17	5	22	6	1	7	6	3	9	2	3	5	6		6	10	2	12	61
100%	229	38	37	75	13	20	33	80	29	109	21	22	43	16	8	24	9	5	14	73	15	88	33	1	34	25	2	27	22	4	26	216
Total	436			125			67			132			143			116			23			103			41			39			75	403

Legend   G = On-going;   T = Terminated;
Alt. = Alternative.

Alt. 1 = Through a Japanese agent/distributor
Alt. 2 = Through a Japanese trading company
Alt. 3 = Through our own branch office
Alt. 4 = A joint venture for marketing/sales purposes
Alt. 5 = A joint venture for production purposes

Alt. 6 = Acquisition of a Japanese company
Alt. 7 = Wholly owned sales subsidiary
Alt. 8 = Wholly owned manufacturing subsidiary
Alt. 9 = R & D laboratory
Alt. 10 = Licensing/franchising rights/technology agreement

n = Actual number of participating companies with respect to ownership.

financial sector; Japan has a large number of banks from the United States, Germany, the United Kingdom, and Switzerland.

Another observation that can be made regards the very high profitability rates shown by some of the 100% owned subsidiaries (over 20%, before taxes). On the other hand, we also find that several companies show losses in their 100% owned subsidiaries. It is quite obvious that a 100% owned subsidiary requires considerable investment, and it may provide high return or it may not; the situation is one of high risk with high return. No other major observations can be made from this study regarding entry channels and profitability.

Table 4.4 confirms our earlier observation that prior to 1971, licensing and the use of a Japanese agent or trading company was quite common. During the period 1971 to 1980, several foreign companies terminated their contracts with Japanese agents or trading companies and established either joint ventures or wholly owned subsidiaries.

Similar tendencies were seen during the period 1981 to 1985. The main reason has been the liberalization of the Japanese market (for FDI to Japan) from 1973 onward. After 1973, 100% owned foreign subsidiaries in most of the business sectors began to be permitted, causing a rapid increase in FDI to Japan. From 1986 onward we find a sharp increase in the termination of relationships with agents, trading companies, and branch offices by foreign companies in Japan. At the same time, we also find a large number of companies terminating either their joint ventures or wholly owned subsidiaries.

The reasons for this behavior by foreign companies have been many. In some cases, companies realized that their decision to form a 100% owned subsidiary or a joint venture was too hasty and that this was not a suitable form for the Japanese market. Moreover, many companies had entered Japan through a joint venture although in the meantime the corporate eye remained focused on forming a 100% owned subsidiary.

In terms of entry channel and termination, we find that the lowest termination ratio is for companies that have formed either a wholly owned manufacturing subsidiary (Q 2, alt. 8) or an R & D laboratory (joint venture or 100% foreign owned; alt. 9). One reason for the low ratio are that these types of channels are established only when a foreign company has obtained a considerable amount of experience in the Japanese market. Also, since an enormous amount of time and investment is also involved, foreign companies are unlikely to make a hasty decision when establishing these two channels.

Branch analysis (see Appendix B4.2) reveals that foreign companies in the chemical, pharmaceutical, machinery, and electronic sectors have used the largest numbers of entry channels, in particular, agents (alt. 1), joint ventures (alts. 4 and 5), and wholly owned sales subsidiaries (alt. 7). Moreover, the ratios show that the number of R & D laboratories (alt. 9) and licensing agreements (alt. 10) is highest in the chemical and pharmaceutical sectors, mainly due to the fact that foreign companies still have an edge over Japanese manufacturers, who

Table 4.4 Cross-tabulation between year of establishment and entry channels

Year of establishment	Alt. 1			Alt. 2			Alt. 3			Alt. 4			Alt. 5			Alt. 6			Alt. 7			Alt. 8			Alt. 9			Alt. 10		
	S	T	G	S	T	G	S	T	G	S	T	G	S	T	G	S	T	G	S	T	G	S	T	G	S	T	G	S	T	G
<1971	56	13	43	31	7	24	43	8	35	28	1	27	31	5	26	6	1	5	20	1	19	2	1	1	5		5	25	1	24
1971–1980	24	15	9	9	9		26	5	21	35	8	27	37	5	32		2	-2	35	3	32	15			7	1	6	17	4	13
1981–1985	13	12	1	9	4	5	22	9	13	17	9	8	10	4	6	3	1	2	14	5	9	10			9		9	11	4	7
>1985	11	15	-4	8	15	-7	19	13	6	46	15	31	27	9	18	6	2	4	17	9	8	8	3	5	13	2	11	11	8	3
19XX	21	3	18	10		10	22	3	19	17	1	16	11		11	8		8	17	1	16	6		6	5	1	4	11	1	10
Total	125	58	67	67	35	32	132	38	94	143	34	109	116	23	93	23	6	17	103	19	84	41	4	37	39	4	35	75	18	57

Legend

S = Entered Japan;   19XX = Year not available;   T = Terminated the channel;   G = on-going channel;

Alt. = Alternative.

Alt. 1 = Through a Japanese agent/distributor

Alt. 2 = Through a Japanese trading company

Alt. 3 = Through our own branch office

Alt. 4 = A joint venture for marketing/sales purposes

Alt. 5 = A joint venture for production purposes

Alt. 6 = Acquisition of a Japanese company

Alt. 7 = Wholly owned sales subsidiary

Alt. 8 = Wholly owned manufacturing subsidiary

Alt. 9 = R&D laboratory

Alt. 10 = Licensing/franchising rights/technology agreement

Note: - sign indicates that there has been minor non-response regarding some entry channels.
Most probably the answers are included in 19XX (year not specified).

are traditionally weak in these sectors. In the non-manufacturing sector, we find that in the financial sector most of the companies entered Japan by establishing their own branch offices (alt. 3).

The results of the cross-tabulations between branches and entry channels are presented in Table 4.5. Regarding use of a Japanese agent (alt. 1), we find the highest termination ratio in the pharmaceutical and machinery sectors. A slightly high termination ratio is also found in the chemical and electronic sectors.

Concerning the channel of using a Japanese trading company, we find the highest termination ratio in the machinery and electronics sectors. The chemical sector also shows a high termination ratio. Moreover, we find a high termination ratio for pharmaceutical companies using a branch office (alt. 3) and acquiring a Japanese company (alt. 6). One of the reasons given for terminating this channel was that the acquisition of a Japanese company was not profitable.

We also find a higher termination ratio for pharmaceutical companies having 100% owned manufacturing subsidiaries (alt. 8) and for companies in the metal sector using licensing agreements (alt. 10). Regarding pharmaceutical companies' terminations, the reasons given were difficulties in obtaining qualified labor, land, and so on. These companies opted for other channels, such as joint ventures. No other significant conclusions can be drawn.

Regarding failures, we find that the termination ratio is slightly higher for the two channels: the Japanese trading company (alt. 2) and joint ventures for marketing purposes (alt. 4). No other significant conclusions can be drawn for the failures regarding their use of entry channels.

The main conclusions that can be drawn regarding investment strategies are as follows: Foreign companies generally entered Japan (especially prior to 1975) by building up their presence step-by-step. The first step was usually to enter Japan through an intermediary (an agent, a trading company, or a licensing agreement), which carries low risks and at the same time offers no control over the operation or direct contact with the market (see Figures 4.3 and 4.4). The second stage was to form a marketing and sales joint venture (especially prior to 1973), a joint venture for manufacturing, a joint R & D laboratory, or a 100% owned subsidiary. The data show that it was only after a certain number of years that companies took these steps, since the risks were considerably higher, even though the rewards and control of the operations were also higher. Some companies at this stage had also acquired a Japanese company for sales or manufacturing purposes.

Moreover, as we mentioned earlier, a large number of companies retained their previous channel even as they moved from one step to another. However, after 1980 we find a large number of foreign companies shifting at a higher pace from one channel to another, depending on the type of product or service. Some companies have an agent, a joint venture, and also a 100% owned subsidiary, depending on their strategic reasons for being in the Japanese market.

Table 4.5 Entry channels based on branches

Branch	Entry channels (Q 2; multiple answers)														
	Alt. 1			Alt. 2			Alt. 3			Alt. 4			Alt. 5		
	S	T	G	S	T	G	S	T	G	S	T	G	S	T	G
Food	5	2	3	4	2	2	4	1	3(1)	5	1	4(1)	4	1	3
Textiles	3	1	2	1	1					3	1	2			
Chemicals	28	13(2)	15	17	7(1)	10	14	3	11(1)	25	4(1)	21(1)	38	8	30(2)
Pharmaceuticals	10	9	1				7	4	3	12	3	9	7	2	5
Metals	4		4	3	2(1)	1	4	2(1)	2(1)	6		6(1)	6	1	5(1)
Machinery	18	10	8(1)	18	13(2)	5	18	6	12	20	7	13(1)	23	6	17(2)
Electronics	21	9(1)	12(3)	8	5(2)	3(1)	9	2	7	18	5(2)	13(1)	16	2(1)	14(1)
Car & car parts	3	2(1)	1	1	1					4	3(1)	1	5	2	3
Other manufactures	11	4	7	5	2	3	4	1	3	12	1	11	12		12
Wholesale and retail trade	8	3	5	5	1	4(1)	7	3	4	17	6	11(2)	1		1
Banks & credit institutes	1		1(1)				26	5	21	3	1	2(1)	1		1
Securities	1	1					12	4	8						
Insurance	4		4				10	2	8	3		3			

(continued)

Table 4.5 (continued)

Branch	Entry channels (Q 2; multiple answers)														
	Alt. 1			Alt. 2			Alt. 3			Alt. 4			Alt. 5		
	S	T	G	S	T	G	S	T	G	S	T	G	S	T	G
Other services	8	4	4	5	1	4	17	5	12	15	2	13	2		2
Total	125(9)	58(4)	67(5)	67(8)	35(6)	32(2)	132(4)	38(1)	94(3)	143(12)	34(4)	109(8)	116(7)	23(1)	93(6)

Legend: S = Entered Japan; T = Terminated the channel; G = ongoing channel; Failure = (between brackets); Alt. = Alternative;
Alt. 1 = Through a Japanese agent/distributor; Alt. 2 = Through a Japanese trading company; Alt. 3 = Through our own branch office;
Alt. 4 = A joint venture for marketing/sales purposes; Alt. 5 = A joint venture for production purposes.

Table 4.5 (continued)

Branch	Entry channels (Q 2; multiple answers)														
	Alt. 6			Alt. 7			Alt. 8			Alt. 9			Alt. 10		
	S	T	G	S	T	G	S	T	G	S	T	G	S	T	G
Food	1		1	3	1	2				1	1		4	2	2
Textiles	1		1	1	1								1		
Chemicals	4	1	3	22	6	16(4)	9		9(1)	19	2	17(1)	21	5	16
Pharmaceuticals	4	2	2	7	2	5	6	2	4	6	1	5	7	2	5
Metals				3	1	2	3		3(1)	3		3(1)	6	3(1)	3
Machinery	4	1	3(2)	29	4	25(1)	10	1	9	3		3(1)	11	1	10(1)

Table 4.5 (continued)

Branch	Entry channels (Q 2; multiple answers)														
	Alt. 6			Alt. 7			Alt. 8			Alt. 9			Alt. 10		
	S	T	G	S	T	G	S	T	G	S	T	G	S	T	G
Electronics	3	1	2	15	1	14(2)	6	1	6	6		5	10	2	8
Car & car parts	1	1		4	1	3(1)	1		1	1		1	1		1
Other manufactures	3		3(1)	3	1	2	4		4	4		4	4	1	3
Wholesale and retail trade	1		1	11	1	10	1		1				4	1	3(1)
Banks & credit institutes							1			1		1	1		1
Securities															
Insurance															1
Other services	1		1	5		5				4		4	4	1	3
Total	23(3)	6	17(3)	103(8)	19	84(8)	41(2)	4	37(2)	39(2)	4	35(2)	75(3)	18(1)	57(2)

Legend: S = Entered Japan; T = Terminated the channel; G = ongoing channel; Failure = (between brackets); Alt. = Alternative; Alt. 6 = Acquisition of a Japanese company; Alt. 7 = Wholly owned sales subsidiary; Alt. 8 = Wholly owned manufacturing subsidiary; Alt. 9 = R & D laboratory; Alt. 10 = Licensing/franchising rights/technology agreement.

**Figure 4.3   Common long-term entry channels used by
foreign companies in Japan**

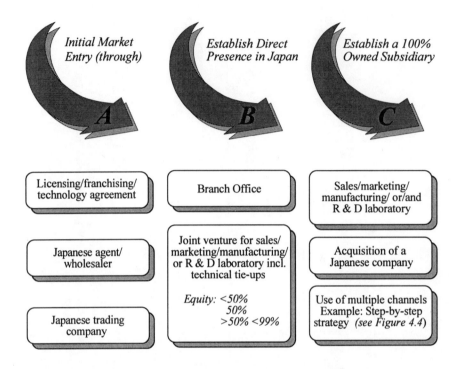

A number of foreign companies that wanted to establish a 100% owned subsidiary in Japan or acquire a Japanese company were not able to do so for a number of reasons, such as exorbitant costs, difficulties in recruiting suitable and well-qualified Japanese personnel, and the lack of a suitable location. These companies eventually settled for the joint venture alternative instead of for the 100% foreign owned subsidiary. However, for these companies, the joint venture with a well-established Japanese company was a short-term strategy tool used mainly to penetrate the market initially.

4.3 MANAGEMENT STRATEGIES

Type of management style

The type of decision making depends on factors such as the type of organization and the size of the company. For example, the greater the distance

Figure 4.4   Way of entering Japan through a step-by-step strategy

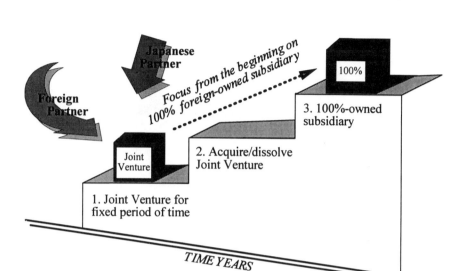

between the headquarters and its subsidiary (and the greater disparity in time zones), the more autonomous or decentralized the subsidiary will be from the headquarters. One of the reasons for an increased delegation of responsibilities in international operations is that communication becomes less frequent as the distance increases despite the availability of modern and efficient communication means.

In Chapter 1, we described in detail the contrast between Western and Japanese management styles.[3] The majority of foreign companies (see App. A, Q 3, 59%; and Figure 4.5), in particular those in joint ventures, use Japanese-style management, whereas wholly owned foreign subsidiaries employ a mixture of Western- and Japanese-style management (see Figure 4.6).

Among wholly owned subsidiaries and joint ventures with over 50% foreign equity, the ratios show that they more often use Western-style management than joint ventures with 50% or less equity. Moreover, generally it is the European companies that use Western management style, according to the ratios, more than US companies (see Appendix B4.3). One of the reasons is that the European companies in this study have a higher number of 100% owned subsidiaries staffed with a large number of expatriates.

It appears that a large number of foreign companies in Japan have, to a great extent, adapted to the conditions prevailing in the Japanese market regarding

Figure 4.5   Type of management style used in Japan

(Q 3)

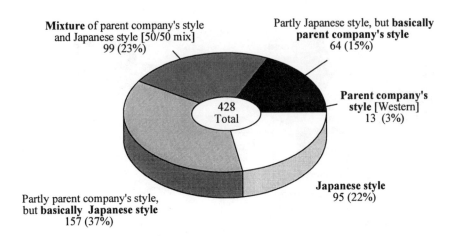

Number of Companies

management in order to compete effectively with their Japanese competitors. Many foreign companies have "Japanized" their company, shifting to a Japanese way of thinking and reliance on a mainly Japanese staff (for more details, consult Chapter 5). In many cases, top managers who are Japanese have authority to run the operation, decision making having been given to the local subsidiary. This way of operating the company removes the language and cultural obstacles that may be present in a company run by expatriates in Japan.

Moreover, our perception, which is confirmed through our extensive case studies, is that the company cultures in the subsidiary in Japan and in the headquarters outside Japan are quite different, leading to friction and conflict between the subsidiary and its headquarters (more details can be found in Chapter 8).

In many cases foreign companies have promoted Japanese managers to most of the high-ranking positions (this holds true especially for many US companies in Japan), and in some cases foreign companies in Japan have no expatriates at all (see Appendix B4.4). This is in contrast to Japanese companies operating outside Japan, which heavily staff the subsidiary with Japanese managers at practically all top managerial positions.[4]

No significant differences could be found between the "Successful," "As expected," and "Failed" companies' management style. It appears that failures show a slightly higher use of Western management style compared to successful companies (see Appendix B4.5).

Figure 4.6   Management style based on ownership

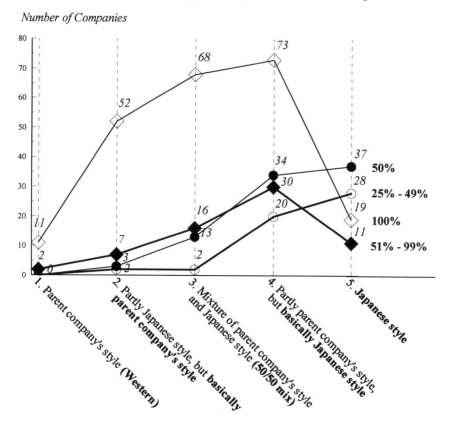

Number of Companies

Regarding the results of the cross-tabulation between management style and nationality of chief executive officers (CEOs), we find that in the "Successful" group it is US companies that have more Japanese CEOs and more often use Japanese management style, conforming to the local conditions prevailing in Japan. On the other hand, European companies have more expatriates and more often use Western management style (see Appendix B4.6). No other major conclusions can be drawn.

Extent of control exercised by the headquarters in the affairs of the Japanese subsidiary

A large number of foreign companies in Japan are decentralized. For over two-thirds of the companies (67%), parent companies provide overall corporate policies and strategy but leave concrete operations to the local subsidiary (see Figure 4.7, Q 4). The headquarters are generally involved in the financial matters of the local subsidiary, product development, and/or R & D activities. The parent companies appear to be mainly interested in formulating the overall strategies, policies, and financial matters; they exert result-oriented control based on the financial performance of their subsidiary in Japan. It seems that to a large extent foreign companies are managed with autonomy within limits.

If we compare the responses of US and European companies, we find very few differences, except that European companies are a bit more controlled by their headquarters, in particular regarding R & D.

We grouped companies' responses according to three performance groups. The results are more or less the same as in Figure 4.7; the companies in the "Successful" and "As expected" groups show similar tendencies, such as similar percentages of responses for most of the alternatives. In the case of failures we find that headquarters exercises a higher degree of control on practically all matters concerning the local subsidiary. However, this conclusion is not strong (see Appendix B4.7).

Regarding the ownership groups (25%<50%; 50%; >50%<100%; 100%), headquarters provide overall corporate policies and strategy to the local

Figure 4.7   Extent of control exercised by the headquarters

n = 423   *(Q 4: multiple answers)*

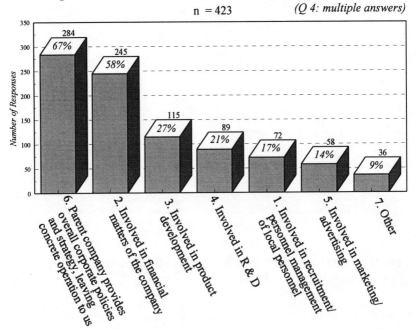

subsidiaries, particularly among the 100% owned subsidiaries (alt. 6). No other significant results can be mentioned (see Appendix B4.8).

Management responsibility in a joint venture

There are 207 foreign companies in this survey that have joint ventures in Japan, with various degrees of equity (see Appendix A); however, only 186 of these answered our question dealing with which partner has management responsibility in the joint venture (App. A, Q 5). Moreover, 26 companies that have a 100% owned subsidiary but either previously had a joint venture or presently have a joint venture (using multiple channels) have also answered this question.

Thirty six percent of the foreign companies mentioned that management responsibility is on a 50-50 basis, equally shared between the Japanese and foreign partner (see Figure 4.8). In 34% of the joint ventures, it is the Japanese partner who has the management responsibility, and in 22% of the cases, management responsibility is shared on the basis of equity contribution. In only 8% of cases is it the foreign partner who has management responsibility for a joint venture. We should note that about 32% of foreign companies have majority equity in joint ventures.

Figure 4.8 Management responsibility in a joint venture

(Q 5)

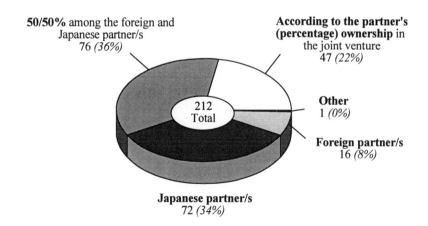

50/50% among the foreign and
Japanese partner/s
76 *(36%)*

**According to the partner's
(percentage) ownership** in
the joint venture
47 *(22%)*

212
Total

Other
1 *(0%)*

Foreign partner/s
16 *(8%)*

Japanese partner/s
72 *(34%)*

Number of Companies

Cross-tabulation between ownership and management shows that in cases where foreign equity is less than 50%, it is generally the Japanese partner who has the management responsibility (55%). Otherwise (in 24% of the cases), it is based on the equity contribution. In 18% of the cases, management responsibility is carried out on a 50-50 basis (see Appendix B4.9).

In a 50-50 joint venture, the management responsibility is divided either accordingly (for 61% of the cases), or on the basis of equity contribution (8%). It is interesting to note that in 30% of the cases it is the Japanese partner who has the overall management responsibility in a 50-50 joint venture.

In cases where the foreign partner has a majority equity we find that in 34% of the cases management responsibility is based on the degree of equity contribution, and in 22% of the cases it is the foreign partner that has management responsibility. However, in 16% of these cases, management responsibility is equally shared, and in 28% of the cases it is the Japanese partner that has the overall management responsibility despite its minority equity holding. No special comments can be made regarding the foreign companies that have a 100% owned subsidiary but previously had or still have a joint venture.

The conclusion that can be drawn in this section is that in a joint venture, the Japanese partner is more likely to have management responsibility for operations in Japan, regardless of the size of its equity contribution. This observation was also confirmed in our case studies.

Some foreign companies mentioned that as long as foreign equity in a joint venture is less than 66.7% (two-thirds), the Japanese partner will generally insist on keeping management control in its hands. This observation is also true for ventures outside Japan, where Japanese companies--in many cases with minority equity holding--will insist in joint venture negotiations on keeping, if possible, control of the overall management.

Special responsibility outside Japan

The headquarters of foreign companies in two-thirds of the cases do not give any special responsibilities to their subsidiaries outside Japan (see Figure 4.9). The size of the Japanese market and/or business activities in Japan are considered sufficient to bear the investment outlays. It can be argued that the size of the Japanese market is so large that most of the foreign companies have to concentrate all their efforts to succeed here.

However, the remaining 34% of the foreign companies have been given responsibilities outside Japan also by their headquarters. The reasons have been that some foreign companies' headquarters see Japan as a gateway to business in other Asian countries, in particular South Korea, People's Republic (P. R.) of China, and Southeast Asian countries, or that they view Japan as a production and exporting base for Asia. Most of the companies that chose alt. 5 (others, in Figure 4.9) referred to their responsibility toward South Korea, Taiwan, and/or P.R. of China.

Generally, foreign companies' Japanese subsidiaries that have been given responsibilities outside Japan are responsible either for East and Southeast Asia or for Asia (mainly East and Southeast) and the Pacific countries. This is true for US companies more than for European companies. Regarding European companies, those from the EFTA countries have the least responsibility outside of Japan. One of the reasons for these differences, as mentioned earlier, is that several European companies are already well established in most Asian countries compared to US companies, which are latecomers to Asia.

It appears that foreign companies in the non-manufacturing sector have been given slightly more responsibilities outside Japan than those in the manufacturing sector (39% compared to 36%). In the manufacturing sector, the companies in the producer goods sector have been given more responsibilities outside Japan (42% compared to 30%). Within the non-manufacturing sector, the financial sector has been given more responsibilities outside Japan (37% compared to 23%).

The reason for the financial sector's (banks, securities, etc.) greater responsibilities outside Japan seems to be that the Japanese financial sector is still restrictive toward foreign financial institutions, and thus foreign institutions

Figure 4.9   Responsibilities given outside Japan

(Q 6)

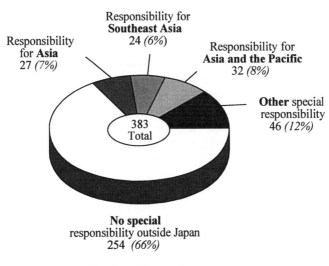

Number of Companies

in Japan can best increase their income by also intensifying their activities in other profitable markets of Asia (e.g., Hong Kong, Singapore, and Taiwan).

Regarding the type of ownership and the responsibilities given outside Japan, we find that fewer 100% owned foreign companies have been given responsibilities outside Japan (28% of the companies) compared to those in joint ventures (44% of those with less than 50% equity, 42% in 50-50 joint ventures, and 32% of those with over 50% equity). This result is contrary to our expectations; we expected the opposite outcome.

The results of the cross-tabulation between performance and Q 6 show that the companies in the "Successful" and "As expected" groups have been given higher responsibilities outside Japan (34%) than the "Failure" groups, which have been given lower responsibilities outside of Japan (29%).

4.4 RELATIONSHIP BETWEEN HEADQUARTERS AND SUBSIDIARY

It is known that foreign companies in Japan face difficulties in maintaining relationships with their headquarters. Foreign companies often have to struggle to communicate with top management at headquarters, who do not understand, for example, what is required to compete in Japan.

Regarding communication problems between the headquarters and subsidiary (Q 20), we find that a large number of companies face problems due to difficulties the headquarters have in understanding the Japanese market, the emphasis headquarters place on short-term profit goals, difficulties of the local staff in communicating directly with their headquarters, and, finally, a lack of desire on the part of headquarters to learn from the Japanese subsidiary's experience (see Figure 4.10). These results are somewhat similar to those of earlier studies carried out by other researchers.

Concerning other problems, some comments have referred to situations in which the subsidiary in Japan is used mainly as a source of headquarters' profits, leading to low morale in the subsidiary; situations in which as soon as sales drop in Japan or there happens to be low demand or a recession, headquarters insists that personnel in the Japanese subsidiary be reduced to maintain the sales and profits levels per employee; slow response from headquarters because most of the correspondence has to be translated into another language; slow response because the organization at headquarters is too large; and difficulty in explaining Japanese law and unwritten rules to headquarters.

A closer examination of the companies that reported problems due to difficulties in headquarters' understanding of the Japanese market or headquarters' over-emphasis on short-term profit goals shows that a large number of these companies are in the manufacturing sector (chemicals, pharmaceuticals, machinery, and electronics) and to a lesser extent in the service

Figure 4.10 Problems between headquarters and local subsidiaries

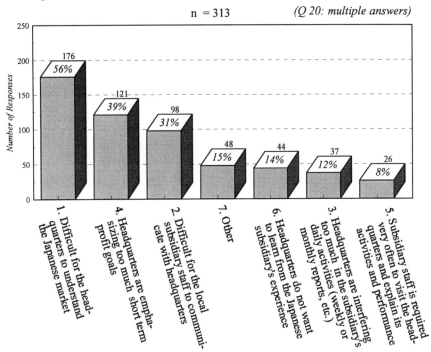

n = 313 *(Q 20: multiple answers)*

sectors (retail and wholesale trade, banking, and various other services). About 70% of the companies have a foreign capital share of over 50%. No special tendencies regarding the year of establishment can be found; however, in the manufacturing sector a large number of companies were established before 1971, whereas in the service sector the majority of the companies were established after 1980 or in some cases after 1985.

The conclusion that can be drawn in this section is that foreign companies in Japan are facing communication problems with their headquarters, but these problems do not necessarily affect the performance of the companies directly. However, they do affect the morale of the local and expatriate employees of the subsidiary. One reason for this problem, in our view, is a lack of knowledge at headquarters of the unique characteristics of Japan: its language, norms and customs, work ethics, and significant differences in business practices (for more details, consult Chapter 8).

4.5 FINANCING STRATEGY

Securing capital in Japan

It is generally considered very expensive to do business in Japan for reasons such as exorbitant land prices, high wages, the high cost of securing well-qualified Japanese staff, the appreciation of the yen, and difficulties in obtaining local financing.

In order to make the Japanese market more accessible to foreign companies, the Japanese government has recently introduced policies for improving the country's investment environment. One of the policy measures is to provide, through a governmental financial institution (the JDB, or Japan Development Bank), a low-interest system for providing loans exclusively for foreign companies with 50% or more foreign equity.

The main means for foreign companies in Japan to obtain capital (see Figure 4.11) are to borrow from Japanese banks, to obtain it from the parent company, to use its own internal financing system, and to borrow from foreign banks in Japan. Only 10% of the companies borrowed funds from the JDB.

One of the main reasons for foreign companies to maintain close contact with Japanese banks is that the banks are then in a position to provide valuable information and are reliable sources of business contacts in Japan (including M & A).

Figure 4.11 Sources for obtaining capital

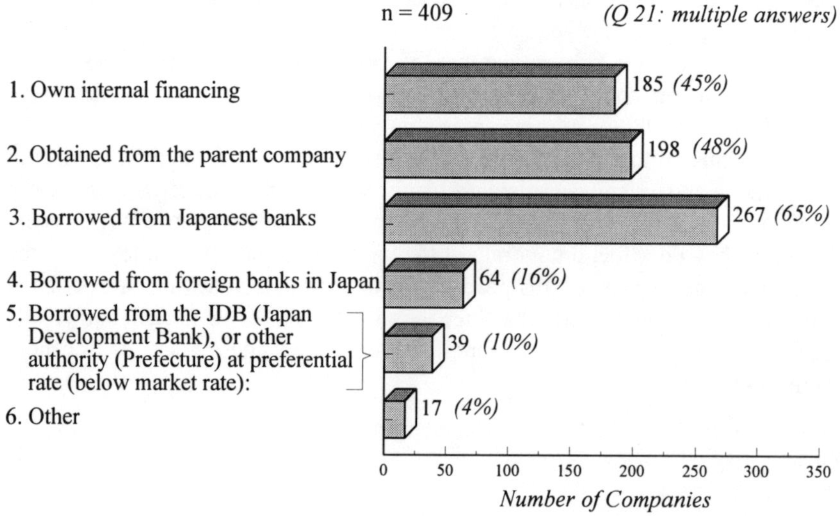

n = 409   *(Q 21: multiple answers)*

1. Own internal financing — 185 *(45%)*
2. Obtained from the parent company — 198 *(48%)*
3. Borrowed from Japanese banks — 267 *(65%)*
4. Borrowed from foreign banks in Japan — 64 *(16%)*
5. Borrowed from the JDB (Japan Development Bank), or other authority (Prefecture) at preferential rate (below market rate): — 39 *(10%)*
6. Other — 17 *(4%)*

Number of Companies

We carried out a cross-tabulation between performance and the sources of capital investment in Japan. It is the successful foreign companies in Japan that more often borrow funds from the JDB, whereas the failures have not made any special use of the JDB funds. The successful foreign companies borrow funds from Japanese banks and at the same time are themselves financially strong, since they are able to a large extent to raise funds internally, whereas the failures appear to face difficulties doing this. The failures are dependent on borrowing funds from Japanese and foreign banks and from their parent company.

One of the reasons for foreign companies' low incidence of borrowing from the JDB is that, according to some of these companies, it is rather difficult to qualify for a loan from the JBD, due to lack of collateral and guarantor plus a rather low financing ceiling (30% to 50% of required financing, with a minimum foreign equity of 50%). Actually, the difference in borrowing rates from the JDB and private financial institutions is rather marginal. Some foreign companies mentioned that they could avoid bureaucratic red tape by avoiding loans from the JDB. According to our studies, the JDB has not been able to properly market its services to foreign companies in Japan directly or through MITI and JETRO, since many foreign companies are not actually aware of JDB activities and the advantages of obtaining preferential or concessional loans from the JDB.

It appears that large companies more often than smaller ones secure JDB loans. Recent recipients of JDB loans, among others, were Daimler-Benz AG, Motorola, Toys R Us, and Volvo.

4.6 CONCLUSIONS

The purpose of making FDI in Japan for a majority of foreign companies is the size and growth of the Japanese market and the importance of Japan in global business. Very few respondents mentioned that their purpose for doing business in Japan was to overcome protectionism.

Regarding investment strategies, we observed that generally foreign companies enter Japan by building up their presence step-by-step over a period of several years. The first step has usually been to enter Japan through an intermediary; the second stage has been to form a marketing and sales joint venture, a joint venture for manufacturing, or a joint R & D laboratory, or else to acquire a Japanese company; and the third step has been to establish a 100% owned subsidiary.

The old strategy of maintaining a 100% owned subsidiary in every country of the world is outdated, at least for Japan. Foreign companies may, depending on their product or service, need a joint venture, a 100% owned subsidiary, technical tie-ups with competitors, or alliances with foreign and Japanese companies in order to be successful in the Japanese market.

Moreover, the use of multiple channels in Japan is quite common. Foreign companies have to be flexible while deciding which channels to use for penetrating the Japanese market. They have to adapt to the conditions prevailing in the Japanese market and invest heavily in the distribution channels. This kind of investment by foreign companies enhances their credibility and commitment to the Japanese market in the eyes of local customers and their own personnel.

We observed that the majority of foreign companies, particularly joint ventures, use Japanese-style management, whereas wholly owned foreign subsidiaries employ a mixture of Western- and Japanese-style management. Top managers in many cases are Japanese, and they have the authority to run the operation. Parent companies of most of the foreign companies provide overall corporate policies and strategy but leave the concrete operations to the local subsidiary. It seems that to a large extent foreign companies are managed with autonomy within limits. This method of operating the company removes the language and cultural obstacles that may be present in a company run by expatriates in Japan.

We found that in the "Successful" group it is the US companies that have more Japanese CEOs, and they are more likely to use the Japanese management style. On the other hand, the European companies have more expatriates and more often use the Western management style. In sum, it is the US companies that more often conform to the local conditions prevailing in Japan.

In a joint venture, the Japanese partner is more likely to have the management responsibility to run operations in Japan, regardless of the size of its equity contribution.

Large numbers of foreign companies in Japan face communication problems with their headquarters, but these problems do not necessarily affect the performance of the companies directly. However, they do affect the morale of the local and expatriate employees of the subsidiary. One reason for this problem, in our view, is the lack of knowledge at headquarters of the unique characteristics of Japan: its language, norms and customs, work ethics, and significant differences in business practices.

Finally, the investment and management strategies have to be tailor-made for the Japanese market.

NOTES

1. See Abegglen, J. C., 1989, p. 7.
2. Note: IMF indicated in 1993 that the People's Republic of China (PRC) is the third largest country in terms of total world GNP (in 1992). However, we question the assumptions by which the GNP per capita was revised by the

IMF, and the government of the PRC has also declined to accept the IMF's dubious way of calculating their GNP.

3. We consider that practically all the respondents understand the meaning of "Japanese management style," since 83% of the respondents to our questionnaire are Japanese.

4. Source: based on Professor H. Yoshihara's survey ("Questionnaire on local presidents and internationalization within Japanese parent companies") sent in November 1992 to 783 Japanese companies listed in the primary market of the Tokyo Stock Exchange that operate subsidiaries in foreign countries. A valid response was obtained from 425 companies (54.3%). Results are expected to be published during 1994 (in Japanese). See also: Ministry of Finance, 1991 (in Japanese).

5 HUMAN RESOURCE MANAGEMENT STRATEGY

Japan is a key market in the global strategy of MNEs and TNCs. In order to be successful, foreign companies have to show their long-term actual commitment by establishing a direct presence in Japan. This might be in the form of offices, production and manufacturing facilities, or R & D laboratories. All of this requires having excellent local personnel, for without them the chances for success in the Japanese market will be meager. In addition, any transfer of technology and know-how from Japan will also be severely constrained.

The issue of human resource management is thus of paramount importance for foreign companies operating in Japan. In Chapter 4, we mentioned that a majority of foreign companies make their decisions regarding human resources in Japan (excluding expatriate recruitment), one of the major differences between Japanese and Western styles of management. Foreign companies have to adapt (at least to a certain extent) to prevailing local conditions in the Japanese market.

In this chapter our interest is entirely devoted to the question of human resource management. We will be looking at the following topics: the number of foreign expatriates in a company and their positions, whether the head of a department is Japanese or an expatriate, training programs offered, criteria for selecting local personnel, recruitment of new graduates for white collar positions, factors given importance by local managers in choosing employment with a foreign company, difficulties in interacting encountered between locals and foreign expatriates, recruitment strategies for local personnel, problems in recruiting Japanese personnel, background information on senior expatriates (function and status, working experience, years stationed in Japan, knowledge of the Japanese language, and planned period of stay in Japan), type of companies from which mid-career local managers have been recruited, Japanese executives on the parent company's board, and the trade unions.

5.1 FOREIGN COMPANIES AS EMPLOYERS

The concept of lifelong employment is changing, and many companies are decreasing their labor force through early retirements. Labor mobility--especially among mid-career managers--is on the rise, and there is an increasing number of layoffs (including some from major Japanese companies) due to the prevailing recession in Japan. All of these factors should make it easier for foreign companies to recruit highly qualified Japanese personnel.

According to a large number of studies, it is rather difficult for foreign companies to recruit Japanese personnel, especially new graduates from well-known universities. Generally, foreign companies compared to Japanese companies face more problems in hiring and retaining Japanese personnel.[1] Several foreign companies in the questionnaire and case studies reported that they spend a great portion of their efforts attracting qualified Japanese personnel.

Despite the economic slowdown, it is still difficult for foreign companies to recruit university graduates in large cities such as Tokyo and Osaka. According to experts, the labor shortage in Japan is expected to prevail for a long time in the future, even if at present it appears that the employment opportunities for Japanese college and university graduates for this year (1993-1994) are more scarce than they were a year ago.

During the last decade, establishing a consistent and attractive hiring program has become easier for many of the larger and more established foreign companies in Japan, but for many potential Japanese employees, the image of foreign companies as unstable still persists.

Nonetheless, most of the foreign companies that established their business in Japan before 1980 have a good track record and are able in some or many cases to expand their contacts with universities and "old Boy/old Girl" networks. However, Japanese college and university graduates' preferences are to join a well-established, large Japanese company.

Many foreign companies in Japan are rather small (though their brand name or CI maybe well known), despite the fact that their parent companies are in many cases MNEs or TNCs. Since most of them are operating on a profit-center concept in Japan, with independent product and service units responsible for their own operating results, foreign companies seem even smaller in the eyes of job seekers.

It is estimated that more than 90% of foreign companies in Japan employ fewer than 300 employees, and at least 80% of foreign companies have less than 100 employees.[2] This small size means that foreign companies have limited access to the Japanese labor market. The ongoing rationalization for small size (layoffs due to the recession) in a number of foreign companies, including some well-known foreign companies in Japan such as IBM and Kodak, has reinforced the negative feeling toward foreign companies. There is a perceived lack of long-term job security and stability in foreign companies in Japan.

5.2 PRESENCE OF FOREIGN EXPATRIATES

Multinational (and transnational) companies generally staff their subsidiaries with local staff and expatriates (from both headquarters and other subsidiaries). The managerial mix depends on the policy and strategy of these companies. Some of the multinationals have a policy of employing no expatriates in their local subsidiaries. On the other hand, a large number of multinationals have a policy of staffing subsidiaries with one or more expatriates in key decision-making positions.

Figure 5.1 shows that in 46% of the responding foreign companies, there were no expatriates. However, 54% of the foreign companies have 1 or more expatriates. The majority of foreign companies have between 1 and 5 expatriates, and in five foreign companies the number of expatriates varies from 52 to 176 expatriates (four companies are in the financial sector and are 100% foreign owned, and one, in the service sector, is 50% foreign owned).

Figure 5.1 Presence of expatriates in foreign companies

n = 398   (Q 7)

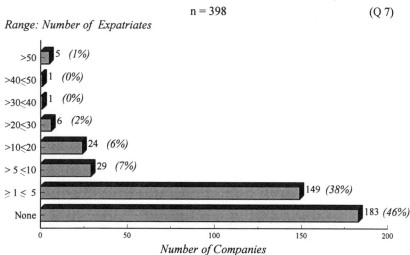

Range: Number of Expatriates

Number of Companies

We carried out cross-tabulation between the type of ownership and the number of expatriates in a company. The result shows that 66% of the companies with expatriates are 100% foreign owned. The lowest number of expatriates is in the minority-foreign-owned companies (6%; see Appendix B5.1).

Concerning nationality of parent company and expatriates, the cross-tabulation shows that European companies have more expatriates (52%) compared to American companies (38%; see Appendix B5.2). One reason for this, in our view, is that European companies in our survey also have a larger number of 100% foreign-owned companies than do US companies.

Table 5.1 shows that the majority of expatriates in the local subsidiary come from their parent companies. Some expatriates have also been dispatched from one of the parent company's subsidiaries outside Japan. In some companies, foreign nationals have been recruited either locally in Japan or from other countries. However, the ratio of expatriates to the total number of employees generally remains rather low. To be more precise, 1,676 expatriates are in 215 foreign companies employing a total of 84,963 persons (expatriates in US companies number 684 [n=81]) and in European companies, 788 [n=111]). The actual ratio of expatriates to the total number of employees is 2%.[3]

The reasons for employing expatriates are many, despite their being expensive to station in Japan. According to several foreign companies, an expatriate is two to four times more expensive as a Japanese manager or top-ranking Japanese executive. Apart from the higher expatriate salary, other fringe benefit costs are considerable (depending on the position), for example, a high bonus, family allowances, a free villa or luxury apartment, free yearly home leave for the entire family, free membership at one or more prestigious and exclusive clubs, education allowances for children, generous pension funds, and installation and repatriation grants.

Some of the reasons given for employing expatriates in a local subsidiary in Japan were:

- Expatriates know the parent company's corporate culture and can easily communicate credibly with headquarters (they also know headquarters' language).
- They make it easier to control the activities of the local subsidiary.
- They help to control and transfer the parent company's technology and know-how.
- Expatriates aid in the transfer of technology and know-how (including market intelligence) from Japan to headquarters.
- They fill the vacancies caused by difficulties in employing high-caliber Japanese personnel.
- Expatriates train local staff to take over their positions after a certain period of time.

**Table 5.1 Distribution of expatriates based on affiliation to parent
company or other subsidiaries outside Japan**

* Total number of expatriates	= 1,676(a)	n = 215 companies
* Number of expatriates from parent companies	= 1,116	n = 199 companies
* Expatriates from other subsidiaries	= 173	n = 46 companies

(a) The remaining 387 expatriates were recruited from other countries or in Japan.

5.3 JAPANESE AND EXPATRIATES IN SENIOR MANAGEMENT POSITIONS

We find that in the majority of the foreign companies, most of the top management positions in all departments are occupied by Japanese (Q 8, see Appendix A). Sixty-three percent of the CEOs (chief executive officers, presidents, or chairmen) are Japanese and 31% are expatriates. In the remainder of companies, the CEOs are both Japanese and expatriates (see Figure 5.2).[4] On the other hand, Japanese companies overseas generally staff most of the top managerial positions with staff from the parent company in Japan.

It appears that the positions expatriates occupy are primarily CEO positions or heads of finance/accounting, R & D, and marketing/sales. The expatriates are most often from the parent company. In personnel departments, the head in most cases is Japanese. One of the main reasons for this is that it facilitates recruitment of Japanese personnel. Moreover, recruitment of local personnel is done mainly by the foreign subsidiary in Japan, with very little interference from the parent company.

In terms of performance, in a majority of the "Successful" companies and also the "As expected" group, the CEOs are Japanese (64% in each group). Regarding the "Failure" group, no specific conclusions can be drawn since practically an equal distribution of Japanese and expatriate CEOs are found (see Appendix B5.3).

The results of the cross-tabulation between CEO and management style (Q 3) show that it can be generally concluded that it is the Japanese CEO who more often implements the Japanese management style. If we compare American companies with European companies, we find that in the American companies the number of Japanese CEOs is higher (over 76%) and that to a large extent they are practicing Japanese management style (see Appendix B4.4 and B4.6).

In European companies, the number of CEO expatriates is higher (over 41%) compared to American companies. The expatriates, to a large extent, practice Western management style or a mixture of Western and Japanese management styles. Some of the European CEOs mentioned that the best way to manage a

Figure 5.2　Distribution of CEOs, Japanese and expatriate

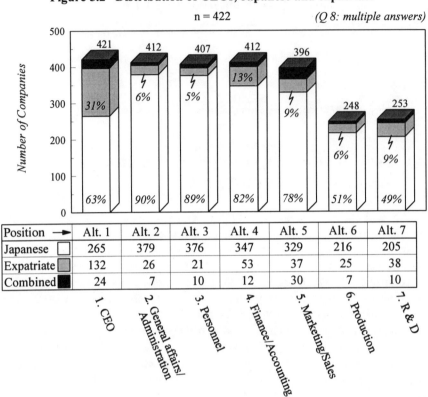

n = 422　　　　　　　　　　　*(Q 8: multiple answers)*

Position →	Alt. 1	Alt. 2	Alt. 3	Alt. 4	Alt. 5	Alt. 6	Alt. 7
Japanese ☐	265	379	376	347	329	216	205
Expatriate ▨	132	26	21	53	37	25	38
Combined ■	24	7	10	12	30	7	10

1. CEO 2. General affairs/Administration 3. Personnel 4. Finance/Accounting 5. Marketing/Sales 6. Production 7. R & D

foreign company in Japan is to use the best of both Western and Japanese management styles.

Successful foreign companies that are 100% foreign owned employ an equal number of expatriate and Japanese CEOs. On the other hand, in the minority-owned foreign companies, we find that all are run by Japanese CEOs (see Appendix B5.4).

A comparison of European and American companies reveals that in the 100% owned American companies, the majority of CEOs are Japanese, whereas in the European companies the majority of CEOs are Europeans. In the case of failures we find that in 100% foreign-owned companies, most of the CEOs are expatriates, especially in the European companies (the sample is, however, too small to draw any definite conclusions).

Cross-tabulation between CEO and ownership gives results similar to those mentioned above. In 100% foreign-owned companies, the number of expatriate and Japanese CEOs is more or less equal, but in American companies the balance is tilted toward Japanese CEOs, and in European companies, toward expatriates (see Appendix B5.5).

Within European companies, it is the Swedish and Swiss companies that employ the largest number (by ratio) of expatriate CEOs. One of the reasons for this is the traditional policy of multinational companies in these two countries of having as far as possible a 100% owned venture as well as an expatriate CEO who can be trusted by the parent company.

We find in our study and also in general that the behavior (operational strategies and rationale) of European companies in Japan and Japanese companies outside Japan are to a large extent very similar. American companies appear to have fewer similarities with European or Japanese companies with respect to ownership and staffing strategies overseas. American companies appear to be more Japanized in their operations in Japan, which are characterized by decentralization and adaptation to the local environment, than are their European counterparts in Japan or Japanese companies operating outside Japan. Ironically, despite the liberal attitude of American-owned companies, they do not seem to be more successful than their more conservative European competitors in Japan.

We carried out cross-tabulation between management style (Q 3), year of establishment, and CEO nationality (Japanese or expatriate; Q 8), but no major observations can be made except, according to the ratios more expatriates hold CEO positions in foreign companies that were established in Japan prior to 1970 and in most of these companies the Japanese management style is practiced. Moreover, cross-tabulation between the management style (Q 3), nationality, and CEO (Q 8) did not reveal any new differences (again, we found that the European companies with expatriate CEOs more often practice Western management style).

Cross-tabulation between management style (Q 3), CEO (Q 8), and business line shows that it is mainly in the financial sector that the number of expatriate CEOs (55%) is higher than the number of Japanese CEOs. At the same time, Western-style management is practiced to a greater extent in this branch. Moreover, due to the recession and the burst of the bubble economy, it is this sector that has had the highest number of firings of employees.

The main conclusions that can be drawn in this section are that generally foreign companies in Japan are highly decentralized (and localized), they have lower numbers of expatriates (even in positions such as CEO or departmental heads), and they employ a large number of Japanese CEOs. This is in contrast to Japanese companies operating outside Japan, for many of the key positions in a majority of these companies are held by Japanese sent from headquarters, allowing tight control by the Japanese parent company.[5]

5.4   TRAINING PROGRAMS

Japanese companies are known for providing intensive on-the-job training (OJT) for their employees. Throughout one's career at a Japanese company, training is given in some form or the other. Compared to most universities in the Western world, where quite specialized and practical courses are offered, Japanese students generally are not exposed to such specialized curricula at their universities. Japanese students are expected to be provided with specialized courses, tailor-made to the specific requirements of a company, only when they join that company.

Foreign companies in Japan that recruit mainly college and university graduates are expected to provide intensive training to these newly recruited employees, especially since foreign companies have a different corporate culture and working environment. However, foreign companies are widely criticized for lacking such training systems in Japan.

Figure 5.3 shows that 83% of foreign companies provide OJT. English language programs for Japanese employees appear to be given very high importance. Technical and managerial training in Japan and abroad is also

Figure 5.3   Types of training programs offered to employees

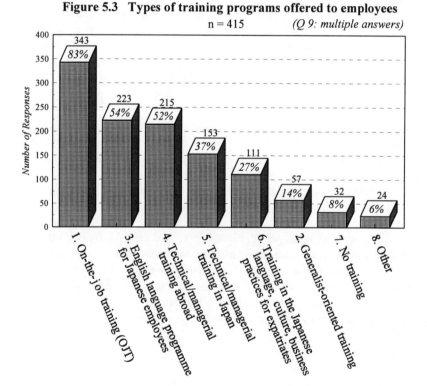

n = 415   *(Q 9: multiple answers)*

offered by a considerable number of foreign companies. Expatriates in a number of foreign companies are given training in Japanese language, culture, and business practices.

A large number of foreign companies provide various incentives to their Japanese employees for learning English (or, in some cases, French). The incentives consist of free tuition, a bonus for passing a certain level of language skill, and others.

Japanese employees are considered to be highly appreciative of receiving training at the parent company. According to foreign companies, training in English is expected to increase Japanese employees' communication with expatriates and with the staff of other subsidiaries and headquarters. Moreover, such training facilitates easier transfer of Japanese personnel to headquarters and other subsidiaries worldwide, and a large number of foreign companies in Japan are multinational and transnational. In addition, transfer of technology and know-how from Japan is also expected to increase.

Foreign companies that do not provide training programs have such a policy either because they rely on mid-career managers or because they simply are not aware of the importance of training in Japan. Moreover, small companies (with less than 50 employees) offer less training both in and outside Japan. Similar results have been reported by a survey carried out by the American Chamber of Commerce in Japan (ACCJ).[6]

5.5 STRATEGY AND POLICY FOR RECRUITING JAPANESE PERSONNEL

Foreign companies are known to face difficulties in general in recruiting staff in Japan, particularly white collar employees. To the Japanese, most foreign companies in Japan are unknown, and most of them are small and very specialized, involved with niche products and services. College and university graduates are known to give importance to the company's image, size, number of years established in the Japanese market, sales growth, and long-term demonstrated commitment in the Japanese market. They show a preference for joining well-known Japanese companies and for job security (desiring lifelong employment), which is considered to be higher at a Japanese company.

Moreover, Japanese companies are generally considered to be male dominated, with most of the managerial positions occupied by males (at least 90%).[7] Foreign companies' recruitment strategies and policies for white collar positions are expected to be somewhat different from those of Japanese companies in terms of selection criteria and employment of males and females, college and university graduates, and mid-career managers.

Selection criteria

Regarding important selection criteria for local personnel, foreign companies' responses are presented in Figure 5.4. It appears that for foreign companies the most important criterion for selecting local white collar personnel is motivation. Other important criteria are experience, personality, education, command of English, and age. Gender (male/female) is not considered an important selection criterion; males and females are given equal preferences. Other criteria refer mainly to ability, talent, initiative, and capacity for teamwork.

Japanese companies are known to give high importance to recruiting new college and university graduates (mainly male), thus giving emphasis to education.[8] Foreign companies behave in a different way for a number of reasons: (1) in joint ventures, a large number of foreign companies do not recruit since the Japanese partner either transfers or dispatches its own personnel on a temporary or a long-term basis; (2) due to difficulties in recruiting high school and college or university graduates, a large number of foreign companies either do not recruit new graduates or put most of their efforts into recruiting mid-career managers; (3) foreign companies give more importance to recruiting brilliant and well-motivated female graduates, who are generally overlooked by the Japanese companies. In addition, because foreign companies recruit

Figure 5.4 Important selection criteria for local personnel

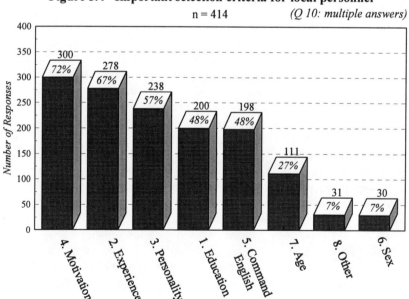

n = 414   *(Q 10: multiple answers)*

relatively more mid-career managers than new graduates, the selection criteria (especially education) are different from the ones used by the Japanese companies.

Recruitment of new graduates for white collar positions

Thirty-three percent of the foreign companies did not recruit at all from new university graduates (Q 11; see Appendix A). Moreover, 62% of the foreign companies did not recruit any high school graduates. Generally speaking, the preference of foreign companies is similar to that of the Japanese companies: to recruit as many university graduates as possible. But this is not so easy for foreign companies in Japan, both because of the prejudice or negative attitude prevailing in Japan toward foreign companies and because of the ignorance of foreign companies regarding effective tools required for recruiting university graduates.

Table 5.2 shows that it is generally large companies that have succeeded in employing new university graduates. Most of these companies are 100% foreign owned or have a majority foreign equity.

Several foreign companies mentioned that they have simply given up recruiting new university graduates and are either recruiting only mid-career managers or graduates from junior colleges, high schools, special schools, and vocational schools. Some foreign companies use a policy of a combination of recruiting new graduates and mid-career managers or of simply moving the operations away from large cities such as Tokyo and Osaka to far-off places in Japan (such as Sendai, Hokkaido or Kyushu), where it is easier to recruit, for example, junior college graduates.

Some foreign companies said that they aggressively recruit young female graduates that either have been overlooked by Japanese companies or have become disenchanted with Japanese corporate life. Several companies

Table 5.2   Employment of university graduates

(Q 11)

Number of employees	Number of companies	In %	Ownership %	Number of companies	In %	Nationality	Number of companies	In %
1 - 50	37	18	25 - 49%	28	14	Europe	95	46
51 - 200	76	37	50%	33	16	USA	97	47
201 - 500	39	19	51 - 99%	35	17	Asia	9	4
501 -	54	26	100%	110	53	Others	5	3
Total	206	100		206	100		206	100

mentioned that they have had to scale back their expansion plans because they could not find enough Japanese personnel. Exorbitant recruitment costs are also a detrimental factor.

Japanese companies themselves, on the other hand, behave in a different way when operating outside Japan. For example, a study shows that most Japanese-owned companies in the United States do not recruit regularly on college campuses nor maintain an active presence there.[9]

In Sweden, for example, it was found that Japanese companies faced problems attracting highly qualified university graduates since student preferences were to join well-known large Swedish companies (e.g., Volvo, ABB, SAS).[10] Moreover, interviews carried out at Japanese companies showed that the turnover of employees was rather high, mainly due to limited career opportunities, such as limited advancement, since the size of the company was small or most of the top positions were occupied by Japanese expatriates; limited autonomy, with most of the decisions made at headquarters in Japan; and limited opportunity for being stationed outside of Sweden. Several interviewees mentioned that Japanese companies were not using a Japanese management style but were behaving like American companies in Sweden, using an American management style characterized by hire-and-fire policies, frequent conflicts with trade unions, top-down decision making (in a pyramid organizational structure), no delegation of authority, and failure to involve local managers in strategic planning.

The conclusion that can be drawn in this section is that since foreign companies in Japan are small in size (despite the fact that most of them are multinationals and transnationals), prospective Japanese employees feel that these global, and in many cases highly successful, companies will give them limited career opportunities, at least in Japan.

It appears to us that most of the foreign companies in Japan have failed in one respect regarding human resource management (HRM): they have not been able to inform themselves or others adequately as to why they are following a strategy of establishing small or minute units based on profit centers. At the same time, they have not done much to remove the tarnished image or reality of the parent company's paramount interest in profitability per employee versus long-term goals of high performance.

Type of companies from which mid-career local managers were recruited

Since foreign companies give considerable importance to recruiting mid-career managers in Japan,[11] we asked the foreign companies from which types of companies mid-career Japanese managers were recruited (Q 17). The results are presented in Figure 5.5.

**Figure 5.5   Type of companies from which mid-career
local managers were recruited**

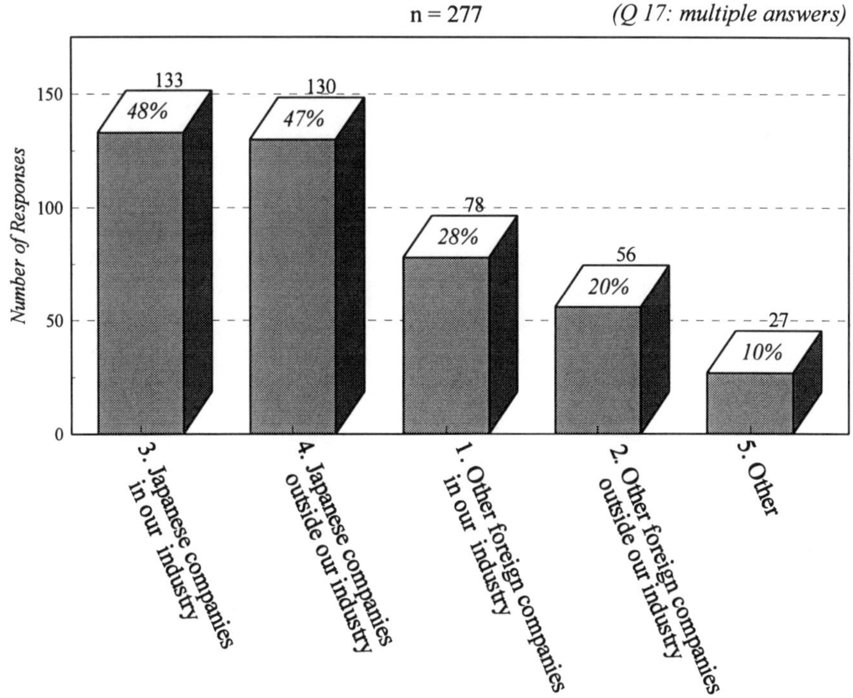

n = 277   *(Q 17: multiple answers)*

Forty-eight percent of the foreign companies recruit mid-career managers from Japanese companies in their own industry (from competitors and via head-hunting). Forty-seven percent of the companies recruit mid-career managers from Japanese companies outside their industry. Twenty-eight percent of the companies recruit mid-career managers from foreign companies in their own industry, and 20% recruit from other foreign companies outside their industry. Figure 5.5 confirms that there is high degree of job hopping among both foreign and Japanese companies.

It appears that there is a large turnover among Japanese personnel in foreign companies. Several foreign companies mentioned that their policy, due to this high turnover, is to avoid recruiting Japanese personnel from other foreign companies, since they question the loyalty of these personnel. Several foreign companies mentioned that if a Japanese manager has changed jobs among more than two foreign companies in a period of a few years, their policy is not to recruit such a manager.

Several companies do not directly recruit mid-career managers. Their policy is either to recruit only new graduates or, in the case of the joint venture, to have their Japanese partner dispatch or transfer its own managers to the joint venture.

The ongoing recession has made it somewhat easier to recruit mid-career Japanese managers to foreign companies in Japan, since a large number of Japanese companies are in the process of laying off personnel or of implementing a policy encouraging the early retirement of well-qualified personnel. Another strategy appears to be to hire a disenchanted mid-career manager from a Japanese company or government institute and count on that employee for new leads to potentially well-qualified Japanese personnel.

However, the cost of recruiting a mid-career Japanese manager is still rather high; foreign companies have to offer a salary of one to several million yen per annum, more than the salary of currently employed managers at the same level. The difference in salaries also leads to disenchantment among the present employees of foreign companies.

Recruitment strategies for local managers

It appears that foreign companies lack an effective employment policy in Japan. Figure 5.6 shows that 73% of the companies recruit employees whenever the need arises, and 50% of the companies are involved in head-hunting for suitable employees, either from Japanese or other foreign companies in Japan.

However, 30% of the foreign companies conduct regular annual recruitment from schools and universities, which is similar to the way Japanese companies recruit, at least in the case of well-known or large Japanese companies. One of the reasons a large number of foreign companies do not follow the traditional Japanese method of recruitment is that most of the foreign companies are small, and many find it to be an expensive method or face other difficulties in implementing regular yearly recruitment.

Some foreign companies mentioned that even if they tried to carry out annual recruitment from the universities, they would not be permitted by Japanese universities to take part in the campus campaign for a variety of reasons, for example, the requirement to recruit a certain number of graduates every year. As there has generally been a shortage of university graduates, the number of Japanese companies seeking this labor has outnumbered the vacancies. However, with the prevailing recession in Japan, the recruitment situation for foreign companies at Japanese universities is expected to improve.

Other recruitment strategies used by foreign companies are offering higher salaries than competitors, television and press advertising, maintaining good contacts with Japanese professors, establishing joint ventures with Japanese companies, and purchasing an agent or distributor in order to obtain manpower.

Figure 5.6   Recruitment strategies for local managers

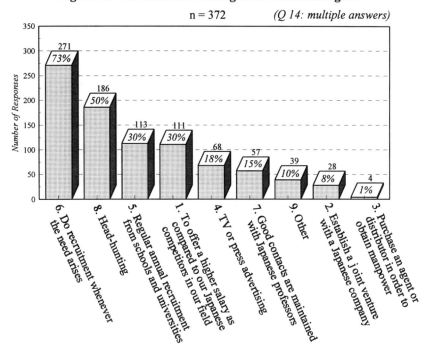

n = 372   *(Q 14: multiple answers)*

Several companies mentioned that since they are not big enough to undertake regular recruitment, they rely on recruitment through their employees' acquaintances, word of mouth, joint efforts with their embassies and chambers of commerce, or direct mailings to potential employees. In the case of joint ventures, companies may obtain employees through transfer from the Japanese partner. However, it is a bit astonishing that the recruitment strategies of joint venture companies in securing well-qualified Japanese employees have not in fact been built entirely upon assistance from the Japanese partner. One of the important reasons given by the foreign companies was that it was very difficult for them to count upon the loyalty of the Japanese staff, who were transferred on only a temporary basis to the foreign joint venture.

Important factors local managers consider in choosing a foreign company

The most important factor to local managerial employees who choose a foreign company as an employer is the greater individual responsibility and freedom in a foreign company (see Figure 5.7). Other important factors are the opportunity to upgrade one's own professional capabilities, higher wages, the reputation and size of the parent company, the opportunity to go abroad, a more objective evaluation of performance, and foreign companies' commitment to the Japanese market. It appears that local personnel, in seeking an employer, seek different things in foreign companies than in Japanese companies.

Better promotion opportunities, shorter working hours, and sexual equality are some other important reasons for choosing a foreign company. Regarding shorter working hours, it is known that generally foreign companies have a five-day working week, with a lower number of overtime hours per day. However, several foreign companies and the case studies show that work accomplishment (job efficiency) is more or less the same in foreign and Japanese companies despite a five-day working week and an average of 2,000 less working hours per year at foreign companies. It is somewhat astonishing that among reasons for choosing a foreign company, employment security was ranked eleventh; lifetime employment was not given special emphasis. One of the reasons could be that it is taken for granted that foreign companies follow a hire-and-fire policy.

Figure 5.7 Main reasons local managers choose a foreign company

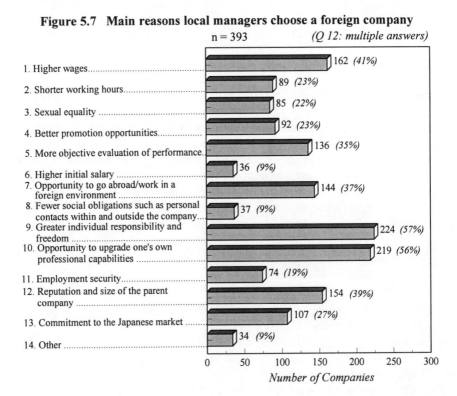

n = 393   (Q 12: multiple answers)

1. Higher wages — 162 (41%)
2. Shorter working hours — 89 (23%)
3. Sexual equality — 85 (22%)
4. Better promotion opportunities — 92 (23%)
5. More objective evaluation of performance — 136 (35%)
6. Higher initial salary — 36 (9%)
7. Opportunity to go abroad/work in a foreign environment — 144 (37%)
8. Fewer social obligations such as personal contacts within and outside the company — 37 (9%)
9. Greater individual responsibility and freedom — 224 (57%)
10. Opportunity to upgrade one's own professional capabilities — 219 (56%)
11. Employment security — 74 (19%)
12. Reputation and size of the parent company — 154 (39%)
13. Commitment to the Japanese market — 107 (27%)
14. Other — 34 (9%)

Number of Companies

Several foreign companies mentioned that their internal surveys (carried out by their personnel departments) showed that apart from the important factors mentioned in Figure 5.7, other reasons Japanese employees chose their company included impartial evaluations of employee ability and work accomplishment, regardless of age, number of years employed, and sex; clearly defined goals to be accomplished; excellent working conditions, including offices that created individual work spaces; accumulation of knowledge and experience; a chance to go abroad; and, for well-known companies, the brand name.

Question 12, in practically all cases, was answered by a Japanese respondent, often a manager, who was involved with questions of recruitment and personnel. In many cases, foreign companies were not able to answer this question because the Japanese employees did not choose the foreign company but were dispatched from the Japanese joint venture partner's company. However, the experience of personnel managers was that transferred Japanese employees highly appreciated in particular the opportunity to upgrade professional capabilities (alt. 10), the greater individual responsibility and freedom (alt. 9), and the opportunity to go abroad (alt. 7).

With the continuing economic slump, Japanese companies are gradually beginning to behave like foreign companies in Japan, emphasizing ability and performance rather than seniority for promotion and increases in salaries. The lifetime employment system for full-time employees is also gradually being discarded by many Japanese companies, and an increasing number of Japanese companies are shedding excess employees.

Problems in recruiting Japanese personnel and relations between the Japanese and expatriates

Foreign companies generally face a tremendous number of problems in recruiting highly qualified Japanese personnel compared to Japanese companies. In our survey, problems that foreign companies face regarding Japanese personnel (see Figure 5.8) include foreign language problems, recruitment of newly graduated university students, recruitment of white collar workers, and lack of long-term loyalty and commitment to foreign companies. Regarding loyalty and commitment, foreign companies face such problems in joint ventures in cases where Japanese personnel are dispatched or transferred on a temporary basis by the Japanese joint venture partner.

Only a few companies mentioned that they themselves or their Japanese personnel face problems due to difficulties in understanding foreign business practices, recruitment of blue collar workers, high labor turnover, or difficulties in understanding foreign social customs.

However, some companies did mention specifically that their Japanese staff face problems in getting along well with expatriates in daily life for a number of

Figure 5.8   Problems in recruiting Japanese personnel

n = 362   *(Q 15: multiple answers)*

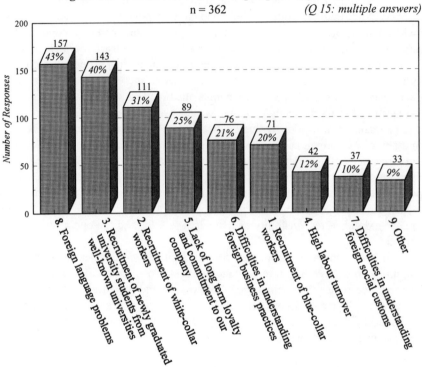

reasons, for example, the use of different languages and the frustration of insufficient communication with headquarters or expatriates due to culture as well as distance. Other problems mentioned by foreign companies are difficulties in recruiting highly qualified, talented, capable Japanese with enough experience and an excellent command of English, especially due to the labor shortage; female workers immediately resigning from the company upon marriage; difficulties in recruiting qualified sales staff; lack of international experience possessed generally by Japanese staff; and their feeling of insecurity in dealing with and living in a foreign environment.

A number of companies mentioned that the Japanese labor standard does not suit foreign companies and will be a constant problem for them in Japan. Problematic Japanese practices include lifetime employment; regular employment of new graduates; a salary system based on the number of years employed instead of ability, achievement, and performance; and rarely dismissing staff when necessary (the lack of a hire-and-fire policy).

Common difficulties encountered by local employees in interactions with expatriates (see Figure 5.9) are language problems, misjudgments caused by cultural differences, expatriates' lack of understanding of the Japanese business environment, and the lack of a long-term commitment on the part of the expatriates toward the local subsidiary.

Several foreign companies mentioned that they do not face any particular problems because all their regular staff members are Japanese who, in most cases, have been transferred by the joint venture partner, with expatriates visiting their companies only on a temporary basis. However, some companies did mention specifically that they face problems due to both Japanese and expatriate arrogance, expatriate failure to utilize Japanese expertise and experience, and expatriates' lack of awareness of the Japanese way of working, for example, Japanese managers maneuver behind the scenes and form a group consensus, whereas expatriates usually work on an individual basis.

Figure 5.9   Common difficulties encountered by local employees

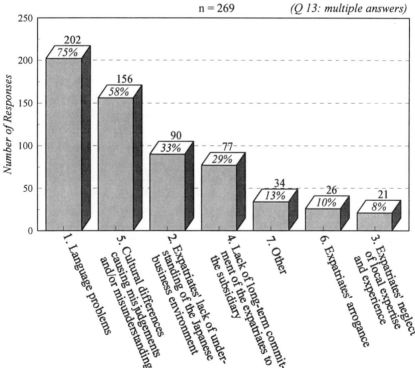

Regarding foreign language problems (Q 15, alt. 8), the observations are practically the same as in the case of Q 13 (alt. 1, language problems). To a large extent, the problems are more obvious in the manufacturing sector (chemicals, pharmaceuticals, machinery, and electronics) and less so in the service sectors (banking, securities, and various other services). Sixty-four percent of the companies have a foreign capital share of over 50%.

In the manufacturing sector, a large number of companies were established prior to 1971 or after 1985, whereas in the service sector most of the companies were established after 1980. We see a contrast if we compare this question (Q 15) with Q 13; both Japanese and expatriate employees face communication problems due to a lack of mastery of the other's language.

5.6 BACKGROUND INFORMATION ON SENIOR EXPATRIATES

Over 182 expatriates hold senior positions in foreign companies in Japan (see Appendix A, Q 16.1), and since it is a well-known fact that very few expatriates can master the Japanese language or have adequate knowledge of Japanese culture, our interest was in investigating the background characteristics of foreign expatriates in Japan.

Sixty-five percent of these expatriates have previously held senior positions at their headquarters (see Appendix A, Q 16.2). The conclusion that can be drawn is that it is very important for the parent companies of foreign companies to dispatch high-ranking expatriates, preferably from headquarters, who at the same time receive the full support of their board.

Seventy-four percent of the expatriates have worked at one or more foreign postings before being stationed in Japan (see Appendix A, Q 16.3). This finding shows that a large number of expatriates have gained working experience by working outside of their headquarters' country prior to being stationed in Japan.

Seventy-one percent of the expatriates have been stationed in Japan for up to five years, and 51% of them have been stationed there for up to three years (see Appendix A, Q 16.4). If we compare these results with the intended period of stay in Japan, we find that 40% of the expatriates plan to stay in Japan about five years (see Appendix A, Q 16.7). These results indicate that generally expatriates stay in Japan for three or more years. This is important because it normally takes some time for an expatriate and his family to adjust to the special conditions prevailing in the Japanese market and to the culture itself. Moreover, it is important to note that frequent replacement of high-ranking expatriates is resented by Japanese employees; this is not a practice that induces harmony but one that leads to confusion.

It is also important to note that very few expatriates (only about 8%) have studied in Japan. Regarding mastery of the Japanese language (see Appendix A,

Q 16.6), about 29% claim to have achieved this. We think this figure is rather low. It is very important for foreign expatriates to be able to master the Japanese language and culture in order to be really successful in Japan. Such mastery appears to be scarce among expatriates in Japan.

5.7 JAPANESE EXECUTIVES ON THE PARENT COMPANY'S BOARD

Appendix A (Q 18) shows that 18% of foreign companies in Japan have Japanese executives on their parent company's board. It is a well-known fact that very few Japanese companies, irrespective of their level of internationalization, have allowed expatriates to obtain positions on their boards.[12] The conclusion that can be drawn is that foreign companies, regardless of size or ownership, and whether of American or European origin, have placed Japanese executives on their parent company's boards (see Table 5.3). This contrasts sharply with practices in Japanese companies, whose behavior we consider highly conservative.

5.8 EXISTENCE OF TRADE UNIONS AND THEIR ROLE

Twenty-four percent of the responding foreign companies reported having trade unions (see Appendix A, Q 19).[13] One of the reasons for such a low figure is that in the case of joint ventures, most of the Japanese employees are members of a trade union only at the Japanese parent company's headquarters. Figure 5.10 shows that 75% of the companies mentioned that an advantage of having a trade union was that it facilitated mutual understanding (better communication) between labor and management.

Table 5.3 Japanese executives on foreign parent company's board

(Q 18)

Number of employees	Number of companies	In %	Ownership %	Number of companies	In %	Nationality	Number of companies	In %
0 - 50	27	36	25 - 49%	8	11	Europe	35	47
51 - 200	24	32	50%	17	23	USA	38	51
201 - 500	10	13	51 - 99%	12	16	Others	2	2
501 -	14	19	100%	38	50			
Total	75	100		75	100		75	100

Figure 5.10   Advantages of having a trade union

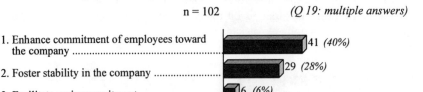

n = 102   *(Q 19: multiple answers)*

1. Enhance commitment of employees toward the company .... 41 *(40%)*

2. Foster stability in the company .... 29 *(28%)*

3. Facilitate easier recruitment .... 6 *(6%)*

4. Contribute to good working environment .... 32 *(31%)*

5. Facilitate mutual understanding between labor and management (better communication) .... 76 *(75%)*

6. Other .... 12 *(12%)*

0   20   40   60   80   100

Number of Companies

Moreover, 40% of the responding foreign companies mentioned that the existence of trade unions enhanced the commitment of employees to the company, 31% of the companies mentioned that trade unions contributed to a good working environment, and 28% mentioned that it fostered stability in the company.

Overall, a positive attitude was found with regard to having trade unions at foreign companies. Practically no company reported having any major industrial disputes or facing high labor turnover. However, it is interesting to note that only 6% of the foreign companies mentioned that trade unions facilitated the recruitment of Japanese employees. Table 5.4 shows that it is more often the large companies (more than 50 employees) that have trade unions.

Japanese executives working for foreign companies in Japan have recently formed an association called FAMA (Foreign Affiliated Companies Manage-

Table 5.4   Existence of trade unions in foreign companies

(Q 19)

Number of employees	Number of companies	In %	Ownership %	Number of companies	In %	Nationality companies	Number of	In %
0 - 50	21	21	25 - 49%	17	17	Europe	44	43
51 - 200	27	26	50%	23	22	USA	58	57
201 - 500	18	18	51 - 99%	20	20			
501 -	36	35	100%	42	41			
Total	102	100		102	100		102	100

ment Association) in order to strengthen their presence and their cooperation and cope with the difficulties of operating a foreign company in Japan. Despite the drawback that only Japanese nationals serving as heads of foreign companies may join the association, it is considered a positive step forward.

5.9 CONCLUSIONS

Foreign companies in Japan are highly decentralized (and localized), they have low numbers of expatriates (including employees in positions such as CEO or departmental heads), and they employ a large number of Japanese CEOs. Regarding performance, foreign companies are successful with both Japanese and expatriate CEOs

Foreign companies generally offer higher wages than their Japanese competitors in order to attract Japanese personnel. They also offer greater individual responsibility and freedom, the opportunity to upgrade professional capabilities, and other advantages. On the other hand, a large number of foreign companies in Japan are small (despite the fact that most of them are multinationals and transnationals), and prospective Japanese employees believe that these global and in many cases highly successful companies will give them limited career opportunities, at least in Japan.

The intense recruitment of Japanese personnel by foreign companies in Japan has eased somewhat, mainly due to the ongoing recession in Japan and the difficulties faced by large Japanese companies in absorbing most of the new university graduates. A large number of Japanese companies are no longer following a policy of lifelong employment. Moreover, the pool of mid-career Japanese managers (both male and female) willing to switch from their present employers has increased considerably, and most foreign companies rely more heavily on mid-career managers than on new university and college graduates.

A recruitment policy must be built upon an extensive network of contacts with universities and the development of an "old Boy/old Girl" network. Despite foreign companies' efforts in these directions, Japanese university graduates generally prefer to join a well-established, large Japanese company, which they expect to provide high job security.

It was observed that some foreign partners in joint ventures (particularly in those where the corporate plan has been to establish a 100% owned subsidiary) face difficulties in securing well-qualified Japanese employees due to the lack of assistance from the Japanese partner. Local employees provided by the joint venture partner are transferred only on a temporary basis to the joint venture; therefore, it is very difficult for the foreign partner to count upon the loyalty of the Japanese staff and to later establish a 100% owned subsidiary.

Most of the foreign companies in Japan, however, have to live with the handicap of being rather small in size. One way to overcome this is to organize all the profit centers (including branch offices and local subsidiaries) under one umbrella, so that the company's appearance in the Japanese market becomes bigger. Another way to overcome this disadvantage is to make the company's brand name or image well known in the Japanese market. Recruiting activities should be an integral part of marketing strategy.

The knowledge of foreign languages by Japanese employees is considered by foreign companies to be weak, thus making the transfer of technology and know-how from Japan to other entities across the globe to some extent difficult. At the same time, it is difficult to work effectively with clients and colleagues of various nationalities. These factors, together with the Japanization of the local operation and the Japanese management style, make the integration of a Japanese operation into the global framework of a multinational, with its global business strategies, somewhat difficult. However, foreign companies have to live with the differences in business culture.

We recommend that short-term objectives such as sales or profitability per employee be disregarded by foreign companies in Japan if they sincerely want to secure high-caliber Japanese personnel; they must give a solid impression that they intend to firmly follow a policy of job security and stability. However, several foreign companies have recently laid off some of their employees due to the prevailing recession in Japan, and this has not provided a positive image in the eyes of local personnel.

In order to establish a positive corporate image among the staff, customers, distributors, and suppliers, a long-term commitment and a large measure of patience is required of foreign companies in Japan. Without this positive image, it will be difficult to attract well-qualified local personnel.

NOTES

1. See Ballon, R. J., 1992; Huddleston, J. N., Jr., 1990.
2. Source: interviews with MITI officials, and MITI, 1993d.
3. Four hundred and thirty-five foreign companies employ 147,023 persons in Japan; the United States employs 73,808, and Europe employs 71,085 employees.
4. Regarding the heads of the production and R & D departments, we should be cautious, since the number of manufacturers is 301; the number of foreign companies possessing their own production units, about 200; and those with R & D units, around 150 (for details, consult Chapter 7). The non-response has been nearly zero by these companies, and therefore it is clear that those with a Japanese head of the production unit constitute 87%; for R & D units, the ratio is 81%. It also appears that some companies that do not possess

their own production or R & D units still have a person responsible for taking care of these matters.

5. Source: MOF, 1991.
6. See ACCJ, and Towers, Perrin, Forster, and Crosby, 1991.
7. See Ballon, R. J., 1992, p. 93.
8. See Sakakibara, K., and Westney, D. E., 1985, pp. 1-20.
9. See Pucik, V., et al., 1990.
10. From the personal experience of one of the authors (Khan, S.) as thesis advisor on this subject to several students at Stockholm University, and the information provided by several Japanese companies based in Sweden.
11. For more details regarding recruiting mid-career managers (including head-hunting), see Nevins, T. J., 1990.
12. Source: based on Professor H. Yoshihara's survey to be published during 1994.
13. In Ballon's study the lower figure of 15% of foreign companies is mentioned as having labor unions. See Ballon, R. J., 1992, p. 46.

6 MARKETING ACTIVITIES OF FOREIGN COMPANIES

In this chapter we will examine the marketing activities of foreign companies in Japan. We have already mentioned in several places in this book that Japan is one of the most dynamic and competitive markets in the world. We will be examining the features of the Japanese business environment, marketing problems, marketing/sales strategy, market position of foreign companies in Japan, marketing expenditures, global standardization, the time lag in introducing major new product models or services, marketing intelligence by foreign companies, the use of profit centers, the development and introduction of unique marketing programs and strategies, and the transfer of successful marketing programs or strategies from Japan. Our study covers both products and services.

6.1 CHARACTERISTICS OF THE JAPANESE MARKET

Earlier, we mentioned the importance of Japan in the global business strategies of foreign companies and the size and growth of the Japanese market. We also mentioned that one of the key factors leading to failure mentioned by foreign companies in Japan has been the severe competition in the Japanese market (for more details, see Chapter 8). Japanese companies dominate many of the market segments very efficiently in terms of brand name, positive CI, product, quality, service, advertising and promotional media, distribution networks, and high market shares.

In the consumer goods sector, the product life cycle (PLC) is considered very short in Japan, and yet the seller needs to maintain high service levels. Moreover, in many industrial sectors, product standards are now set by Japanese companies, and this was previously a monopoly of European and American companies. The general price level in Japan is considerably higher than that in all other OECD countries, and some foreign companies consider the high price level both an impediment and an inducement to conducting business in Japan.

In Chapter 5 we discussed the problems faced by foreign companies in recruiting highly qualified Japanese personnel and concluded that the recruitment strategy should be an integral part of the marketing strategy. Headquarters of foreign companies have strategically delegated marketing and sales functions to their subsidiaries in Japan. Only 14% of the foreign companies reported that some control was exercised by their headquarters regarding the marketing and advertising functions of the subsidiary in Japan (Q 4; see Figure 4.7). The heads of marketing and sales departments in most foreign companies are Japanese (91%; see Figure 5.2).

6.2 THE BUSINESS ENVIRONMENT IN JAPAN

Figure 6.1 shows that 70% of the foreign companies found the Japanese market very competitive and another 25% found the market competitive. Only 5% of the foreign companies claimed that the Japanese market was not competitive, and all of these companies were dispersed in most of the branches.

A large number of foreign companies found that the Japanese market was huge and growing (despite the slowdown of the economy), they were able to differentiate their products and services, and new models and services were introduced with a high frequency. There was a high degree of marketing innovation, mainly among manufacturers of products with very short PLCs. About 15% of the companies reported that the frequency with which new models and services were introduced was low; however, the branch analysis regarding these companies revealed that only 64% of the companies were in the manufacturing sector, and others were dispersed over most of the branches. Regarding product differentiation, it appeared that, particularly in the producer goods sector, the product or service was custom-built, and this offered foreign companies opportunities for introducing a higher profit margin differential.

The majority of the companies did not find that their expansion in the Japanese market was hampered by the appreciation of the yen. One important reason was that virtually no foreign company reduced its price in the Japanese market even when it became cheaper to import raw materials, and semi-finished and finished products due to the appreciation of yen. Some companies even mentioned that they had been able to remit higher profits to their parent company with the appreciation of yen.[1]

On the other hand, Japan was considered to be the costliest place to do business. Therefore, some foreign companies mentioned that the appreciation of the yen had helped them to reach at least the break-even point in a reasonable

Figure 6.1 The business environment in Japan

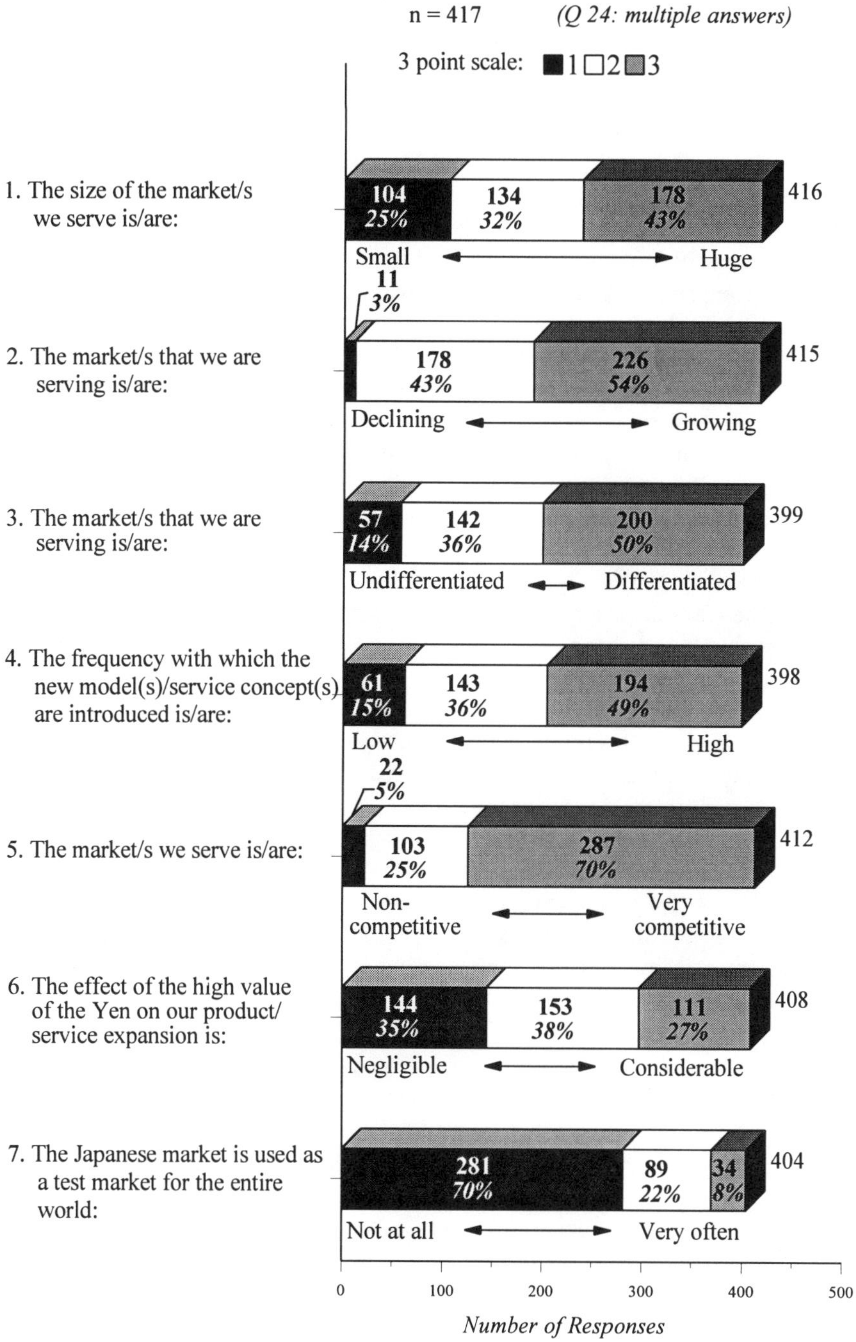

n = 417   *(Q 24: multiple answers)*

3 point scale: ■1 □2 ▨3

1. The size of the market/s
   we serve is/are:

   | 104 25% | 134 32% | 178 43% | 416 |

   Small ◄————————► Huge
   11
   3%

2. The market/s that we are
   serving is/are:

   | 178 43% | 226 54% | 415 |

   Declining ◄————► Growing

3. The market/s that we are
   serving is/are:

   | 57 14% | 142 36% | 200 50% | 399 |

   Undifferentiated ◄——► Differentiated

4. The frequency with which the
   new model(s)/service concept(s)
   are introduced is/are:

   | 61 15% | 143 36% | 194 49% | 398 |

   Low ◄————► High
   22
   5%

5. The market/s we serve is/are:

   | 103 25% | 287 70% | 412 |

   Non-   Very
   competitive ◄——► competitive

6. The effect of the high value
   of the Yen on our product/
   service expansion is:

   | 144 35% | 153 38% | 111 27% | 408 |

   Negligible ◄——► Considerable

7. The Japanese market is used as
   a test market for the entire
   world:

   | 281 70% | 89 22% | 34 8% | 404 |

   Not at all ◄——► Very often

0   100   200   300   400   500

Number of Responses

period of time. Twenty-seven percent of the companies reported that they were considerably affected by the high value of the yen mostly in the manufacturing sector (70%). Branch analysis revealed that those companies that entirely relied on procurement of raw materials within the Japanese market were the ones that were most affected by the appreciation of the yen (mainly companies in the chemicals, machinery, and electronics).

Generally we find in the marketing literature that the Japanese market is used in many cases as the test market for the entire world.[2] Several authors go so far as to state that if one is successful in the Japanese market, then the company will also be successful in the rest of the world. In our study, it appears that despite the tough competition prevailing in the Japanese market (Q 24, alt. 7), foreign companies generally did not use Japan as a test market for the entire world.

Specifically, 70% of the foreign companies did not use the Japanese market as a test market for the entire world. Companies that did mention the alternative "Very often" concerning using Japan as a test market for the entire world were mainly found in the manufacturing sector, especially in producer goods: chemicals, machinery, and electronics. The majority of these companies were established prior to 1986, with over 50% foreign capital.

The reason given by the companies for not using Japan as a test market was that Japan is a special market with very high-quality standards. It was believed that in some ways the standards do not make sense, for instance, in terms of the extra cost that buyers have to pay, at least outside of Japan, especially in the industrial goods sector. Several manufacturers mentioned that the Japanese intermediate goods buyers were fussy about the material in which the goods (pipes, iron, and steel) were packed, for example, if there were oil spots on the wooden crates in which the goods were packed, they refused to take delivery.

In the consumer goods sector, several manufacturers mentioned the extravagance in the Japanese practice of using several layers of packaging materials; in many European countries and the United States such practices may lead to a boycott of products by environmentally conscious consumers. On the other hand, some companies did mention that the stringent quality controls imposed on them by quality-conscious Japanese buyers have highly improved their competitive position globally.

6.3 MARKETING PROBLEMS

Regarding marketing problems encountered by foreign companies in Japan, the most important problems mentioned (see Figure 6.2) were the fact that Japanese customers are very demanding of and sensitive to product quality, difficulties in recruiting marketing/sales staff, Keiretsu (especially in the financial sector), and complicated and multitiered distribution channels.

Difficulties in recruiting qualified Japanese staff for marketing and sales positions, among others, have already been highlighted in the previous chapter.

Other problems that some foreign companies faced in Japan were rigid technical requirements and regulations concerning imported products; difficulties in adapting to Japanese customs, habits, and tastes; difficulties in acquiring distribution channels; and the inability to acquire Japanese companies.

It is quite astonishing that only 12% of the foreign companies reported difficulties in acquiring Japanese companies or distribution channels. This factor has been given wide coverage in the massmedia and also in the ACCJ and the EC surveys[3] which refer to the complexities and difficulties of foreign companies in this regard. However, it is quite clear that high land prices, high stock prices, and the strength of the yen (105 yen = $1 in March 1994) make the sales price of many Japanese companies prohibitive for foreign companies in Japan.

Concerning difficulties in adapting to Japanese customs, habits and tastes, foreign companies found that Japanese customers were among the most demanding in the world. It is quite obvious that if foreign companies want to be successful on the Japanese market, they have to pay greater attention to the demands and sensitivities of Japanese buyers toward product quality.

Figure 6.2 Marketing problems encountered in Japan

n = 362   *(Q 25: multiple answers)*

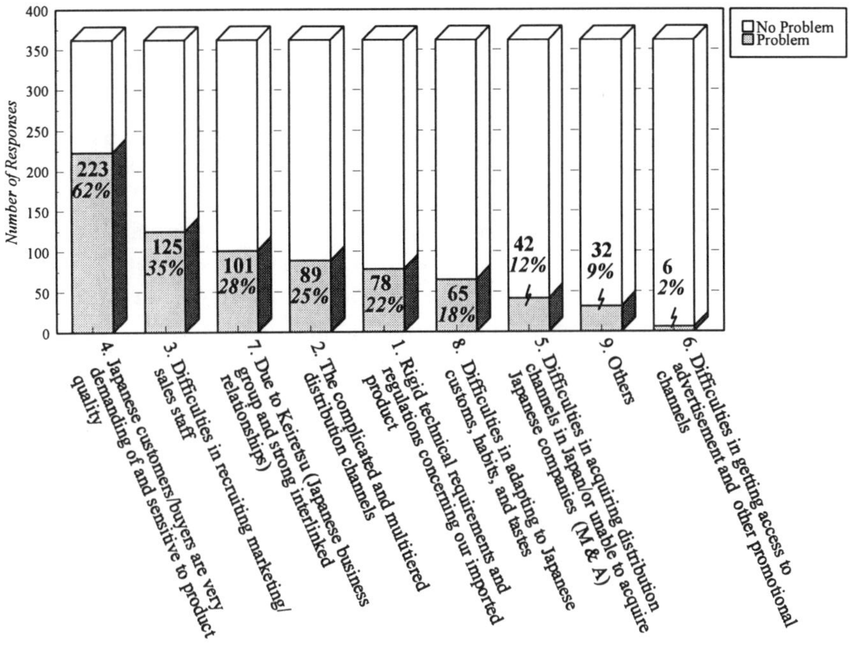

Cross-tabulations using several factors such as branch, performance, size, ownership and year established were used to analyze two well-debated problems, complicated and multitiered distribution channels in Japan (alt. 2) and Keiretsu (alt. 7). Cross-tabulation showed that 28 companies faced problems due to both multitiered distribution channels and Keiretsu. This figure is rather low, representing less than one-third of those who responded to this question.

Regarding complicated and multitiered distribution channels, 84% of the companies reporting this as a problem were in the manufacturing sector (with 57% of these in the consumer goods sector). A large proportion of the companies were in food, chemicals, pharmaceuticals, electronics, and machinery sectors. It appears that companies that established their businesses in Japan after 1970 faced more problems, especially in the service sectors. Regarding ownership, 72% of foreign companies had a capital ratio of over 50%. Sixty-nine percent of the "Successful" or "Very Successful" companies were in this group. A majority of the foreign companies were of small in size, with fewer than 200 employees (70%).

Concerning problems due to Keiretsu, 53% of companies reporting this were in the manufacturing sector (with 59% of these in the producer goods sector). Companies in both the manufacturing and service sectors faced similar problems; however, the service sectors (banking and insurance) appeared to be facing more problems than the manufacturers. Regarding performance, 63% of the successful foreign companies reported facing the problem of Keiretsu, and 60% of the companies were 100% foreign owned. Moreover, 60% of these companies were established in Japan before 1981, and 70% of them had fewer than 200 employees.

Several foreign companies mentioned that loyalty to a Keiretsu (or large business groups) was extremely important in selling products or services to a member of this group. For instance, if a foreign company wanted to sell machine tools to, say, Toyota, then it was extremely important that the CEO and all the salesmen drove Toyotas, since the procurement department officials of Toyota carried out a seller loyalty evaluation at least yearly, and this included such factors as the type of cars driven by senior executives of the supplier. Several foreign executives mentioned that due to fear of retaliation, they preferred driving a Japanese-made car to driving a foreign-made one.

Some foreign companies mentioned that the Japanese Ministry of Health and Welfare controls and various other regulations in the pharmaceutical sector were excessive, absurd, and discriminatory toward foreign companies in Japan. Few foreign companies mentioned that Japanese government officials were intervening too much in import procedures. It is interesting to note that a majority of the foreign companies did not report facing problems due to government regulations.

Foreign companies in the securities branch mentioned that they faced problems regarding the level of service offered to Japanese customers, since customers were spoiled by excessive service provided by their Japanese competitors.

Several foreign companies mentioned that they had difficulty making their corporate name (corporate image) or brand name well known in Japan. The Japanese customers' product preferences were known to be toward foreign or domestic companies that had a well-established image (positive CI) or brand name. Some foreign companies mentioned that Japanese buyers placed importance on product appearance rather than function.

Some foreign companies mentioned that the merit of Japanese customers was that they remained customers for a long time when high-quality products or services were provided to them at a competitive price. Generally speaking, we found that most companies facing problems in the Japanese market had an ownership of 50% or more foreign capital. It appeared that in joint ventures with 50% or less foreign capital, the Japanese joint venture partner was in a position to resolve many problems.

6.4 MARKETING AND SALES STRATEGIES

Figure 6.3 shows that 62% of the responding foreign companies had developed special products (models) or service concepts for the Japanese market, and 43% of them were exploiting their product and market niches. Seventy-two percent of the companies that chose alternatives 1 and 5 were manufacturers (the majority were in the producer goods sector), and there was much buyer-seller interaction, with custom-built products requiring extensive post-sales services. Regarding performance and ownership, for both alternatives, 74% of the companies were in the "Success" group. Sixty-eight percent of the companies that chose alternative 1 and 77% of those choosing alternative 5, had a foreign equity of over 50%.

The special characteristics of the Japanese market confirm our notion that foreign companies' marketing and sales strategy had to be based on product and service adaptation based on Japanese buyers' tastes, preferences for high quality, and various other requirements.

Foreign companies exploited their market niches, which were mainly in narrow market and product segments, sometimes with limited competition from their Japanese rivals due to technological barriers to newcomers. Foreign companies' marketing strategies were based on product and service differentiation from their competitors, and a large number of companies had a majority equity in the ventures (62% of the companies were 100% owned).

Thirty-eight percent of the foreign companies had adopted their headquarters' slogan, product concept, and/or corporate image (CI) in the Japanese market. A large number of foreign companies were of medium to large size; over 62% of

Figure 6.3 Marketing and sales strategies

n = 373   *(Q 26: multiple answers)*

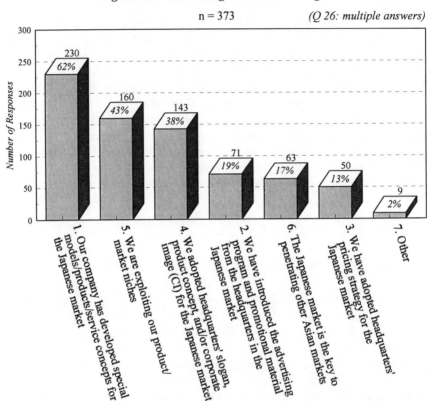

the foreign companies had more than 50 employees. Regarding ownership, 61% of the foreign companies were 100% foreign owned.

Some other marketing and sales strategies used by foreign companies were the introduction of advertising and promotional material from headquarters (standardization strategy), using the Japanese market as the key to penetrating other Asian markets, and adopting headquarters' pricing strategy for the Japanese market.

6.5 MARKET POSITION IN JAPAN

Regarding the market position of foreign companies in Japan, 54% of the foreign companies reported that their company and/or brand name were well known in Japan (see Figure 6.4), and 47% of the companies described themselves as market leaders in terms of quality. Forty-five percent of the foreign companies' products or services were highly price competitive, and 38% of the foreign companies were market leaders in product or service development. Several of them held substantial market shares in their segments.

Moreover, 33% of the companies had developed an exclusive sales and service network (including spare part centers and service stations), matching service levels many cases offered by Japanese competitors (the majority of these were in the producer goods sector), and 28% of the companies were using a joint venture partner's distribution channel. Other important factors were efficient systems for exchanging market information with headquarters and quick delivery time.

For example, regarding alternative 7, 77% of the companies were in the manufacturing sector (a majority of these were in the producer goods sector) and also belonged to the "Success" group. Seventy-one percent of the companies had over 50% foreign equity. Fifty-four percent of the companies were 100% foreign owned. Moreover, 70% of the foreign companies had fewer than 200

Figure 6.4 Foreign companies' market positions in Japan

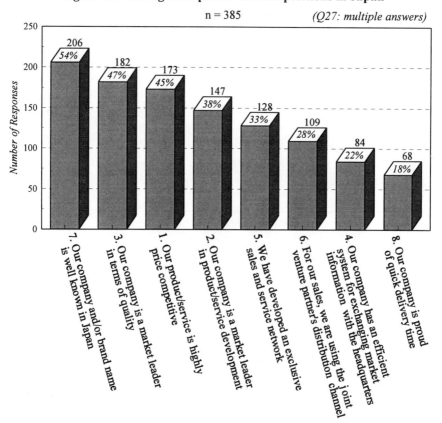

employees in Japan. Generally, we found that the response rate to various questions was lower from companies with less than 50% foreign capital. In the total sample, the percentage of minority-owned foreign companies was only 12%.

The conclusion that can be drawn is that generally successful foreign companies must be highly competitive in the Japanese market in terms of CI or brand name, sales and service network, and leadership in quality of product, service development, price, or delivery time. Whenever possible, the joint venture partner's distribution channels should be used. Moreover, foreign companies need to have repair and after-sales services (spare part centers and service stations), since they are indispensable for, among other things, protecting the brand image of a company.

6.6   EXPENDITURE ON MARKETING

Thirty-eight percent of the foreign companies reported yearly expenditures on marketing of about 3% or less than 3% of their total sales (see Figure 6.5). However, 22% of the companies said yearly marketing expenditures were in the range of 5% to 10% of their yearly sales, and 25% of the foreign companies reported marketing expenditures of over 10% of their yearly sales. We find that foreign companies' marketing expenditures in Japan were higher compared to those of many foreign companies operating in other OECD countries.

The reasons given were that advertising and promotion is rather expensive in Japan and that much promotional and advertising material had to be specially designed (with translation and printing costs) for the Japanese market. The

Figure 6.5   Yearly expenditure on marketing as percentage of total sales

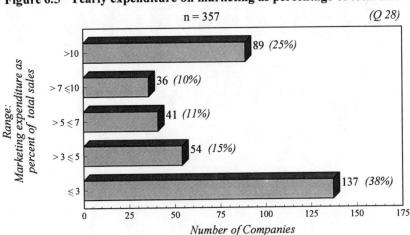

amount of personal selling was extremely high, that is, face-to-face contact between buyer and seller was extensive and intensive, as was frequent training of marketing and sales staff. Also, as the next question revealed, half of the foreign companies in Japan were not using globally standardized products and/or services for the Japanese market, so they were not able to utilize economies of scale in marketing.

Companies in the financial sector reported that their marketing expenditures were rather low in Japan, less than 1% of their earnings. Moreover, several foreign companies mentioned that they thought they should spend more on marketing but were unable to do so at the time either because their profits were too low (or they were incurring losses) or because they had not fully established themselves in the Japanese market.

A close examination of the companies with yearly marketing expenditures of over 10% of their sales revealed that 69% of the companies were in the manufacturing sector (62% of these were in the consumer goods sector), 67% of the companies were in the "Success" group, 83% of the companies had over 50% equity (64% of the companies were 100% foreign owned), and 39% of the companies had more than 200 employees. It was interesting to note that nine in the "Failure" group had marketing expenditures of over 10% of their sales.

6.7 GLOBAL STANDARDIZATION

The pros and cons of global standardization within the context of international marketing strategy have been debated intensively both inside and outside the academic world.[4] Competition in the Japanese market is considered to be some of the fiercest in the world. Therefore, it is quite natural that foreign companies will gain a competitive advantage if they are responsive to local needs and requirements when performing such activities as product and service adaptation, pricing, distribution, advertising and sales promotion, and after-sales service.

In the consumer goods and service sectors, we found that some well-known global companies who rarely follow localized adapted marketing but instead use standardized global marketing to provide economies of scale have, at least in Japan, made product/service and marketing adaptations. Examples are Coca Cola, McDonald's, and Kentucky Fried Chicken.

In this study, 50% of the foreign companies reported that they were not following a strategy of global standardization of product/service (including marketing activities) in the Japanese market. At the same time, another 50% of the companies, followed a global standardization strategy (see Appendix A, Q 29).

The standardization strategy was generally followed by manufacturers (76%, with a majority in the producer goods sector). Moreover, we found that in the following branches, companies relatively more often did not follow the strategy of standardization of products or services: food processing, pharmaceuticals, wholesale and retail trade, banks and credit institutes, and insurance companies. We found that in these branches the level of marketing innovation carried out by foreign companies in Japan was rather high.

European companies appeared to follow more often (50%) the standardization of product or service as compared to US companies (43%). In the group of companies that were not following a standardization policy, we found that 53% of the companies were from the United States, and 42% were European. Regarding performance and size of companies, no major differences were found between those companies that did and those that did not follow a standardization strategy.

It is quite clear that cultural differences, the distance between the United States and Europe, and the Japanese language make it rather difficult to centralize the translation and printing of advertisements and promotional materials at the headquarters of the foreign parent company. In order to be successful, these activities to a large extent have to be carried out in the Japanese market.

The same holds true for service support activities (spare part centers or service stations, etc.). These have to be located as often as possible in Japan (including such activities for the entire Asian region); otherwise it is extremely difficult to establish long-term relationships with Japanese buyers, especially in industrial goods, which require complex and specialized services.

6.8 TIME LAG IN PRODUCT AND SERVICE INTRODUCTION

About 50% of the companies (with the majority in the producer goods sector) reported that there was no particular time lag in introducing their products and services in the Japanese market compared to their home market (see Appendix A, Q 30). Several companies in this group developed products or services in the Japanese market especially for Japanese buyers or specially tailored their products or services for the Japanese market.

Another 50% of the foreign companies (with the majority in the producer goods sector) mentioned that there was a time lag between introducing their major product models or services in their home market and doing so in Japan. The time lag varied from a couple of months to over a year. A variety of reasons were given for this delay. In the pharmaceutical branch, there was a general delay due to testing procedures of new drugs and registration. In the case of automobiles, new models were thoroughly checked and clearance took some time. Several companies accused Japanese authorities of purposefully delaying the assignment of patent rights so that Japanese competitors could develop similar products and establish a foothold first.

Some companies in the financial sector reported that the Ministry of Finance took more time than usual when giving permission to introduce new service concepts that were highly successful in their other major markets. The purpose assumed was protection of the weaker domestic financial market.

Some foreign companies mentioned that there was a delay in introducing a product or service in the Japanese market due to distance from headquarters and testing of the product or service in Europe and the United States prior to launching it in the Japanese market, especially if some modifications had to be made for the Japanese market. Some companies accused their headquarters of being too slow in introducing their new products or services in the Japanese market. Higher preference was given by the headquarters to the markets of Europe and the United States, giving Japanese competitors the breathing time to develop similar products or services before these foreign companies could enter the Japanese market. By the time the foreign companies did introduce their new developments in Japan, the product or service was no longer new to Japanese buyers.

Cross-tabulation between global standardization (Q 29) and the time lag in introducing new major products or services (Q 30) did not reveal any major differences. About 25% of the companies that had standardized their products or services had faced a time lag in introducing their major new developments in the Japanese market, and another 26% of the companies that had standardized their products or services had not faced a time lag in introducing those in the Japanese market. In addition, 24% of the foreign companies that had not standardized their product or service did not face any time lag in introducing their new offering in the Japanese market.

Finally, it is quite clear that in order to be successful in the Japanese market, foreign companies have to introduce their new product models or service concepts as soon as possible; however, in most cases it did take some time to introduce new models, due to distance, market research, the need for product adaptation, regulations and technical requirements, and registration.

6.9 MARKET INTELLIGENCE

It is well known that Japanese companies keep a very close eye on their competitors, whether Japanese or foreign. The fiercely competitive market in Japan has encouraged the development of effective data collection, analysis, and feedback for strategic and corporate planning and other purposes. The seller also maintains very close face-to-face contact with the buyer and transmits information from the field directly to the marketing and sales department on a daily basis. It is not a joke to say that the Japanese seller rarely forgets the birthday of his or her clients.

Regarding foreign companies in Japan, we found that 85% of the foreign companies collected data from their clients (see Figure 6.6). This was considered to be quite effective as a method for carrying out market intelligence in Japan because the clients were in contact with competitors and thus were in a very good position to provide accurate information on rivals regarding product quality, price, delivery time, and level of service. Branch analysis revealed that 73% of companies that collected data from clients were in the manufacturing sector, with a majority in the producer goods sector. The dominant industries and services were chemicals, pharmaceuticals, machinery, electronics, and banks and credit institutes.

Sixty-three percent of the foreign companies used the traditional method of collecting data about their competitors: using printed materials such as journals, annual reports, and newspapers. Most of these companies kept full-time Japanese staff members busy translating Japanese printed materials. Some companies mentioned that nearly a quarter of the world's written material was produced in Japan; therefore, possessing Japanese language knowledge themselves

Figure 6.6   Type of market intelligence

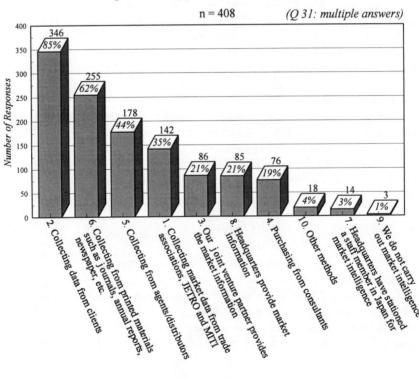

or having qualified Japanese staff members, put them in a position to obtain highly valuable information about their competitors in Japan. Such information was rather difficult to obtain from written materials in Europe or the United States. In other words, it was easier to carry out industrial espionage in Japan than elsewhere, provided one could master the Japanese language.

Other market intelligence methods used by foreign companies in Japan were to collect data from agents and distributors, trade associations, JETRO, and MITI; to obtain information through a joint venture partner; and to have headquarters provide market information or purchased information from local and foreign consultants in Japan. Very few foreign companies in Japan stationed staff members from headquarters specifically for market intelligence. One of the reasons was the high cost of stationing an expatriate in Japan. Only three companies reported that they did not carry out any market intelligence in Japan.

Some foreign companies reported that Japan's industrial organizations discriminated against them in not letting them become members because they were wholly owned foreign subsidiaries. Foreign companies, in particular in the financial, insurance, pharmaceutical, and food industries, mentioned they were facing difficulties in obtaining industrial information, since membership in such organizations was exclusively reserved for Japanese companies. Some foreign companies claimed that it was the Keiretsu (industrial groups) that were behind this type of discrimination.

The Japanese advisory panel to the Fair Trade Commission proposed in March 1993 that Japanese industrial organizations should not discriminate against foreign companies in Japan when considering them for membership because this is considered to be a barrier limiting foreign access to domestic markets. In Europe and the United States, Japanese companies do not face this type of discrimination. The US administration, in Structural Impediments Initiative talks, has attacked Japan for being lax on antitrust policies, for this is considered one of the barriers impeding foreign companies' entry into the Japanese market.

6.10 PROFIT-CENTER AND CROSS-SUBSIDIZATION APPROACHES

It is a well-known fact that European and American companies generally organize their business units using a profit-center approach for each product and service group, that is, each product or service is responsible for showing profits and for providing a contribution to headquarters (covering general administration costs, and the like). Foreign companies in Japan generally face heavy pressure from their headquarters to show profits for every product and service and every market segment at an early stage, for the companies follow short-term profit maximization strategies and objectives.

On the other hand, Japanese companies generally claim to follow a policy of cross-subsidization in which the profitability of each product and service group is not what is of paramount importance, but the total profitability of the entire company. Japanese companies generally face lower pressure to show immediate profits and to pay high dividends, thus they can pay greater attention to long-term objectives.

Fifty-eight percent of the foreign companies mentioned that they were using a profit-center approach (see Appendix A, Q 32). They were organized as a division within a company or belonged to a large independent entity. In several cases, foreign companies mentioned that they were selling only one range of product or services (using narrow market segments), and therefore they had no other alternative but the profit-center method. Seventy percent of the companies were in the manufacturing sector in this group, with a majority in the producer goods sector.

Fifty-six percent of the companies that were not using profit centers were following a policy of cross-subsidization within their division or entity (again, a majority of these companies were in the producer goods sector). One of the main reasons was the high cost of doing business in Japan. The total profitability of the entire Japanese subsidiary was important, not the profitability of each individual product or service group. Some foreign companies mentioned that the Japanese taxation system forced them to consolidate the entire operation under one umbrella. This method was also convenient for them, since corporate taxes are exorbitant in Japan, and if some products or groups were showing losses within one or more divisions, then they could offset them against the high profits of other products or services before paying corporate taxes. However, in internal evaluation, they followed more or less a profit-center approach, with heavy pressure on their product/sales managers to show profits. Seventy-six percent of the companies in this group were in the manufacturing sector.

Another advantage of organizing all the subsidiaries and product/service groups in Japan under one umbrella was that it facilitated local recruitment, since the size of a company was given great importance by prospective Japanese employees. Several of the companies mentioned that this policy was only of a cosmetic nature, since in day-to-day business the product/service groups and different subsidiaries in Japan do not consult with each other very often and do not necessarily report to the president or CEO of the company in Japan, but directly to the subsidiary's headquarters outside Japan.

Finally, several companies mentioned that they followed a mixture of both approaches. The overall tendency appears to be to use profit-centers, since this method facilitates performance and evaluation of each product/service group in Japan.

6.11 INTRODUCTION OF UNIQUE MARKETING PROGRAMS

Seventy percent of the foreign companies had successfully developed and introduced a unique marketing program or strategy that was tailored for Japanese buyers (see Figure 6.7). Several companies mentioned that due to differences in culture, tastes, and habits, they had to develop and introduce a special marketing program or strategy suitable for the Japanese market. Ignoring this adaptation would lead to failure in the Japanese market. Foreign companies had to be highly innovative in marketing in the Japanese market if they wanted to achieve success.

Seventy-two percent of the foreign companies that had successfully developed and introduced a unique marketing program or strategy were in the manufacturing sector, with a majority in the producer goods sector. The major industries were food processing, chemicals, pharmaceuticals, machinery, electronics, wholesale and retail trade, banks and credit institutes. Regarding ownership, 66% of the companies had more than 50% foreign equity. Fifty-three percent of the companies were from the United States, and 42% were from Europe.

Table 6.1 shows that successful foreign companies developed and introduced a unique marketing program or strategy slightly more often than the failures. The number of years of establishment in the Japanese market do not correlate with any significant differences with respect to the introduction of a unique marketing program or strategy. Generally, 70% of the foreign companies had introduced unique marketing programs. Regarding nationality, we found that companies from most countries represented had introduced unique marketing programs. Companies from a few countries had spent little or no effort in introducing unique marketing programs, for example, those from Denmark, Finland, Panama, Hong Kong, Poland, Singapore, India, and Korea.

Figure 6.7 Introduction of a unique marketing program/strategy

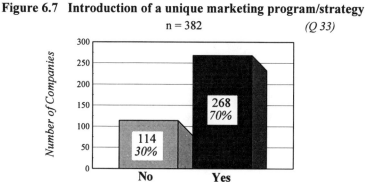

n = 382   (Q 33)

Table 6.1   Introduction of a unique marketing program/strategy based on performance   (Q 48)

Alternative (Q 33)	Sample 1 Number of companies	In %	Sample 2 Number of companies	In %	Sample 3 Number of companies	In %
NO	70	26	32	39	9	36
YES	200	74	50	61	16	64
Total	270	100	82	100	25	100

Legend
Sample 1 = Very successful and successful; Sample 2 = As expected;
Sample 3 = Very unsuccessful and unsuccessful.

In the food processing industry, all foreign companies had introduced unique marketing programs or strategies in Japan. Generally, it was the companies in the manufacturing and services sector that had introduced a unique marketing program or strategy in the Japanese market. Banks and credit institutions introduced slightly fewer unique marketing programs or strategies, one possible reason being that several of the banks and credit institutions are established in the form of representative offices in Japan and therefore do not need to actively market their services in Japan.

Cross-tabulation using Q 29 (global standardization) and Q 33 (introducing a unique marketing program/strategy) shows that 38% of the companies that had globally standardized their products or services had also developed and introduced a unique marketing program or strategy for the Japanese market, as compared to 12% of those that had not globally standardized their products or services.

6.12   TRANSFER OF SUCCESSFUL MARKETING PROGRAMS AND STRATEGIES TO HEADQUARTERS

Twenty-six percent of the foreign companies reported that they had transferred a successful marketing program/strategy to their headquarters or to other subsidiaries outside Japan (see Figure 6.8). This finding shows that the marketing innovations made by foreign companies' subsidiaries in Japan flow back to the parent company and its subsidiaries outside Japan, constituting both a vertical and a horizontal flow of marketing know-how. The Vernon and Wells product cycle model (PCM)[5] cannot entirely explain this feature of foreign companies in Japan. A large number of American and European companies have developed marketing programs or strategies specifically tailored for the Japanese market, and they have also been able to transfer parts of these to their

Figure 6.8 Transfer of a successful marketing program/strategy to headquarters

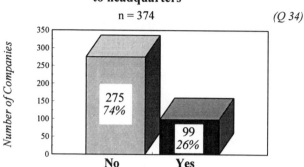

n = 374   (Q 34)

parent companies and/or to other subsidiaries outside Japan (for more details, see Chapters 8 and 9).

Table 6.2 shows that about 29% of successful and 28% of failed companies transferred a successful marketing program or strategy outside Japan. Eighty-one percent of the foreign companies who did this are in the manufacturing sector, with a majority of them (64%) in the producer goods industries. Regarding ownership, 55% of the foreign companies were 100% owned. Fifty-eight percent of the foreign companies had fewer than 201 employees. The very low rate of transfer in the non-manufacturing sector is due to the fact that the service sector is still weak in Japan compared to the United States and Europe.

Foreign companies that had been established longer in Japan had more often transferred a successful marketing program or strategy outside Japan. Forty percent of the foreign companies that were established in Japan before 1971 had transferred a successful marketing program or strategy outside Japan, and only 13% of foreign companies that established themselves in Japan after 1985 had done so (see Appendix B6.1).

Table 6.2 Transfer of successful marketing program/strategy to headquarters based on performance   (Q 48)

Alternative (Q 34)	Sample 1 Number of companies	In %	Sample 2 Number of companies	In %	Sample 3 Number of companies	In %
NO	186	71	66	80	18	72
YES	76	29	16	20	7	28
Total	262	100	82	100	25	100

Legend
  Sample 1 = Very successful and successful; Sample 2 = As expected;
  Sample 3 = Very unsuccessful and unsuccessful.

One of the reasons why companies that had established themselves in the Japanese market recently had transferred a lower number of successful marketing programs and strategies outside Japan is that it generally takes several years for a foreign company to establish itself properly in the Japanese market.

We find in Europe and the United States the general notion that Japanese companies are excellent in production technology and R & D but somewhat weak in marketing know-how. However, in our study we see that about one-fourth of the foreign companies had transferred a successful marketing program or strategy outside Japan. This is quite an interesting result, and it implies that European and American companies can no longer take for granted their monopoly on introducing unique marketing programs or strategies on their own continents.

European companies had transferred more successful marketing programs/strategies outside Japan than had American companies (54% compared to 45%). Some European companies had transferred a higher percentage of their successful marketing programs/strategies than American companies, for example, the Netherlands (46%), Sweden (41%), and Germany (33%), in contrast to the US (25%; see Appendix B6.2).

The branch comparison showed that 81% of the successful marketing programs/strategies that had been transferred outside Japan came from the manufacturing sector, in particular in textiles (50%), chemicals (42%), electronics (28%), and machinery (27%), as shown in Appendix B6.3. It is in the manufacturing sector that customer responsiveness and quality, among others, are extremely important factors in marketing consumer and industrial goods and services successfully in Japan. It appears that successful foreign companies, particularly, in the manufacturing sector, had been able to transfer programs outside Japan to increase their competitive edge.

Some foreign companies, particularly, in the services sector, mentioned that due to cultural differences between Japan and Western countries they believed that it would take some time before they were able to transfer a successful marketing program or strategy from Japan to headquarters or other subsidiaries outside Japan. The Japanese financial sector, as mentioned earlier, is internationally still weak, thus only minor transfers have taken place until now.

Cross-tabulation between Q 29 and Q 34 shows that only 6% of the companies that had not globally standardized their products or services had transferred a successful marketing program or strategy outside Japan. On the other hand, 24% of the companies that had developed and introduced a unique marketing program or strategy in the Japanese market (Q 33) had also transferred that successful marketing program or strategy outside Japan.

6.13   FINANCIAL INSTITUTIONS' ACTIVITIES

In this section we will mention briefly the position of financial institutions in the Japanese market. Some specific questions concerning financial institutions were asked (see Appendix A, Q 23). Financial institutions represented about 14% of the companies that took part in the survey.

The types of services provided to customers in Japan (Q 23.1) were mainly portfolio management, advisory services, banking, foreign exchange, options, futures swaps, trade financing, corporate lending, inward investment to Europe, brokerage, stocks and bonds, M & A business, and insurance.

Regarding the type and degree of competition faced in Japan (Q 23.2), most of the foreign financial institutions faced strong and severe competition from both Japanese and other foreign institutions, specifically, from about 150 Japanese and 40 major foreign-affiliated institutions. Some institutions claimed that the existence of cartels made the competition intense and that the competition was therefore unfair. For some respondents, the major competitors were foreign financial institutions in Japan.

The strengths on which foreign institutions compete with their Japanese competitors (Q 23.3) were the AAA-rating of the parent bank; the global network of the parent company or global strength; headquarters' long experience, more than 100 years in some cases; headquarters' well-trained staff in Japan; headquarters' expertise in all the world markets; sophisticated banking products; expertise in customer and market knowledge; occupying market niches; and using overseas home base connections to obtain an upper hand over other competitors.

Regarding discrimination faced in the Japanese market by foreign financial institutions (Q 23.4), a large number of foreign institutions mentioned that they did not face any special discrimination in the Japanese market. The CEOs of many of these institutions were Japanese, recruited as mid-career managers from well-known Japanese securities companies or from the Ministry of Finance. These CEOs had difficulty understanding the wide coverage given by the mass media and various chambers of commerce to the administrative guidelines leading to unfair competition in the Japanese market. However, personal interviews and some answers to the questionnaire revealed that some Japanese executives, and the expatriates in particular, faced the following problems:

- Unfair competition, cartel-like situations in which the big four Japanese securities institutions (Nomura, Daiwa, Nikko, and Yamaichi) dominate or have simply monopolized the market.
- Japanese city banks exchange their views regularly with each other but keep foreign institutions out of these meetings.
- Dissatisfaction with some of the regulations of the Bank of Japan (BOJ) and the Ministry of Finance (MOF), and administrative guidelines (including

oral directives) and excessive regulations that make it difficult to enter the Japanese market.
- The fact that they are forbidden to sell services in Japan that are normally sold in the United States and Europe.
- Relationship-oriented business practices, such as the strong ties between Japanese financial institutions and Japanese companies that make it difficult for foreign institutions to do business.
- Re-financing is difficult for foreign banks, even those whose parent banks have an AAA rating, and bank guarantees of foreign bank branches in Japan are not accepted even if the parent bank has an AAA rating.
- The actual credit standing of the bank is sometimes ignored, in contrast to the experience of even small Japanese banks, so that funding costs are higher in Japan.
- The high cost and problems in obtaining a license in Japan.
- It takes a considerably longer time for a foreign company to become a member of the Tokyo Stock Exchange (TSE) than for a Japanese security company to join the European or US stock exchanges.

6.14 CONCLUSIONS

It appears to us that foreign companies have been following a bypass strategy, since the number of foreign companies in Japan is not remarkably high. They have been avoiding the second largest market in the world for a number of reasons. It is a known fact that the Japanese distribution system is complicated and multitiered, and the existence of strong business groups with tightly interlinked relationships (such as the Keiretsu) who follow exclusive business practices may also cause problems for foreign companies in Japan. Many foreign companies complain that there are a number of barriers that make it difficult to penetrate the Japanese market. At the same time, it is the costliest market of the OECD countries. On the other hand, we found that despite these problems, most foreign companies taking part in this survey were successful in Japan.

In many ways the Japanese market is unique, particularly due to differences in culture, taste, and habits. Therefore it is not easy to standardize a product, service or a marketing strategy. Foreign companies have to adapt to the peculiarities of the Japanese market.

Building a positive corporate image takes time; this can be clearly seen, for example, in the automobile industry sector. Sweden's Volvo and Germany's Mercedes, BMW, and Audi have spent huge amounts of money and time in building a positive corporate image in Japan. Foreign companies have to show, among other things, a long-term commitment in order to succeed in the Japanese market.

A large number of foreign companies successfully exploited their market niches, which were mainly in narrow market and product segments with limited competition from their Japanese rivals. Many foreign companies had developed an exclusive sales and service network, and many were using a joint venture partner's distribution channels effectively. Successful foreign companies in Japan paid great attention to the demands and sensitivities of Japanese buyers toward product quality.

Many foreign companies had a high degree of autonomy. European companies compared to US companies appeared more often to follow a global standardization of product/service and more frequently to transfer a successful marketing program or strategy outside Japan.

One of the reasons companies that had established themselves in the Japanese market recently had transferred a lower number of successful marketing programs/strategies outside Japan was that it generally takes several years before a foreign company can properly establish itself in the Japanese market.

Foreign companies have to be innovative in the Japanese market because of the fact that Japanese customers are the most demanding and quality sensitive in the world. Global standardization of marketing programs/strategies is difficult in the Japanese market, but marketing innovation done in Japan and the transfer of marketing know-how from Japan to headquarters and to other subsidiaries outside Japan are rewarding for many foreign companies. In addition, these activities give a competitive edge to foreign companies in Japan.

NOTES

1. We should note that in several foreign companies a part of the salary of their CEO is based on sales, profits, stocks, and the inventory of the local subsidiary.
2. See, among others, Kotler, P., et al., 1985.
3. See ACCJ and A. T. Kearney, Inc., 1991; Commission of the European Communities, 1991.
4. See Takeuchi H., Porter, M. E., 1986, pp. 111-146.
5. Vernon, R., and Wells, L. T., Jr., 1991.

7 PRODUCTION AND RESEARCH & DEVELOPMENT

In order to be successful in the Japanese market it is vital for foreign companies to have a local production base and local R & D operations. In Chapter 6 we concluded that it was of utmost importance for foreign companies to adapt their products and services to Japanese market requirements if they were to be successful. One way of showing commitment to Japanese buyers, particularly, in the industrial producer goods sector, where tailor-made products or applications are developed and modified in cooperation with buyers, is to establish production facilities and R & D units in Japan.

7.1 INTRODUCTION

Global companies (MNCs and TNCs) cannot ignore Japan since Japan is part of the triad with the United States and Europe. Large numbers of foreign companies from Europe and the United States have technical leads over their Japanese competitors in several key industrial sectors or product/service niches, and for these companies, the Japanese market provides tremendous opportunities not only for selling in the Japanese market but also for improving technology and know-how. The reverse flow of this expertise outside Japan further enhances the companies' global competitiveness, increasing global synergy, in the field of production and R & D.

Japan is known for its production efficiency, and foreign companies that establish a production base in Japan can learn and acquire its production system and know-how. If they succeed in achieving this, their delivery security will increase, and this will strengthen their competitive edge in Japan as well as show firm commitment to the Japanese market to their buyers, suppliers, subcontractors, and local employees. Our interest in this chapter is to discover the reasons foreign companies carry out production in Japan and whether any difficulties are faced in meeting the specific requirements of customers, in the performance of foreign companies' factories, or in the transfer of Japanese production techniques to headquarters.

Japan has already overtaken practically all of its main competitors in several high-tech segments, including semiconductors, ICs, biotechnology, new materials, various sectors in the field of consumer and industrial electronics, robots, and telecommunication.

By establishing an R & D base in Japan, foreign companies are able to participate in a market where new technologies and know-how are continuously being developed. For foreign companies to be successful in Japan, they have to become part of the Japanese research network, or "insiders"--to work with various relevant Japanese laboratories, research institutions, universities, and manufacturers.

Technologies developed in Japan by foreign companies can considerably improve their competitiveness globally and at the same time facilitate the recruitment of highly qualified and talented Japanese personnel in other departments as well as R & D and production.

The purpose of this chapter is also to explore wider issues concerning the parent-subsidiary relationship with respect to R & D autonomy and personnel. R & D topics include innovative activities undertaken by a company, the share of employees engaged in R & D, the expenditure on R & D, the number of patents obtained in Japan, the transfer of R & D results to the parent company, and autonomy in conducting R & D. In the present study, a large number of foreign companies with production facilities and R & D in Japan are in the producer goods sector (see Appendix A for details).

7.2   REASONS FOR HAVING PRODUCTION FACILITIES IN JAPAN

Two hundred seven foreign companies out of 301 companies selling manufactured products reported having production facilities in Japan.[1] Sixty-five percent of the foreign companies reported that there were advantages to having production facilities in Japan: lower costs for the manufacture of customer-specified products in Japan, shorter delivery times, increased ease in meeting Japanese quality and specific product requirements, and quick pre- and after-sales services (see Figure 7.1). A majority of these companies were in the producer goods sector, and 56% of the companies overall had over 50% foreign equity.

Forty-seven percent of the companies mentioned that having production facilities in Japan enabled them to show their commitment to their customers,

Figure 7.1   Reasons for having production facilities in Japan

n = 207 of which: M1 = 66; M2 = 136; N1 = 3; N2 = 2 *   *(Q 35: multiple answers)*

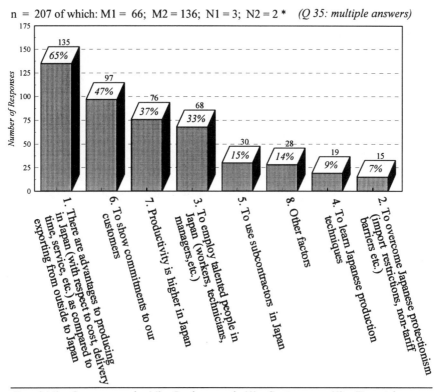

*Note: * M1 = Consumer goods; M2 = Producer goods; N1 = Service sector; N2 = Financial sector*

and 36% of the companies also mentioned that the productivity at their Japanese factories was considerably higher than at their factories outside Japan. Several foreign companies mentioned that their Japanese factories were used as success models by their parent companies and other subsidiaries outside Japan.

Other important reasons for having production facilities in Japan were as follows: to employ talented Japanese engineers and technicians; to use Japanese subcontractors, and to learn from Japanese production techniques.

Very few foreign companies, however, reported that their purpose in having production facilities in Japan was to overcome Japanese protectionism. The companies that chose alternative 2 (overcoming Japanese protectionism) were mainly in the food, chemicals, and pharmaceuticals sectors, and the majority (60%) were European. Moreover, most of these companies were in the "Success" group. This factor again underlines how inaccurate is the picture presented by the mass media and the ACCJ, EC Commission, and various chambers of commerce in Japan, as it clearly exaggerates Japanese protectionism as an impediment to doing business in Japan or as a barrier blocking foreign access to the Japanese market.

Regarding the final alternative (other factors), the specific reasons mentioned for having production facilities in Japan were: quality control was excellent in Japan; the particular market needs, modifications, and requirements of Japanese customers could be met more smoothly; logistics were improved; delivery was quicker; technical and tailor-made specifications could be met more effectively; it was easier to attract talented Japanese staff; special types of packaging could only be manufactured in Japan; unique Japanese tastes in foods could be more easily satisfied; and high-quality Japanese parts, components, and materials could be utilized. Several foreign companies mentioned that they imported the required machinery from outside Japan but did the actual manufacturing in Japan because this was highly efficient in terms of productivity. In the pharmaceuticals sector, it was more convenient to manufacture the products in Japan because otherwise it was necessary to obtain permission for every imported raw material from the Ministry of Health and Welfare.

7.3 FACTORY PERFORMANCE IN JAPAN VERSUS THAT IN PARENT FACTORIES OUTSIDE JAPAN

We found that overwhelmingly the foreign companies (61%) reported that the performance of their factories in Japan was higher or much higher than that in their parent companies' factories outside Japan (see Figure 7.2). The factors taken into consideration in evaluating performance were productivity, cost, precision and quality, machine tool designs for NCs and CNCs, and delivery times.

Only 10% of the companies reported that the performance of their factories in Japan was lower than the factories of their headquarters outside Japan. In these cases, common reasons given were the lack of availability of qualified local staff and difficulties in obtaining suitable land close to their buyers. Both of the companies that reported having a much lower performance from their factories in Japan (Q 36) were in the "Success" group of manufacturers. Companies that chose alternative (lower performance) were mainly in the machinery and electronics sectors, most of them in the "Success" group, and a large number of them (56%) were from the United States.

Sixty eight percent of the successful or very successful foreign companies reported a higher or much higher performance in Japan, whereas only 46% of the failures reported such results (see Table 7.1). However, only 7% of the foreign companies in the "Success" group reported having a lower performance from their factories in Japan compared to their parent companies. This observation again shows how important it is for foreign companies to have production facilities in Japan in order to be successful.

Figure 7.2   Performance of factory in Japan compared to that of parent's factory outside Japan

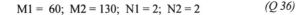

M1 = 60; M2 = 130; N1 = 2; N2 = 2   *(Q 36)*

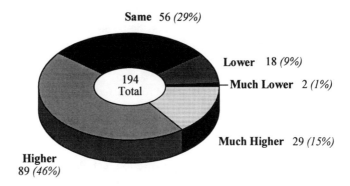

Same 56 *(29%)*

Lower 18 *(9%)*

—**Much Lower** 2 *(1%)*

Much Higher 29 *(15%)*

Higher
89 *(46%)*

194
Total

Number of Companies

Some foreign companies mentioned that due to the fact that productivity and quality levels were considerably higher at their factories in Japan (with nearly zero defect rates and quicker deliveries) as compared to those at their parent company, they received a large number of visitors (managers and technicians) from their headquarters and other subsidiaries. The visitors came to observe this phenomenon and to find out, among other things, the secret behind the higher productivity and product quality in Japan.

Table 7.1   Performance of factory compared to parent's factories outside Japan, based on performance criteria   (Q 48)

Alternative (Q 36)	Sample 1 Number of companies	In %	Sample 2 Number of companies	In %	Sample 3 Number of companies	In %
1 = Much lower	2	2				
2 = Lower	7	5	8	19	2	18
3 = Same	34	25	16	39	4	36
4 = Higher	67	49	15	37	5	46
5 = Much higher	26	19	2	5		
Total	136	100	41	100	11	100

Legend
  Sample 1 = Very successful and successful; Sample 2 = As expected;
  Sample 3 = Very unsuccessful and unsuccessful.

7.4 THE TRANSFER OF JAPANESE PRODUCTION TECHNIQUES TO THE PARENT COMPANY AND OTHER SUBSIDIARIES

Thirty-five percent of the foreign companies reported that they had transferred Japanese production techniques from their factories to their parent company or to other subsidiaries outside Japan (see Figure 7.3).

Table 7.2 shows that generally the successful foreign companies had been responsible for transferring a bulk of Japanese production techniques (equipment and know-how) outside Japan; 77% of the transferring companies were successful ones. Among the 70 transferring companies, only 4% of them were failures.

Figure 7.3   Transfer of production techniques to parent company

n = 204 of which: M1 = 63; M2 = 137; N1 = 2; N2 = 2   *(Q 37)*

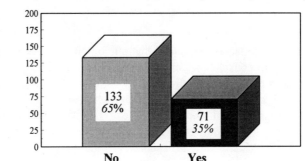

Table 7.2   Transfer of production techniques to parent company, based on performance criteria   (Q 48)

Alternative (Q 37)	Sample 1 Number of companies	In %	Sample 2 Number of companies	In %	Sample 3 Number of companies	In %
No	89	62	28	68	9	75
Yes	54	38	13	32	3	25
Total	143	100	41	100	12	100

Legend
 Sample 1 = Very successful and successful; Sample 2 = As expected;
 Sample 3 = Very unsuccessful and unsuccessful.

The foreign companies that had transferred production techniques had also been established longer in the Japanese market (see Appendix B7.1). Eighty-two percent of the foreign companies that transferred production techniques had established themselves in Japan prior to 1981. Ratios showed that manufacturers in the chemicals, car and car parts, pharmaceuticals, and electronics sectors had been responsible for most of the transfers of production techniques (see Appendix B7.2). It is in these areas that Japan is presently highly competitive globally, despite the fact that Japan is generally considered to be weak in the chemicals and pharmaceuticals sectors.

Eighty percent of the companies in this group had 50% or more foreign equity. Regarding nationality, we find that foreign companies from the United States and Europe were responsible for practically all transfer of production techniques from Japan (see Appendix B7.3). Foreign companies from the United States alone were responsible for fully 59% of the transfer of production techniques outside Japan. Other major countries transferring such techniques were Germany, the Netherlands, Switzerland, and Sweden. We see that the Vernon and Wells (1991) model of PCM needs some revision if it is to take into account the reverse transfer of production techniques.

Most foreign companies that transferred Japanese production techniques mentioned that they had done this once; in several cases transfer had occurred over 50 times. The types of transfer had been related to such things as product development and improvement (including new products and designs), various types of production techniques and know-how (including new manufacturing processes), production equipment, and designs. Some companies mentioned that Japan is now one of the major sources in the triad for a whole range of production techniques. For example, Volvo of Sweden, which previously transferred its production techniques to Japan, has been recently acquiring, among other things, production know-how from Japan, and transferring it back to its parent company in Sweden.

7.5 DIFFICULTIES IN PERFORMING PRODUCTION ACTIVITIES IN JAPAN

A large number of companies mentioned that they have had difficulties in performing production activities in Japan, mainly due to high land prices, high wages, and lack of qualified staff (see Figure 7.4). These results are in line with earlier studies. For example, companies mentioning high land prices were, in a majority of cases, established in Japan prior to 1986, and have a present foreign capital ratio of over 50% (the main industries were chemicals, pharmaceuticals, machinery, and electronics).

Other problems faced were difficulties in obtaining suitable land or production sites, particularly, in the vicinity of buyers; too strict environmental regula-

Figure 7.4   Difficulties while performing production activities in Japan

n = 179 of which: M1 = 51; M2 = 125; N1 = 2; N2 = 1   *(Q 38 : multiple answers)*

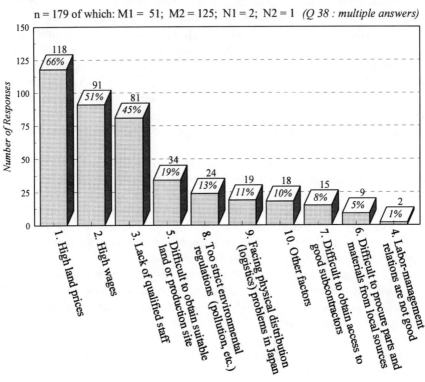

tions; physical distribution problems; difficulties in obtaining access to good subcontractors; difficulties in procuring parts and materials locally; and (for two companies) problems due to labor-management relations. A majority of the foreign companies reported that in Japan their company faced a minimal number of labor-management problems. Japanese workers were considered to be the most diligent in the world.

Several foreign companies mentioned that they faced difficulties with the recruitment of well-qualified graduates from Japanese universities; severe legal regulations regarding pollution controls; a lack of product modification capability by the parent company; a lack of understanding by headquarters as to the high product quality requirements of Japanese buyers; restrictions on innovation by the parent company; too much interference by the Japanese government; cultural differences between headquarters and the subsidiary, leading to tremendous problems in product development; and high energy costs and corporate taxes.

Foreign companies that chose alternatives 1, 2, and 3 were mainly in the food, chemicals, pharmaceuticals, machinery, and electronics sectors. Practically all the companies were in the "Success" group, and some were in the "As expected" group. Regarding ownership, most foreign companies had 50% or more foreign equity (alt. 1, 86%; alt. 2, 87%; alt. 3, 90%). Concerning alternative 4, both companies responding were 100% foreign owned.

7.6 REASONS FOR CONDUCTING R & D IN JAPAN

According to JETRO, the number of research centers established by foreign manufacturing companies increased from 76 in 1984 to 123 in 1989.[2] Activities in these research centers were strengthened during the period, and the number of researchers and R & D budgets increased by 2.6 and 2.3, respectively. The R & D activities of foreign companies, aimed at the expansion of sales in the Japanese market, included the development of new products designed for the Japanese market as well as support for sales activities in Japan such as technical services. The number of foreign companies conducting R & D in Japan was modest in absolute numbers; they represented some of the leading MNCs and TNCs.

Most of the companies that answered our question on reasons for conducting R & D in Japan (see App. A, Q 47) were actually conducting R & D in Japan at the time (88%, or 138 companies out of 157 companies answering the question).[3] Figure 7.5 shows that for 83% of the foreign companies, one reason for conducting R & D in Japan was to adapt to the needs of the Japanese market promptly; they were involved in Japan-specific R & D and product modification research. For 56% of the foreign companies, a purpose of conducting R & D was to establish an integrated system of R & D, production, and sales. For 50% of the companies, one purpose was to apply the parent company's technology and product innovation in Japan.

Other important reasons for conducting R & D in Japan were to generate global synergy in R & D by exchanging R & D results with the parent company and other subsidiaries; to employ Japanese researchers and technicians; to profit from the Japanese environment, which is favorable to product innovation and development; and to improve R & D capabilities, reflecting the fact that Japanese R & D has advanced in several areas.

Exceptionally few foreign companies mentioned that their purpose for conducting R & D in Japan was to monitor technology (alt. 8) or to establish an R & D base in Asia (alt. 9). Those foreign companies that chose alternatives 8 and 9 were mainly from the chemicals sector, medium to large in size (with over 50 employees), and owned 50% or more foreign equity (alt. 8, 90%; alt. 9, 100%). In the case of alternative 8, the majority of foreign companies were from Europe

Figure 7.5   Reasons for conducting or intending to conduct R & D in Japan

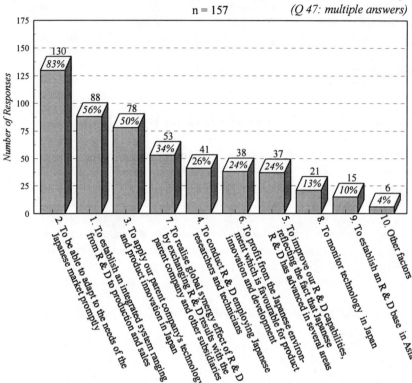

(65%), and in the case of alternative 9, the majority of the foreign companies were from the United States (57%).

Several foreign companies had established technology centers (including technical centers) in Japan. In these centers, customers could collaborate with the company to develop and test new products and processes and to modify products according to their needs. In addition, the company could demonstrate equipment (eliminating one need to travel to Europe or the United States), do test production of customers' products, and provide training in operation, repair, and maintenance. Examples are the recently established Ford R & D center for electronic automotive components and Tetra Pak Technical Center, established by a market leader in liquid packaging.

Several foreign companies mentioned that they were actively collaborating on research projects with Japanese universities, research institutes, and manufacturers, and transferring the R & D results to their headquarters and other subsidiaries. They were also able to raise the morale of their Japanese engineers by dispatching them to the parent company's R & D centers. An important reason for conducting R & D in the pharmaceuticals sector was that Japanese law required that clinical trials be done in Japan prior to obtaining registration licenses for new medicines.

It is quite clear that the purpose of establishing an R & D unit (or plans for establishing an R & D unit) is not low cost, since Japan is one of the most expensive countries in which to carry out such activities. Despite the risks, there are great strategical advantages to be gained, such as globalizing the technology base in the triad, increasing the level of innovation, and the synergetic effects of exchanging R & D results with the parent company and other subsidiaries.

It is quite apparent that Japan is a leading center of innovation for a broad range of technologies, some of which are available nowhere else in the world. Therefore, the focus for most foreign companies in the Japanese market will naturally be the development of new products and processes at the developmental or applied level in order to adapt to the needs of the Japanese market promptly and be competitive in and outside Japan. For example, the R & D department of Eastman Kodak of the United States has successfully developed products (such as the Kodak Imagelink Scanner 500) especially geared to the Japanese market.

7.7 INCEPTION OF R & D ACTIVITIES IN JAPAN

Figure 7.6 shows that 45.8% of the companies in the manufacturing sector were carrying out R & D in Japan. Fifty percent of the foreign companies conducting R & D were established in Japan before 1981 (see Figure 7.7). It is interesting to note that 23% of the companies conducting R & D were established after 1985 in Japan. Regarding performance, 75% of the foreign companies were in the "Success" group, 21% in the "As expected" group, and 4% were in the "Failure" group. Fifty-five percent of the companies conducting R & D were from the United States, and 42% of them were from Europe. Regarding ownership, 56% of the companies had over 50% foreign equity. In cases where both production and R & D activities were carried out by the same company, about 34% of the companies were 100% foreign owned.

Regarding the size of the companies as measured by the total number of employees in Japan, we found that 42% of the companies conducting R & D were large or very large, with over 200 employees. Only 29% of them had less than 51 employees.

In the consumer goods sector, European companies had an edge over American companies, whereas in the producer goods sector it was the American companies that had an edge in carrying out R & D in Japan. In the consumer goods sector, European products had a higher quality image than American products in Japan. According to the Japanese, buying an American car, for ex-ample, would make one a regular customer of a particular repair station in

Figure 7.6   Manufacturing companies conducting R & D in Japan

Base = 301 Manufacturing Companies   *(Q 39)*

NO   163 *(54.2%)*

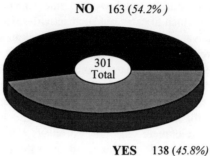

YES   138 *(45.8%)*

Japan. Generally, we found that most of the R & D was carried out by American companies, followed by Germany, the Netherlands, Switzerland, France, the United Kingdom, and Sweden.

Foreign companies that were conducting R & D in Japan were mostly in the following branches: chemicals, electronics, machinery, pharmaceuticals, car and car parts, and food processing.

Foreign companies doing R & D could be divided into two groups, based on the questionnaire and the case studies. One group of foreign companies was conducting limited R & D in order to meet Japanese customers' specific requirements. The other group of foreign companies was conducting long-term

Figure 7.7   Inception of R & D activities in Japan

n = 138 of which: M1 = 51; M2 = 83; N1 = 4   (Q 39)

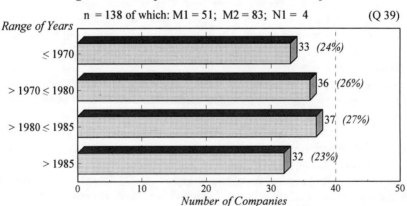

R & D with the aim of transferring technology and know-how from Japan. At the same time, these companies hoped to obtain global synergy and economies of scale by concentrating certain types of R & D in Japan and coordinating it with R & D activities carried out at headquarters and other subsidiaries. A recent example worth mentioning here is BASF (from Germany), which opened its new materials R & D laboratory for metal and ceramics injection molding and electro-conductive and magnetic polymers. The main purpose was to develop new products and technologies targeted for the Japanese as well as the world market.

Several foreign companies are carrying out production and R & D with their Japanese competitors, buyers, and suppliers in such forms as tie-ups, design-ins, and other cooperative and strategic alliances.[4] Recent examples of such alliances are: Cannon and Motorola (United States), Toyota and General Motors (United States), Mitsubishi Motors and Jurid (Germany), Suzuki Motor and Varity (Canada), Hitachi and Texas Instruments (United States), and Toshiba and Microsoft (United States).

7.8 NUMBER OF RESEARCHERS AND TECHNICIANS

Regarding the number of researchers and technicians, we found that 77% of the foreign companies had up to 50 persons engaged in R & D, and 24% of them had five or fewer persons (see Appendix A, Q 40). Thirty-eight percent of the foreign companies also had expatriates engaged in R & D; however, the majority of these companies had only between one and five expatriates.

The total number of researchers and technicians in 133 companies was 10,515, and the total number of expatriates involved in R & D in the 36 companies who had them was 147 (the total number of researchers was 8,363 in these companies). Expatriates accounted for 2% of the researchers and technicians in these 36 companies. In 97 foreign companies with R & D units, there were no expatriates. Clearly, most foreign companies rely entirely upon Japanese researchers and technicians for conducting R & D in Japan.

It appears that the number of foreign companies with more than 50 researchers and technicians is not very large in Japan, 23% of the total. Similarly, the number of expatriates engaged in R & D is not large, but in 50% of the companies having at least one expatriate, he or she happened to occupy the position of head of the R & D department and was involved with administrative duties, among others. Most of the companies employing expatriates in R & D were very large: 50% of them had over 500 employees in Japan, and only 17% of them had fewer than 50 employees.

Regarding foreign companies with more than 50 researchers and technicians, the majority of the companies were in the chemicals, pharmaceuticals, and electronics industries, and the majority (58%) were in the consumer goods sector. A large number of companies were from the United States (58%), and 58% of them were 100% foreign owned. No special tendencies were found regarding foreign companies with more than five expatriates other than the fact that all of them except one were 100% foreign owned, and slightly more of them were European.

7.9 EXPENDITURE ON R & D

Figure 7.8 shows that 50% of the companies conducting R & D had an average expenditure on R & D as a percentage of total sales of over 4%. Moreover, 11% of the companies had R & D expenditures of over 10% of their sales. A large proportion of R & D expenditures was on research personnel, equipment, the laboratory, and land (laboratory premises), which costs an exorbitant amount in Japan.

The average expenditure of foreign companies for R & D as a percentage of total sales was 4.79%. This ratio is very high compared to the Japanese companies' average spending for R & D in the manufacturing industry, which was 3.36% in FY 1990 (for details, see Chapter 2).[5]

Figure 7.8   Average expenditure for R & D as percentage of total sales

n = 125 of which: M1 = 45; M2 = 77; N1 = 3   *(Q 41)*

Range: Average Expenditure
for R & D in percent

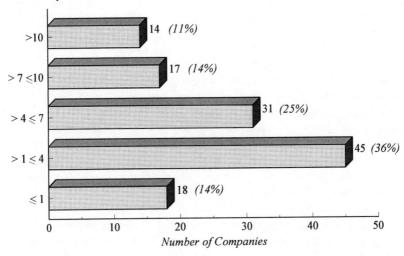

Number of Companies

A large number of foreign companies with expenditures for R & D in the range of over 7% and less than or equal to 10% of sales were in the consumer goods sector (59%) as well as a majority of the companies in the pharmaceuticals and chemicals sectors (in cosmetics, for example). Fifty-three percent of the companies were European, and all the companies in this group had 50% or more foreign equity. Sixty-five percent of the companies had over 200 employees.

Those companies that had R & D expenditures of over 10% of their sales had the following characteristics: a majority of them were in the pharmaceuticals sector, nearly 50% were active in the consumer goods sector, 57% were American, all of them had 50% or more foreign equity, and 57% of them had over 200 employees.

Regarding average expenditures for R & D as a percentage of total sales, we found that the highest average expenditure was in the pharmaceuticals industry (8% of the total sales), followed by the machinery (5.5%), chemicals (4.02%), and electronics (3.32%) industries.

Several foreign companies mentioned that it was very expensive to conduct R & D in Japan, but that in order to maintain competitiveness and show commitment to the Japanese market, they had to incur such expenditures. Moreover, by having production and R & D facilities in Japan, they could consider themselves full insiders there.

7.10 TYPE OF R & D ACTIVITIES AND FUND ALLOCATIONS

We found that practically all foreign companies allocated funds to development research (100%) and 76% of them also conducted applied research, but only 32% of the companies allocated any funds to basic research (see Appendix A, Q 42). The majority of foreign companies were carrying out product modification research in order to meet Japanese customers' specific requirements. The expenditures were lower on basic research, since most of this was conducted at headquarters or in other subsidiaries outside Japan.

Regarding those companies that indicated that they were conducting basic research in Japan, we found that the majority of them were active in the producer goods sector (71%), a majority were from the United States (54%), and most of them were in the chemicals, pharmaceuticals, machinery, and electronics sectors.

In Japan's own manufacturing industry (FY 1991), about 6.8% of the funds were allocated for basic research, 21.7% went to applications research, and 71.5% were for development research.[6] It is well known that Japanese companies place a very heavy emphasis on applied and developmental research.[7] Foreign companies appear to follow the tendency that prevails in the

Japanese market. However, in the long run we believe that as foreign companies become "insiders," the amount of their basic research in Japan will also increase.

7.11 NUMBER OF PATENTS OBTAINED IN JAPAN

Figure 7.9 shows that 70% of the foreign companies had obtained patents in Japan. Twenty-eight percent of the foreign companies reported that they had obtained more than 10 patents in Japan. Successful companies had obtained the largest number of patents (78%), 35% of the companies had obtained more then 10 patents, and only 43% of the failures had obtained between 1 and 10 patents (see Appendix B7.4). Sixty-eight percent of the companies that obtained patents were active in the producer goods sector, where products are developed specifically for individual buyers.

Foreign companies that had established themselves in Japan before 1971 had also obtained a large number of patents in Japan (52%), and the lowest number of patents had been obtained by companies that had established themselves in Japan after 1985 (7%). The conclusion that can be drawn is that it takes several years after the establishment of production facilities and R & D units on the Japanese market before a foreign company is in a position to obtain patents in Japan.

Figure 7.9   Number of patents obtained in Japan

n = 132 of which: M1 = 46; M2 = 82; N1 = 4   *(Q 43)*

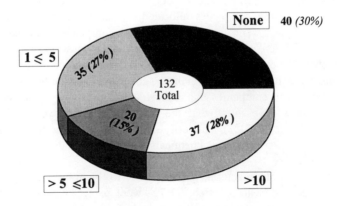

Number of Companies

Branch analysis reveals that a majority of the foreign companies that obtained patents in Japan were to be found in the chemicals, pharmaceuticals, machinery, and electronics industries. American companies had obtained the largest number of patents, followed by those from Germany, Switzerland, and the Netherlands.

We found that foreign companies with production facilities and R & D units are highly innovative in Japan. The results are quite encouraging and show how important it is to conduct production and R & D in Japan.

7.12 AUTONOMY FROM HEADQUARTERS IN CONDUCTING R & D ACTIVITIES IN JAPAN

We find that 26% of the companies reported that their R & D activities were completely autonomous from their headquarters, and another 37% mentioned having autonomy from headquarters to a large extent (see Figure 7.10). Only 8% of the companies reported that their R & D activities were controlled by their headquarters.

Table 7.3 shows that in all three performance groups, approximately two-thirds of the foreign companies had been given a high degree of autonomy from their headquarters in carrying out R & D activities in Japan; 61% of the

Figure 7.10 Autonomy from headquarters in conducting R & D activities in Japan

n = 147 of which: M1 = 53; M2 = 90; N1 = 4   *(Q 44)*

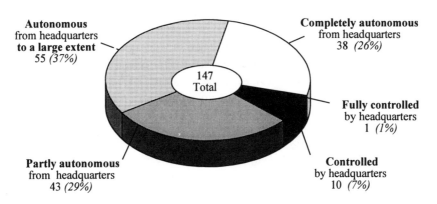

Number of Companies

Table 7.3   Autonomy from headquarters in conducting R & D
            activities, based on performance criteria   (Q 48)

Alternative (Q 44)	Sample 1 Number of companies	In %	Sample 2 Number of companies	In %	Sample 3 Number of companies	In %
1 = Completely autonomous from the headquarters	29	27	7	24	2	29
2 = Autonomous from the headquarters to a large extent	40	37	11	38	3	43
3 = Partly autonomous from the headquarters	34	31	9	31		
4 = Controlled by the headquarters	6	5	2	7	1	14
5 = Fully controlled by the headquarters					1	14
Total	109	100	29	100	7	100

Legend
  Sample 1 = Very successful and successful; Sample 2 = As expected;
  Sample 3 = Very unsuccessful and unsuccessful.

companies reporting complete autonomy from their headquarters were from the United States (alt. 1). Companies reporting being controlled by their headquarters (alts. 4 and 5) were active mainly in the consumer goods sector (91%, with a majority in the pharmaceuticals industry), and 64% of these were European.

Cross-tabulation between complete autonomy in conducting R & D in Japan (Q 44, alt. 1) and companies that obtained more than 10 patents in Japan (Q 43, alt. 4), showed that 32% belonged to both groups. This result shows that a correlation can be found between complete autonomy and number of patents obtained in Japan, but there is a need to investigate this point in depth before definite conclusions can be drawn.

Several foreign companies mentioned that in order to avoid overlap in R & D with subsidiaries outside of Japan and the parent company, they consult and coordinate R & D activities with each other and decide who will carry out which type of activity. In most cases, foreign companies' research activities were closely coordinated with the parent company in order to obtain synergies in R & D and be competitive globally.

It is interesting to note that in order to successfully carry out R & D activities, there is a need for a greater amount of autonomy from headquarters. Some of the reasons were to be able to carry out Japan-specific R & D, which was, in many cases, different from that in other OECD countries, and to be competitive in meeting the challenge from their rivals in Japan. However, we should be cautious in drawing conclusions, since the responses to our questionnaire were received only from foreign companies' subsidiaries in Japan, and they emphasized local autonomy in conducting Japan-specific R & D.

We found, as already mentioned, that foreign companies have to adapt to the requirements of their Japanese customers, develop product and service together with their customers, meet the stringent product/service quality requirements prevailing in the Japanese market, and at the same time transfer technology from Japan and become competitive globally.

7.13   REVERSE TECHNOLOGY TRANSFER

An overwhelming 64% of the foreign companies reported that they had transferred R & D results from Japan to their headquarters or to other subsidiaries outside Japan (see Figure 7.11). Table 7.4 shows that in all three performance groups, about two-thirds or more of the companies had transferred R & D results outside Japan. Seventy-six percent of these companies had more than 50 employees in Japan, and 46% of the companies had over 200 employees in Japan.

When we closely scrutinized the year that foreign companies established themselves in the Japanese market, we found that the companies that had established themselves in Japan prior to 1971 had transferred a large amount of R & D results outside Japan (55% of the transferring companies). The longer the company had been established in the Japanese market, the more R & D results had been transferred outside Japan. Foreign companies that had established themselves in the Japanese market recently (after 1985) had transferred the

**Figure 7.11   Transfer of R & D results to parent company
or other subsidiaries**

n = 150 of which: M1 = 54; M2 = 90; N1 = 4; N2 = 2   *(Q 45)*

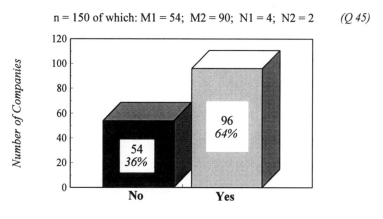

Table 7.4   Transfer of R & D results to parent company or other subsidiaries, based on performance criteria   (Q 48)

Alternative (Q 45)	Sample 1 Number of companies	In %	Sample 2 Number of companies	In %	Sample 3 Number of companies	In %
No	37	35	11	37	2	29
Yes	69	65	19	63	5	71
Total	106	100	30	100	7	100

Legend
  Sample 1 = Very successful and successful; Sample 2 = As expected;
  Sample 3 = Very unsuccessful and unsuccessful.

fewest R & D results outside Japan (only 7% of the transferring companies; see Appendix B7.5).

Branch analysis reveals that 34% of the companies that transferred R & D results outside Japan were from the chemicals industry, and the other notable industrial sectors transferring R & D were pharmaceuticals, machinery, and electronics (see Appendix B7.6). Foreign companies mentioned a large number of product fields in which they transferred R & D results to their headquarters or other subsidiaries outside Japan, for example, medicinal products, various types of chemicals (such as carbon fiber), packaging material and know-how, electronic parts and components, measuring instruments, and machine tools (CNCs and NCs).[8] Regarding nationalities, we found that US companies had been responsible for 57% of R & D transfer, followed by Germany, the Netherlands, the United Kingdom, Sweden, Switzerland, France, and Italy (see Appendix B7.7).

Several foreign companies mentioned that in their global operations, Japanese engineers and technicians were played an important role. The Japanese engineers and technicians were frequently dispatched to assist in production- and R & D-related matters at headquarters and other subsidiaries outside Japan.

Cross-tabulation between the companies that transferred R & D results (Q 45) and degree of autonomy (Q 44) shows that 63% of the companies that transferred R & D results had autonomy in carrying out R & D in Japan, and only 4% of the such companies were controlled by their headquarters (Q 44). Similarly, when we carried out cross-tabulation between the companies that transferred R & D results and those that obtained patents in Japan (Q 43, one or more patents), we found that 67% of the companies that transferred R & D also obtained patents in Japan.

These results clearly show that the more autonomy the foreign companies had, the more their R & D results were transferred from subsidiaries in Japan to headquarters or to other subsidiaries outside Japan. Moreover, those companies that transferred R & D results also obtained a larger number of patents in Japan.

The indication is that subsidiaries must have autonomy in R & D in order to be innovative in obtaining patents and making R & D advancements and that subsidiaries that do have such autonomy transfer their R & D results, thus making the parent company competitive globally and obtaining synergy in conducting R & D in the triad.

Cross-tabulation with the number of employees engaged in R & D showed that 65% of the companies that transferred R & D results had more than 10 researchers and technicians engaged in R & D in Japan. Moreover, approximately 50% of the companies transferring R & D results spent on average over 4% of their total yearly sales on R & D.

As we described earlier, existing theories mention that one of the main purposes for conducting R & D in Japan (and elsewhere, outside of the home country) by foreign companies was to apply the parent company's technology, assuming thereby that it was the parent company that was transferring R & D resources to its subsidiary in Japan. The phenomenon of reverse technology transfer cannot be explained adequately by existing theories.

We found in this study that a foreign company's subsidiary could also be a source of new product development and innovation in Japan, with US and European companies, either parent companies and/or other subsidiaries, receiving the new product or innovation from its subsidiaries in Japan.[9]

Our results show that technology transfer is not a one-way transfer from the parent company to its foreign subsidiary but a two-way transfer in which technology is also transferred from subsidiary to parent company or other subsidiaries outside of Japan.[10] We are refuting in this book, at least to some extent, the Vernon and Wells[11] model of one-way technology transfer. Moreover, the existing literature on international trade theory is full of serious shortcomings in that it fails to treat reverse technology transfer satisfactorily. We expect that this study will lead to new developments in the theory of multinational companies (for details, see Chapters 8 and 9).

7.14 DIFFICULTIES IN CONDUCTING R & D IN JAPAN

The results concerning difficulties confronted by foreign companies in conducting R & D in Japan were in line with earlier studies (see also App. A, Q 38, production).

The three most important concerns (see Figure 7.12) were difficulties in recruiting well-qualified Japanese personnel, the high cost of conducting R & D, and the infrastructure. Only 13% of the companies chose alternative 7 (worry about patent protection in Japan).

Regarding difficulties in recruiting well qualified Japanese personnel, we found that 65% of foreign companies experiencing these had over 50% foreign

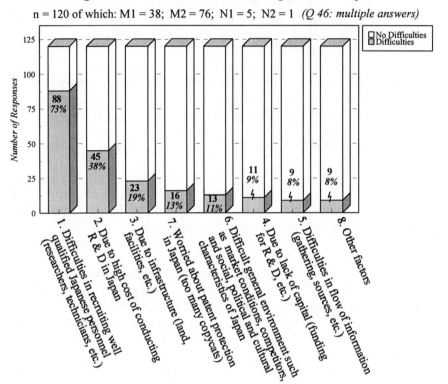

Figure 7.12   Difficulties in conducting R & D in Japan

n = 120 of which: M1 = 38; M2 = 76; N1 = 5; N2 = 1 *(Q 46: multiple answers)*

equity, and they started their business activities prior to 1980. In contrast, only 10% of foreign companies with minority equity reported having recruitment problems. It appeared that the minority-owned foreign companies faced fewer problems in recruitment because this was taken care of by the local partner.

Alternative 7, on patent protection, is highly debated in and outside Japan; however, we found that only 16 companies reported facing such problems.[12] The majority of these companies were in the chemicals and pharmaceuticals sectors (75%), and a large number of them were from Europe (56%). It is well known that foreign companies in the chemicals and, in particular, in the pharmaceuticals sectors do possess world patents in certain high-tech fields and applications, and they were concerned about patent protection. Some foreign companies mentioned that they had problems due either to the lengthy time required by the Japanese Patent Office (JPO) for processing their patent applications or to the scope of patent protection in Japan.

Some foreign companies mentioned that coordinating headquarters' and the subsidiary's R & D in Japan was a major obstacle to overcome. Other foreign companies mentioned that raw materials available in Japan were too expensive. Still another group of foreign companies mentioned that they were doing quite well in applied research but were facing problems in basic research, since that was monopolized by headquarters, and also that they had difficulties recruiting qualified and talented staff in Japan. However, a large number of companies appeared to be satisfied with the R & D support they were receiving from their headquarters.

Regarding flow of information (alt. 5) and difficult general environment (alt. 6), we found that a large number of companies that chose these were in the consumer goods sector. The desire of foreign companies was to be in the proximity of their customers, but this was not easy, either due to exorbitant costs or to difficulties in obtaining land or labor.

The conclusion that can be drawn is that foreign companies have to be well established in Japan with a good CI before they are in a position to employ well-qualified Japanese personnel to conduct R & D in Japan.[13] Foreign companies in the transition period have the possibility of employing mid-career technicians or of head-hunting researchers and technicians. These options should be slightly easier due to the slump prevailing in Japan.

Once a foreign company is able to recruit well-qualified Japanese personnel, they are in a better position to attract other well-qualified Japanese researchers via "old boy/old girl" networks. As soon as foreign companies overcome their initial problems, it is expected that they will experience success in the Japanese market, and will begin to be counted as "insiders."

The recent layoffs by Japanese companies makes it somewhat easier to attract well-qualified Japanese researchers and technicians, as mentioned earlier. However, the actions of some of the foreign companies have reinforced the hire-and-fire image of them in the minds of Japanese personnel, for example, the sudden cancellation of the employment contracts of newly recruited university graduates by some foreign companies in Japan.

7.15 CONCLUSIONS

We found that investment in production facilities and R & D units is extremely costly in Japan due to reasons such as high land prices and wages, that this makes it financially risky to pursue such activities, and that there are difficulties in attracting qualified personnel. More and more foreign companies were realizing that it is strategically necessary to carry out production and R & D locally, and were either opening or expanding units in Japan based on joint ventures and strategic alliances or units that were 100% foreign owned.

A large number of foreign companies conducting R & D and production had been established for a long time in Japan, and they had been able to expand their contacts with universities, sometimes via "old boy/old girl" networks. One common strategy was to hire a mid-career researcher or production manager from a Japanese company, foreign company, government research institute, or university and count on that employee for new leads to potential production and research personnel. Over 80% of the foreign companies' heads of R & D and production departments were Japanese.

We found in this study that only a small amount of basic research was carried out by foreign companies in Japan and that the concentration of research efforts was mainly on applied and development work, with the research conducted primarily by Japanese staff. In order to obtain global synergy in R & D, research was coordinated with the parent company and its subsidiaries, but at the same time a large amount of autonomy was given for R & D based on Japanese customers' requirements and various other research efforts deemed necessary in the context of the global network of the parent company.

One of the main reasons that foreign companies conduct R & D and carry out production in Japan is to come up with new products and processes in order to improve the competitive advantages of the parent company globally, both in production and R & D. Not only was Japan seen by foreign companies as a technology leader in production and R & D, but Japanese production and R & D personnel were seen as providing quality guidance and effort in and outside Japan.

Moreover, foreign companies viewed Japan as an essential international center for R & D because Japan is the second largest market in the world, with very high quality R & D and standards of production.

We have been able to show clearly in this study that foreign companies in Japan have been making innovations, have obtained a large number of patents, and have experienced a high degree of autonomy from their headquarters. They have also been transferring R & D results and production know-how to their headquarters and other subsidiaries, thus supporting the parent company in realizing global synergy effects of R & D and in production.

Finally, we have been able to refute--at least to some extent--the Vernon and Wells[14] model of one-way technology transfer. Moreover, we have shown that the existing literature on international trade theory is full of serious shortcomings in that it fails to treat reverse technology transfer satisfactorily. This study is expected to lead to new developments in the theory of multinational companies, as discussed in more detail in Chapter 9.

NOTES

1. The actual number of foreign companies with production and R & D facilities is slightly higher, but we faced a minor non-response for most of the
   questions. Five companies in the non-manufacturing sector also answered.

The main reason for this is that several companies in the non-manufacturing sectors have production and R & D facilities related to their businesses, e.g., soft drink and beverage manufacturers and fast food chain restaurants. Several foreign companies are involved in both manufacturing and non-manufacturing activities. In order to avoid double counting we placed the foreign companies in only one of the groups, the one representing their major business activities.

2. Source: JETRO, 1992.

3. Practically all the foreign companies that gave an answer to this question were conducting some type of R & D in Japan. Some of the companies that did not possess R & D laboratories, had subcontracted R & D to their subcontractors, universities, and research institutes.

4. Consult also Ohmae, K., 1985a, pp. 11-18.

5. In FY 1991 the average spending on R & D as percentage of total sales in the Japanese manufacturing industry rose to 3.47%. Source: Management and Coordination Agency, 1993.

6. Note: refers to mainly corporate R & D. For details see Management and Coordination Agency, 1993, p. 150.

7. See Mansfield, E., 1988, pp. 1769-1774.

8. Due to the confidentiality promised to foreign companies, the entire list of specific R & D results cannot be published in this book.

9. Readers are advised to consult also a recent book describing the case history of Applied Materials in Japan, their success in high-tech fields, and the significant contribution of their subsidiary in Japan toward the emergence of Applied Materials as a global growth company in the 1990s: Morgan, J. C., and Morgan, J. J., 1991.

10. Note: the old notion of Japan as an imitator and not an innovator does not hold true today.

11. Vernon, R., and Wells, L. T., Jr., 1991.

12. Similar results were found in ACCJs and A. T. Kearney, Inc., 1991, p. 20.

13. Eastman Kodak (in Japan, and several other foreign companies) in 1993 refused to offer newly recruited university graduates promised jobs in their R & D departments, due to the prevailing slump in the Japanese market. This action, unfortunately, has further tarnished the foreign companies' image in the Japanese market.

14. Vernon, R., and Wells, L. T., Jr., 1991.

8 KEY SUCCESS FACTORS AND ADVICE TO FOREIGN COMPANIES

In this chapter, we will give a final review of the key success factors in foreign companies in Japan, and based on these factors we will provide advice to foreign companies that are already present in Japan or are planning to invest in Japan.

8.1 INTRODUCTION

In Chapter 1, we mentioned that this research focuses entirely on the micro-level management problems of foreign companies in Japan. Further, in Chapter 3 we discussed the performance of foreign companies in Japan. Emphasis was placed on financial criteria in measuring a company's performance in Japan. In this chapter we will take an in-depth look at the key factors for success in the Japanese market based on both financial and non-financial criteria. At the same time, we will mention key factors for failure. We will also provide practical advice to foreign companies that are already established in Japan or are planning to invest in Japan regarding what they should and should not do in order to avoid failure in the Japanese market.

8.2 FACTORS CONDUCIVE TO THE SUCCESS OR FAILURE OF FOREIGN COMPANIES IN JAPAN

In this section we will present foreign companies' views about which factors contribute to their success and their failure in the Japanese market. It should be noted that we are not attempting to develop a success formula for foreign companies in Japan, as success depends on numerous factors that are not fully covered in this research, such as the relative efforts of competitors, chance, and so forth. Our expectations are that by shedding light on the factors affecting the success or failure of foreign companies in Japan, we may be able to help those companies formulate more effective strategies.

Foreign companies were asked to give their own views regarding their success or failure in the Japanese market. They identified key factors out of a list of 15 success factors and 15 failure factors. Further, they could list additional factors in those cases where the list did not contain the factors they considered most crucial.

A wide number of success and failure factors were mentioned by the respondents (see Figure 8.1). Regarding success factors, we found that foreign companies referred often to the following factors: excellent products or services, highly qualified and talented Japanese personnel, excellent technology and know-how, parent company's total support, well-known company and brand names, right timing for investment in Japan, excellent Japanese joint venture partner, overall commitment to the Japanese market, and excellent marketing capabilities.

The failure factors mentioned were too many competitors, difficulties in reaching satisfactory corporate profit levels in a short time period, lack of well-known company and brand names, inferior marketing capabilities, lack of highly qualified and talented Japanese personnel, and lack of overall commitment to the Japanese market.

It is interesting to note that the factors indicated as facilitating success in Japan are in most cases at least partly controllable by the companies, whereas the factors that have caused failure are most often uncontrollable.

We will present a brief discussion regarding the success and failure factors. The success factors can be grouped into three clear, distinctive groups. First, the majority of the foreign companies mentioned that one of the most important reasons for their success in the Japanese market was their company's excellent, high-quality products or/and services (adapted and modified according to Japanese requirements), which, combined with other factors such as excellent technology and know-how, well-known company and brand names, and excellent marketing capabilities, contributed highly to their success.

Second, the companies highlighted the crucial role in their success played by their qualified and talented Japanese personnel and/or excellent Japanese joint venture partner. Third, a high level of support by the parent company, and choosing the right time for investing in Japan combined with having an overall commitment to the Japanese market led to success in Japan.

Foreign companies attributed their failures to the highly competitive Japanese market, with its large number of local and foreign competitors. Japan, as we mentioned in previous chapters, is considered to be one of the most competitive markets in the world.

Figure 8.1   Key success and failure factors in the Japanese market

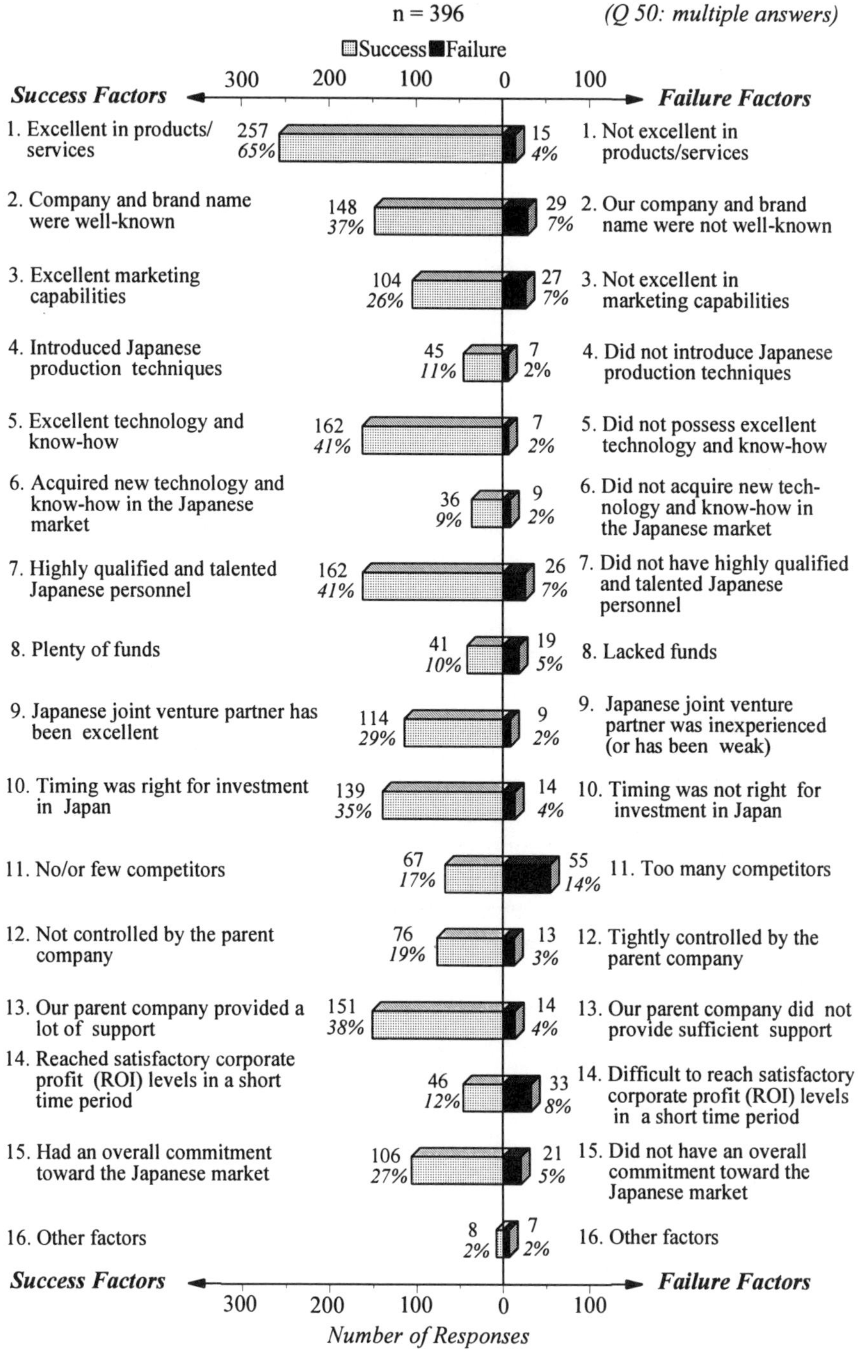

n = 396   (Q 50: multiple answers)

☐Success ■Failure

Success Factors	300	200	100	0	100	Failure Factors

Success Factors	Success	Failure	Failure Factors
1. Excellent in products/ services	257 / 65%	15 / 4%	1. Not excellent in products/services
2. Company and brand name were well-known	148 / 37%	29 / 7%	2. Our company and brand name were not well-known
3. Excellent marketing capabilities	104 / 26%	27 / 7%	3. Not excellent in marketing capabilities
4. Introduced Japanese production techniques	45 / 11%	7 / 2%	4. Did not introduce Japanese production techniques
5. Excellent technology and know-how	162 / 41%	7 / 2%	5. Did not possess excellent technology and know-how
6. Acquired new technology and know-how in the Japanese market	36 / 9%	9 / 2%	6. Did not acquire new technology and know-how in the Japanese market
7. Highly qualified and talented Japanese personnel	162 / 41%	26 / 7%	7. Did not have highly qualified and talented Japanese personnel
8. Plenty of funds	41 / 10%	19 / 5%	8. Lacked funds
9. Japanese joint venture partner has been excellent	114 / 29%	9 / 2%	9. Japanese joint venture partner was inexperienced (or has been weak)
10. Timing was right for investment in Japan	139 / 35%	14 / 4%	10. Timing was not right for investment in Japan
11. No/or few competitors	67 / 17%	55 / 14%	11. Too many competitors
12. Not controlled by the parent company	76 / 19%	13 / 3%	12. Tightly controlled by the parent company
13. Our parent company provided a lot of support	151 / 38%	14 / 4%	13. Our parent company did not provide sufficient support
14. Reached satisfactory corporate profit (ROI) levels in a short time period	46 / 12%	33 / 8%	14. Difficult to reach satisfactory corporate profit (ROI) levels in a short time period
15. Had an overall commitment toward the Japanese market	106 / 27%	21 / 5%	15. Did not have an overall commitment toward the Japanese market
16. Other factors	8 / 2%	7 / 2%	16. Other factors

Success Factors	300	200	100	0	100	Failure Factors

Number of Responses

Moreover, the companies mentioned that it is difficult to reach satisfactory corporate profit levels in a short time period in Japan. This confirms again the fact that it takes some time before a company can start showing profits in Japan due to the high cost of doing business, competition, the need for product adaptation and modification, and so on. In several cases, the lack of recognizable company image or brand name was considered to be another factor leading to failure in the Japanese market.

It is somewhat surprising that only a very few companies mentioned financial resources (Figure 8.1, alt. 8) as an important factor for success or failure in Japan. Moreover, not a single foreign company mentioned that the reason for its failure in the Japanese market had been that the Japanese market is a closed one. Only a small number of companies criticized restrictive Japanese governmental regulations or cumbersome bureaucracy.

Furthermore, foreign companies that failed in the Japanese market or were facing problems generally blamed a combination of several factors, such as lack of product adaptation and modification, short PLC, passive sales activities, inferior marketing capabilities, lack of highly qualified and talented Japanese personnel, lack of overall commitment to the Japanese market, difficulties in understanding what the buyer needed, psychic and physical distance between the parent company and the Japanese market (this included communication gaps), cultural differences, peculiar business manners, small size of the subsidiary in Japan, or small size of the parent company, rendering it unable to make the necessary large-scale investment required for the Japanese market.

The United States claims nearly 50% of the companies participating in our study; thus the majority of the companies mentioning key success and failure factors were from the United States. We carried out cross-tabulations on nationality and success factors in the Japanese market. The results are more or less the same as those just mentioned (see Appendix B8.1). However, an inter-regional comparison (United States/Europe) shows that European companies, compared to US companies, more often attributed their success to an overall commitment to the Japanese market (alt. 15; Europe 56%, US 38%). In contrast, US companies placed more weight on the following factors: excellent marketing capabilities (alt. 3; United States 54%, Europe 41%), excellent Japanese joint venture partner (alt. 9; United States 61%, Europe 36%), right timing for investment in Japan (alt. 10; United States 54%, Europe 39%), and no or few competitors (alt. 11; United States 61%, Europe 39%).

The result of the cross-tabulation on nationality and failure factors in the Japanese market (App. B8.2) shows that European companies more often blamed their failures on a large number of competitors (alt. 11; Europe 55%, United States 40%), whereas US companies put the blame on incorrect timing for investment in Japan (alt. 10; United States 64%, Europe 14%), tight control by the parent company (alt. 12; United States 77%, Europe 23%), or not having an overall commitment to the Japanese market (alt. 15; United States 62%, Europe 38%).

We also carried out cross-tabulations on industrial sectors (manufacturing, services, and financial institutions) and success and failure factors in the Japanese market. The results do not provide any new success and failure factors. The chemicals, machinery, electronics, pharmaceuticals, and services sectors reported that the factors already mentioned played a key role in their success or failure in the Japanese market. In all branches, fierce competition in the Japanese market was considered as a detrimental factor leading to failure.

Cross-tabulation between the year of establishment in Japan and success and failure factors in the Japanese market, and cross-tabulation between business line and key success and failure factors again do not reveal any new factors affecting foreign companies' performance in Japan.

8.3 KEY FACTORS FOR SUCCESS IN THE JAPANESE MARKET

Japan's enormous trade surplus is widely criticized, and efforts are being made to increase exports to Japan. In some sectors (e.g., semiconductors), specific quantitative import targets have been set up for the Japanese market. However, the success in meeting these targets or increased exports and FDI to Japan will depend on the efforts made by individual foreign companies either already in Japan or planning to enter Japan.

The experiences of participating foreign companies in Japan shows that successful penetration of the Japanese market--which on the one hand is an integral part of OECD but on the other hand is rather unique both in terms of language, culture, and business practices--required well-planned, tailor-made strategies. As we noted earlier, Japan is to a large extent an open market, free from tariff and non-tariff barriers in most industrial sectors. However, it is also quite clear that there are certain obstacles, impediments, and barriers to entering some sectors (particularly non-manufacturing ones). The difficulties already mentioned, for example, put foreign SMEs (small and medium-sized enterprises) compared to TNCs and MNCs at an even greater disadvantage in competing successfully in Japan.

For the coming decades Japan will remain a market requiring specialized strategies that will be in many ways different from those required in western Europe or the United States. In the next sections, we present the key factors for success that most of the 436 foreign companies participating in this study experienced (see Q 52): investment and management strategies, local management and organizational framework, marketing mix strategies, reverse flow of know-how from subsidiary to parent company, and ways of hedging against the pitfalls of failure in the Japanese market. It is important to note that throughout this chapter "foreign companies" refers to successful foreign companies unless otherwise noted.

Investment strategies

Entry channel strategies. Foreign companies have entered the Japanese market through many channels. One alternative has been forming a joint venture with (preferably) 50% or more foreign equity. For several foreign companies, a Japanese partner was their key to success in Japan. However, foreign companies have to decide whether a partnership is really necessary, and must make a great effort to carefully selecting a good and reliable local partner before linking up. In certain sectors, such as food and food chains (grocery stores), we found that a Japanese partner was necessary in order to understand the market, establish long-term links with clients, and so forth.

Another successful alternative for foreign companies has been the 100% foreign-owned subsidiary. Initially, if required, the subsidiary was staffed with management and technical staff from headquarters.

A third successful alternative has been to start an enterprise as a joint venture for a fixed time period (build up the presence step-by-step) and then acquire the Japanese joint venture partner or terminate the joint venture, focusing from the beginning on 100% foreign ownership. Foreign companies following this strategy considered the joint venture to be a short-term strategic tool, useful mainly for initially penetrating the market. We found that some foreign companies, particularly if they possessed a specialized niche product (or service concept), focused from the beginning of their venture in Japan on becoming a fully owned subsidiary. For these companies, in many cases a joint venture was a short-term strategy.

However, it is important to note that it is not easy to terminate a joint venture and start a 100% owned subsidiary in a short time span, since the process of establishing one's own brand image (or CI), recruiting loyal local personnel, acquiring land and buildings, and overcoming language and communication barriers takes much time.

Successful foreign companies' headquarters laid down clear, explicit aims, objectives, and goals right from the beginning regarding sales channels for the Japanese market. We found several companies that were facing confusion and not functioning satisfactorily because their headquarters were not able to clearly define aims and objectives regarding sales channels. This problem was noticed mainly in joint ventures, where the Japanese partner was satisfied but the foreign partner found total resistance from the local joint venture partner concerning sales of products (of the foreign partner) that competed with the Japanese partner's product varieties. Thus, the joint venture could not grow in terms of sales and revenues. Moreover, the board of directors of the joint venture was not receiving clear directives from the parent company (of the foreign partner) regarding which policies to pursue in Japan.

Apart from the three alternatives mentioned, foreign companies have found success in the Japanese market by using dealers, wholesalers, or exclusive agents; selling directly through retailers; and employing a trading company. (Strategic alliances are discussed later.) Earlier we mentioned the advantages and disadvantages associated with various entry alternatives both in terms of risks and returns.

The use of multiple channels. The use of multiple channels in Japan is quite common. We found several companies using two or more channels. Foreign companies that established a joint venture or a 100% owned subsidiary had at the same time a licensing agreement, an agent, trading company, or another type of channel, depending on the specific type of product/service and/or special buyers. Moreover, a large number of foreign companies retained previous channels even as they moved from one channel to another, depending on their strategic reasons for being in the Japanese market.

In order to meet the stringent demands of Japanese customers, foreign companies in the manufacturing sector were required, for example, to have a marketing/sales and manufacturing subsidiary and an R & D laboratory in Japan. This kind of investment by foreign companies enhances credibility and commitment to the Japanese market in the eyes of the local customers and local personnel.

Foreign companies generally encountered problems with most of the entry channels. The problems, in our opinion varied with the type of entry strategy chosen by a foreign company in Japan. For example, joint ventures may feel more comfortable with respect to recruitment of local personnel, lower financial risks, ease in borrowing funds, access to markets and distribution channels, production or R & D activities, and obtaining land. On the other hand, they have to sacrifice total control of their operation, lack direct access to customers, and risk losing control of a product or technology. In addition, they risk being taken over by the partner, having conflicts with the local partner, and not obtaining the total commitment and loyalty of local transferred employees. Profits may also be lower.

The distribution channels are considered to be complicated in Japan, and they are multitiered. Foreign companies showed flexibility in choosing one or more entry channels in Japan and in taking a long-term perspective. Our study has clearly shown that a foreign company can be successful whether it chooses a middleman, establishes a joint venture, or has a 100% owned subsidiary.

The old strategy, particularly among MNCs and TNCs, of always maintaining a 100% owned subsidiary in every country of the world is outdated, at least for Japan. Foreign companies may (depending on product/service) need a joint venture, a 100% owned subsidiary, technical tie-ups with competitors, or alliances with foreign and Japanese companies in order to be successful in the Japanese market.

Generally speaking, foreign companies follow a step-by-step strategy for establishing an excellent sales and distribution network in the Japanese market, since it takes time to establish long-term relationships with buyers (and/or suppliers and subcontractors). It takes some time before well-qualified, loyal local personnel can be recruited. It also takes time to establish brand image (brand awareness) or corporate image and thus to show a long-term commitment to the Japanese market. In order to create a market for their type of product/service, step-by-step expansion with a long-term perspective in the Japanese market is followed by successful companies. Foreign companies, even if they are active in upper niches, usually face severe competition in Japan. For these companies, establishing good long-term personal relationships with customers, suppliers, and subcontractors in Japan has taken time.

Several of these foreign companies investigated many factors prior to selecting one or more entry channels, including whether they had competitive prices, whether the quality level of their product/service would meet Japanese standards (zero defect), whether the time required to build one's image (corporate or brand) was acceptable, the extent of product/service adaptation required, the extent of product testing and modification, and the time necessary to educate the market about its advanced products. Also investigated were the facilities for providing excellent pre- and after-sales services, the achievement of punctual delivery time, and the effects of yen appreciation, which provides certain competitive advantages and disadvantages, since the price level is considerably higher in Japan than elsewhere for both domestic and imported products/services.

Strategic alliances.   Successful strategic alliances among foreign and Japanese companies are gradually increasing in number. These include a large number of R & D and production tie-ups among foreign and Japanese companies, who in several cases are competitors in various product fields and markets.

It is a known fact that production, R & D, marketing, and/or distribution alliances some times lead to mergers and acquisitions (M & A). It appears that foreign companies are a bit reluctant to form strategic alliances with Japanese companies because of a fear of being acquired by the Japanese partner or losing their technology. Some foreign companies mentioned the fear that entering into an alliance with a Japanese company could cause the loss of their distinct identity.

In our opinion, strategic alliances among foreign and Japanese companies are of mutual benefit for all parties involved, and this option should not be overlooked by foreign companies. Alliances are particularly attractive for SMEs lacking knowledge about Japanese markets and contacts. Foreign companies spent considerable time, for example, in building joint strategic and product planning departments, and in creating management teams for planning and coordination, joint quality projects, and shared marketing and distribution network.

Regarding acquisitions, we believe that despite the strength of the yen (about 105 yen = $1 in March 1994), the time is particularly good for foreign companies to buy Japanese companies, due to the fall of share prices on the Tokyo Stock Exchange and the fall in real estate values during 1992-1993. Moreover, as the Japanese economy continues to deteriorate or experience recession, sellers are also under pressure to change their attitudes, for instance, less concern than before is given to where the capital comes from (foreign or domestic).

Foreign companies have to carefully evaluate the two alternatives available to them in the Japanese market, outright takeover (which is rather difficult in Japan) or acquiring only a certain percentage of a Japanese concern, retaining the existing management, and at the same time seizing effective control of the company. Foreign companies have to give serious attention to M & A compared to other alternatives for entering the Japanese market (particularly for acquiring distribution channels or production bases).

Several foreign companies in this study established technology and capital cooperation with Japanese companies and have successfully penetrated the Japanese market. For example, Mercedes-Benz Japan Co., which is a 100% owned foreign company, has been highly successful in selling luxury cars in Japan by establishing cooperative agreements with Yanase Company and Mitsubishi Motors Corporation. BASF (parent company from Germany) provided the capital and technology to its 100% owned subsidiary in Japan to establishing a joint venture with 50% foreign equity. The Japanese JV partner provided talented personnel, including distribution and sales personnel, and outlets. This joint venture has also been highly successful in Japan. Other successful JVs are those of Coca Cola, McDonald's, and Motorola (with Toshiba).

Time frames. Generally speaking, it is very difficult to make huge profits in the Japanese market, particularly, in a short time period. In many cases, with similar levels of investment outlays, it takes a longer time to reach satisfactory profit levels in Japan than in the United States and Europe. The main reasons for the longer time period necessary to reach a satisfactory level of ROI is the high cost of doing business in Japan. However, it is interesting to note that a large number of foreign companies have stated they are making profits in Japan and remitting these to their headquarters outside Japan (see Appendix A, Q 53).

Generally, foreign companies in our study had a long-term view of Japan and a firm long-term business plan with a total commitment from headquarters to the Japanese market. It appears that these foreign companies were flexible, pragmatic, patient and persistent, and did not expect profits too early. Moreover, in the initial stages of their operation, these companies did not place ROI as the top priority. They settled down seriously, and carefully weighed the joint venture alternative with that of the 100% owned subsidiary. They acted as a Japanese company, with a clear vision, and had a sustainable competitive advantage with adequate and committed resources.

Management strategies and issues

Local management and organizational framework. Practically all the foreign companies in this study have, to a large extent, adapted to the conditions prevailing in the Japanese market regarding management in order to compete effectively with their Japanese and foreign competitors. Many foreign companies have Japanized their company, using the Japanese way of thinking and a mainly Japanese staff. Joint ventures, in particular, use Japanese-style management, whereas wholly owned foreign subsidiaries in some cases employ a mixture of Western and Japanese-style management. In a majority of the cases, top managers are Japanese who have authority to run the operation (CEOs and divisional heads); decision making in day-to-day operations has been given to the local subsidiaries. This way of operating the company removes the language and cultural obstacles that may be present in a company run by expatriates in Japan. Moreover, several foreign companies in Japan have Japanese executives on their parent company's board.

A large number of foreign companies in Japan are decentralized, with their parent companies providing overall corporate policies and strategy but leaving the concrete operations to them. The parent companies appear to be interested mainly in formulating overall strategies, policies, and financial matters of the subsidiary in Japan; to a large extent foreign companies are managed with autonomy, within limits.

Generally, headquarters of foreign companies have not given any special responsibilities to their subsidiaries outside Japan. They consider the size of the Japanese market and/or business activities in Japan sufficient to bear the investment outlays. We argue that the size of the Japanese market is so large that most of the foreign companies have to concentrate all their efforts to succeed in it.

We found that several foreign companies in Japan faced communication problems with their headquarters, but these problems did not necessarily affect the performance of these companies directly. However, they did affect the morale of the local and expatriate employees of the subsidiary. One reason for this problem, in our view, is the lack of knowledge at headquarters of the unique characteristics of Japan: its language, norms and customs, work ethics, and significant differences in business practices.

Foreign companies consider it a prerequisite to have excellent local personnel, for without them the chances for success in the Japanese market will be meager. In addition, any transfer of technology and know-how from Japan will be severely constrained. The issue of human resource management is thus of paramount importance for foreign companies operating in Japan. A majority of the foreign companies make their own decisions regarding human resources in Japan, excluding expatriate recruitment. Foreign companies adapt, at least to a certain extent, to prevailing local conditions in the Japanese market.

Advancement opportunities are given to talented staff in order to try to secure qualified Japanese staff. Local staff are trained both in Japan and abroad, given full trust and authority, and encouraged to take initiatives. All of this leads to higher morale among local employees, and the Japanese management structure facilitates attracting talented staff.

Most foreign companies show commitment to the Japanese staff and to lifetime employment. At the same time, they implement a long-term management strategy. These companies encourage their Japanese staff to establish communication networks with headquarters.

In a joint venture, these foreign companies try their utmost to obtain the loyalty of the transferred employees of the Japanese joint venture partner, or else they try to directly employ at an accelerated pace excellent Japanese personnel who understand the company's strategies so that they can reduce the reliance on temporary transferred personnel.

Generally, few foreign companies can expect to recruit students graduating from Japan's elite universities. Therefore, in order to recruit good personnel, foreign companies either do mid-career recruitment (sometimes hiring women) or offer an attractive employment package, such as more holidays, more free time, training in and outside Japan, greater individual responsibility and freedom, a less rigid attitude toward employment compared with most Japanese companies, and slightly above-market salaries. Moreover, foreign companies band together in order to improve recruitment, for example, the Swedish Embassy organizes joint recruitment seminars for Swedish companies in Japan.

Foreign companies also recruit employees from their customers, since this type of hiring helps to cement relations between businesses. The recruitment policy is built upon an extensive network of contacts with universities and the development of an "old boy/old girl" network. Foreign companies spend considerable amount of time and money making their brand name or image well known in the Japanese market, and recruiting activities are an integral part of their marketing strategy.

In order to enhance a positive corporate image among staff, customers, distributors, and suppliers, a long-term commitment and a large measure of patience is demonstrated by foreign companies in Japan. Without this positive image, foreign companies find that it is difficult to attract well-qualified local personnel.

Large foreign multinationals are in most cases rather small in Japan, and since most of them operate by a profit-center concept, they are even smaller in the eyes of potential job seekers. This small size leads to limited access to the Japanese labor market. In order to facilitate recruitment of local personnel, we argue, it is important for foreign companies to place all their profit centers (including divisions, subsidiaries, and so forth) under one umbrella, since the size of the foreign company (together with reputation) plays an important role in recruitment. Local prospective employees generally are looking at what a company can offer not in the short term, but in the long term. Therefore, successful foreign companies first explain their long-term strategy to these prospective employees.

We realize that these recommendations are easy to recommend but difficult to implement, since MNCs and TNCs have global networks, and their subsidiaries are interlinked and cannot function effectively separately. However, we argue that in the case of Japan, a separate strategy that is unique to the Japanese market needs to evolve if companies are to be successful in the second largest market in the world.

We personally recommend that short-term objectives such as sales or profitability per employee be disregarded by foreign companies in Japan if they sincerely wish to secure high-caliber Japanese personnel and to give the solid impression that they intend to follow firmly a policy of job security and stability.

Expatriates and their adjustment to the local environment. Foreign companies generally carefully select and dispatch expatriates to fill mainly top managerial positions in their Japanese subsidiaries. Several foreign companies argue that a foreign CEO (if this is the only alternative available) should be cautious, open-minded, and trustworthy in the eyes of the Japanese. Headquarters should set the goals for the CEO and then keep out of the way and provide full support. These expatriates usually stay a long while in order to fully adjust to Japan, and are encouraged to learn the Japanese language. We argue that expatriates sent to Japan should be familiar with the Japanese market and should be top-class executives from the highest ranks (at least directors) in the parent company.

We observed that foreign companies that dispatched very young executives to occupy top positions in Japan or executives with working experience from developing countries, in many instances, had problems in Japan. Local Japanese personnel were reluctant to work with colonial-minded expatriates or foreign executives who appeared to be immature or childish in their appearance and behavior. Japanese employees preferred foreign executives with a fatherlike appearance and working experience from OECD countries (preferably from Europe or the United States).

Several foreign companies recommended that expatriates should think and act for the long term as Japanese do. They should know that Japan is a high-cost and very competitive market. They should overcome the Japanese language barrier, since the language barrier is one of the greatest demerits in doing business in Japan. Expatriates should give importance to Japanese needs and wants and listen carefully to the market signals. Building market confidence and taking rapid and adequate measures that fit the needs of the market are also important, as is very good understanding of the Japanese commercial rules and customs, legal system, and human relationships, as well as the nature of the Japanese people. In summary, expatriates should respect the Japanese culture and national character.

Marketing mix strategies

Competition in Japan is considered to be the severest in the world, and at the same time, Japan is considered to be the costliest place to do business among the OECD countries. One of the key failure factors mentioned by foreign companies in Japan was the severe competition in the Japanese market. It takes time for foreign companies to build an image in Japan based on price, quality, prompt delivery, total customer satisfaction, and service and maintenance support. The headquarters of foreign companies have strategically delegated the marketing and sales function to the subsidiary in Japan.

Foreign companies find that Japanese customers are among the most demanding in the world, and therefore they face difficulties in adapting to Japanese customs, habits, and tastes. It is quite obvious that in order for these companies to be successful in the Japanese market, they have to pay great attention to the demands and sensitivities of Japanese buyers toward product quality. Some companies did mention that the stringent quality controls imposed on them by image- and quality-conscious Japanese buyers have highly improved their competitive position globally. Moreover, the fiercely competitive market in Japan has encouraged them to develop effective data collection, analysis, and feedback for strategic and corporate planning and other purposes.

In order to develop brand and corporate image, foreign companies have to incur high expenditures for marketing support, service centers, advertising, promotional activities and public relations. We found that foreign companies' marketing expenditures in Japan were higher than those of many foreign companies operating in other OECD countries.

Some foreign companies, for example, in the service sector, mentioned that they had problems regarding the level of service offered to Japanese customers, since these customers were spoiled by excessive service provided by Japanese competitors.

Foreign companies had developed special products (models) or service concepts for the Japanese market, and several foreign companies were exploiting their product and market niches with higher product quality and service levels compared to Japanese competitors. These market niches were mainly in narrow market/product segments with limited competition from Japanese rivals due to technological barriers to newcomers. Foreign companies' marketing strategies were based on product/service differentiation from their competitors.

Moreover, these foreign companies continuously introduced new, high-quality products (offering new features, functions, and model varieties) with price levels corresponding to Japanese needs, employing a strategy similar to that used by their Japanese competitors.

A large number of foreign companies had high quality and technologically advanced products that were rather expensive in Japan. Further, these companies had developed sales and service networks in Japan, so they could justify such high customer expenditures.

Not only do foreign companies adapt and modify their products, but they also target the correct market segment. Modifications could be minor or very simple, such as changes in design, color, size, packaging appearance and materials, and taste, or they could require that the entire production line be rebuilt. Meeting these requirements could be expensive, but the profit margins meant the investment would ultimately pay off. However, over-modification could be disastrous. Foreign companies generally try to find out what and how to adapt by identifying, for example, Japanese customers' needs and requirements.

Successful foreign companies have set up a system for prompt response to the market and customers' needs as they change, and they are also prepared for prompt countermeasures. They treat suppliers, subcontractors, and distributors as partners, showing them that they have a long term commitment to the Japanese market. They utilize Japanese technical skills, obtain perfection in TQC, and invest heavily in human resources and in distribution channels.

Moreover, these foreign companies have a clear vision of the Japanese market and a sustainable competitive advantage; they are always one step ahead of their competitors. They are consistent, have adequate and committed resources, take intelligent risks, spend time building confidence, keep an eye on market tendencies, and obtain early access to sales networks. In other words, successful foreign companies have consistent long-term marketing strategies and a good understanding of the peculiarities of the distribution system. They try to live with and find the positive side of working with Keiretsu, cooperating with these business circles if deemed necessary.

We found that some well-known global companies in the consumer goods and service sectors who rarely follow locally adapted marketing methods, using standardized global marketing instead to receive the economies of scale advantage, have, at least in Japan, made product/service and marketing adaptations.

Furthermore, many foreign companies developed and introduced unique marketing programs or strategies tailored for Japanese consumers. Several companies mentioned that due to differences in culture, tastes, and habits they had to develop and introduce a special marketing program/strategy suitable to the Japanese market, for ignoring the need for adaptation would have led to failure in the Japanese market. Therefore, foreign companies had to be highly innovative in marketing in the Japanese market in order to achieve success. Generally, it is the companies in the manufacturing and service sectors that have introduced unique marketing programs or strategies in the Japanese market. Banks and credit institutions have made slightly fewer introductions of unique marketing programs/strategies in the Japanese market.

Several foreign companies reported that they had transferred a successful marketing program/strategy to their headquarters or to other subsidiaries outside Japan. This observation shows, again, that innovations made by foreign companies' subsidiaries in Japan flow back to the parent company and its subsidiaries outside Japan.

Foreign companies were innovative in the Japanese market because of the fact that Japanese customers are the most demanding and quality sensitive in the world. Global standardization of marketing programs/strategies is difficult in the Japanese market, but marketing innovation done in Japan and the transfer of marketing know-how to the headquarters and other subsidiaries outside Japan is rewarding for many foreign companies. Such activities also give a competitive edge to foreign companies in Japan.

The Japanese distribution system is complex, and it is premature to claim that it is biased against foreign products. Actually, few foreign companies mentioned that they were facing problems due to the complicated and multitiered distribution channels or to Keiretsu. While some foreign companies possibly were able to bypass established distribution channels, most companies in our study went through established routes (several third parties), at least in the majority of the industrial sectors. We argue that foreign companies have to contact an industrial association in order to find out which types of distribution channels function in their branch, since these channels vary from branch to branch.

Many foreign companies complain that there are a number of barriers that make it difficult to penetrate the Japanese market. However, we found that despite these problems, most foreign companies taking part in this survey were successful in Japan.

Market research. Several foreign companies mentioned that they faced problems when they launched new products without sufficient market research. Therefore, we argue that market research should be of the same quantity and quality as that of Japanese companies when they make inroads in a foreign market. Foreign companies should try to learn from the Japanese enterprises entry strategies for foreign markets. Foreign companies generally prepared high-quality market and feasibility studies. In so doing, they were able to cooperate more effectively with Japanese companies as their partners, customers, or suppliers.

We found that a number of foreign companies that had carried out insufficient feasibility studies and market research faced problems in the Japanese market.

For example, several foreign companies lacked explicit strategies for choosing their entry channel from various other channels available to them in the Japanese market.

Therefore, we recommend that all foreign companies in Japan do their homework as well as the successful ones do, studying in depth the actual circumstances of the Japanese market, such as customers' tendencies and user needs. They should obtain thorough knowledge of the market characteristics, carefully study the peculiar and complicated Japanese distribution system and rely less on outside consultants and more on their own staff for market research. Foreign companies should very critically scrutinize market and feasibility studies.

8.4   REVERSE FLOW OF KNOW-HOW FROM SUBSIDIARY TO PARENT COMPANY

In the past, Japan was attractive only on the basis of its size, growth, and profitability (ROI). Today it is even more attractive as a place to obtain production and technology know-how and patents in order to transfer them to headquarters and/or subsidiaries outside Japan. In the previous section, we mentioned the development and transfer of marketing programs from Japan.

Several foreign companies mentioned that in their global operations Japanese engineers and technicians played an important role. Japanese engineers and technicians were frequently dispatched to assist in production- and R & D-related matters at headquarters and other subsidiaries outside Japan.

The effects of the prevailing strict industrial standards, demanding consumers, severe competition, high-quality standards, and the need for product/service modifications and adaptations to the Japanese market, to name a few factors, have been that a large number of foreign companies in Japan have become innovation centers for their parent companies. For many foreign companies, success is measured not only in terms of, for example, market share or ROI, but also in terms of innovation made by their subsidiaries in Japan and then transferred to the parent company or other subsidiaries.

Foreign companies in Japan have generally become part of the Japanese research network, or "insiders"; they work with various Japanese laboratories, research institutions, universities, and manufacturers. Moreover, one way of showing firm commitment to the Japanese market and to buyers, suppliers, subcontractors, and local employees is to have production facilities and R & D units in Japan.

In this study, a large number of foreign companies had developed their own marketing programs, production methods, and new technologies (including patents). At the same time, several of these companies had successfully transferred this know-how to the parent company or other subsidiaries outside Japan.

This is an interesting phenomenon of reverse transfer of innovation, since foreign companies initially entered Japan with the parent company providing the Japanese subsidiary with most of the know-how in order to compete successfully in the Japanese market.

Furthermore, the flow of this know-how outside Japan enhanced the company's global competitiveness, creating global synergy in production and R & D. At the same time, technology development facilitated the recruitment of highly qualified and talented Japanese personnel in all departments, not only in R & D and production. In addition, the morale of these foreign companies' Japanese engineers was raised by dispatching them to the parent company's R & D centers.

Foreign companies also reported that the performance of their factories in Japan was higher or much higher than their parent company's factories outside Japan. Generally, the successful foreign companies were responsible for transferring the bulk of Japanese production techniques outside Japan.

Foreign companies' R & D activities were aimed at the expansion of sales in the Japanese market and included product modification research, development of new products designed for the Japanese market, and support for sales activities, such as technical services.

Foreign companies' purpose for establishing an R & D unit was not low cost, since Japan is one of the most expensive countries in which to carry out such activities. These companies saw that despite the risks, there were wider strategical advantages to be gained, such as globalizing the technology base in the Japan, United States, and Europe triad, increasing the level of innovation, and obtaining synergetic effects by exchanging R & D results with the parent company and other subsidiaries. A large number of foreign companies conducting R & D had an average expenditure on R & D as percentage of total sales of over 4%, and many of these companies had obtained patents in Japan. Moreover, most of these companies reported that their R & D activities were either completely or to a large extent autonomous from their headquarters.

It is interesting to note that in order to successfully carry out R & D activities, there was a need for a greater amount of autonomy from headquarters. Two of the reasons were to be able to carry out Japan-specific R & D, which was in many cases different from that in other OECD countries, and to be competitive in meeting the challenge from rivals in Japan.

We found that a foreign company's subsidiary could also be a source of new product development and innovation in Japan, with the US or European parent company and/or subsidiary outside Japan receiving the new product or innovation from its subsidiary in Japan.

Our results showed that technology transfer by foreign companies is not a one-way transfer from the parent company to its foreign subsidiary, but a two-way transfer in which technology is also transferred from subsidiary to its parent company or other subsidiaries (outside Japan/rest of the world). This subject is further discussed in Chapter 9.

8.5 AVOIDING PITFALLS THAT CAUSE FAILURE IN THE JAPANESE MARKET

In this final section we provide further practical advice to foreign companies that plan to invest in Japan or have recently entered the Japanese market.

Before we go further, let us say that it has become quite clear to us that there is widespread mistrust and ill feeling between Japanese personnel and expatriates at a large number of foreign companies with 50% or more foreign equity. It appears that the Japanese employees want to occupy the top-ranking positions and run the operation of the subsidiary with autonomy from the headquarters.

Some Japanese managers even mentioned that they felt that headquarters was treating Japan like a poor Southeast Asian developing country by dispatching expatriates in large numbers to occupy most or all of the key managerial positions and run the operations in a foreign language. Local employees were promoted and judged on the basis of foreign language skills. Several Japanese managers mentioned that headquarters needed to recognize the uniqueness of Japan.

Foreign companies' transfer pricing policy and the suppression of profits in order to avoid high corporate taxes in Japan was also criticized by several Japanese respondents. Some Japanese managers mentioned that expatriates were antagonizing Japanese personnel with their excessive authoritative behavior, or hegemonic attitude.

On the other side, headquarters, particularly in TNCs and MNCs with global networks, wanted to control the operations of the subsidiary, at least to some extent, with an expatriate dispatched from headquarters who understood headquarters' language, and corporate culture and could easily communicate with its staff members. At the same time, these MNCs and TNCs wanted to promote and transfer talented Japanese staff to other subsidiaries of the parent company outside Japan.

These conflicts are not unusual; they are found in almost all countries with FDI. However, our feelings are that the dimension of this problem is great in Japan, since Japan is on the one hand an economic superpower (surrounded by poor developing countries), and on the other hand, a conservative and still somewhat closed society in terms of language, culture, and homogeneity. The presence of expatriates, particularly those occupying top ranking positions, and high interference by headquarters are accepted only grudgingly by Japanese personnel, and are considered below their dignity or somewhat humiliating, since they are still not used to working side by side with people of a large number of nationalities as are the Europeans and Americans.

Some Japanese managers claim that expatriates have a colonial mentality, especially those expatriates directly transferred from other developing countries in Asia (including NIEs), South America, or Africa as top-ranking directors in the Japanese subsidiary. The only advice that we can give is that foreign companies should try to understand this problem and be sensitive to these types of feelings and issues. They should also try to find remedies as many foreign companies in Japan have, for example, by entrusting management to the local staff; having minimum numbers of expatriates occupy top managerial positions; having those expatriates who have been working in developing countries first transferred to headquarters, then, after a certain period, to the Japanese subsidiary; and transferring expatriates with experience in working at headquarters (occupying top-ranking positions), western Europe, or the United States. Pretending that such problems do not exist will only aggravate them further and lead to low morale among local employees and high labor turnover.

It is important for foreign companies to promote Japanese managers to higher positions, training them by stationing them at headquarters and subsidiaries outside Japan. In this way, Japanese managers could occupy top managerial positions in Japan. This method will minimize the foreign companies' problems in Japan in term of costs, recruitment, and conflicts among local personnel and expatriates. It is not appropriate to transfer and place an expatriate at a top managerial position mainly on the basis of knowledge of the English language and headquarters' way of working; the expatriate should also have acquired at least some knowledge of Japanese language, business manners, customs, culture, and history.

It is interesting to note that a large number of expatriates and several Japanese respondents cast doubt on the idea or would hesitate in establishing a joint venture in Japan, despite the fact that a large number of such ventures are classified as successful. Foreign companies appear to worry about losing control to the Japanese joint venture partner. The respondents are more biased toward the 100% owned foreign subsidiary.

Advice to foreign companies in key areas

Management Style

- Do not place an expatriate in a top managerial position when he or she is not familiar with the Japanese situation, lacks means of communication with Japanese society, lacks knowledge regarding the Japanese culture and economy, or antagonizes Japanese personnel.

- Avoid an excessively Western management style and hegemonic strategy, or authoritative behavior.
- Do not have plural managers, since the practice leads to confusion and low morale among employees.
- Do not enforce the parent company's cultural values or standards, impose a foreign way of thinking, or insist on doing things as at headquarters.
- Do not have a shortsighted, self-centered policy or distrust Japanese staff.
- Do not bring in too many expatriates, since friction among local personnel and expatriates is bound to increase.
- The parent company should not interfere too much in the affairs of the local subsidiary or hold a too strong grip on the subsidiary, since extensive interference from the headquarters is not appreciated by the Japanese personnel.
- Do not control Japanese staff using a foreign language, manage the subsidiary using a foreign language, overvalue English-language capability at the expense of business knowledge, or judge local employees' capabilities mainly on the basis of language skills.
- Do not employ those who change jobs frequently.

Corporate Goals and Objectives

- Do not seek short-term profits, pursue a short-term profit strategy, expect returns similar to those in the home country, or expect instant success and profits.
- Do not put blame on the peculiarities, exclusiveness, or the uniqueness of the Japanese market when business is not moving satisfactorily. In other words, make efforts to satisfy the demands of the Japanese market (with high quality, prompt service, and on-time delivery).
- Do not withdraw (or perform a short-term evacuation) from Japan when business does not seem to go well, especially after obtaining capable Japanese staff.
- Do not hastily reduce staff or lay off personnel during a recession for reasons such as a fall in sales-per-employee or profit-per-employee ratios.
- Do not manipulate the accounting system in order to show lower profits or make losses and thus avoid taxes, abusing transfer pricing.
- Do not leave management entirely to the local partner in a joint venture, particularly one with 50% or more foreign equity.
- Do not base success entirely on financial goals or ratios, evaluate success entirely on the basis of short-term profitability, or judge a local branch on weekly, monthly, or quarterly bases.
- Do not change top management every two or three years.
- Do not frequently change policies and strategies.
- Do not use the same policies and strategies as in the home country.

- Do not leave Japan because it's a difficult market.
- Do not go alone unless you have unlimited funds and time.
- TNCs and MNCs usually tend to impose their administrative policies on the local company, but they should avoid doing this in Japan.
- Japan is an expensive market, but at the same time it is not recommended that foreign companies handle Japan from other developing countries in Asia; etc.

Distribution Channels

- Avoid using an agent, particularly a big agent, since agents give limited attention and commitment to foreign companies' products. Foreign companies need a dedicated Japanese organization (trading company, agent, subsidiary, or joint venture) that can give first priority to their product or service.

8.6 CONCLUSIONS

The first conclusion that can be drawn is that, generally, successful foreign companies are highly competitive in the Japanese market in terms of corporate image (CI) or brand name, sales and service network, and market leadership in quality or product/service development, price, and delivery time. Whenever possible, the joint venture partner's distribution channels are used. Moreover, foreign companies provide repair and after-sales services (spare part centers and service stations), since they, among other factors, are indispensable for protecting the brand image of a company.

Foreign companies have been successful in the Japanese market through using several entry alternatives, such as the 100% owned subsidiary, joint venture, dealers, wholesalers, and exclusive agents, and through selling directly through retailers, employing a trading company, and forming strategic alliances. The use of multiple channels in Japan is quite common.

Most foreign companies in Japan have, to a large extent, adapted to the conditions prevailing in the Japanese market regarding management in order to compete effectively with Japanese and foreign competitors. Many foreign companies have Japanized their company, adopting a Japanese way of thinking and relying mainly on Japanese staff, even as CEOs and department heads. Most foreign companies are managed with autonomy, within limits.

Moreover, many foreign companies view Japan as an essential international center for R & D, because Japan is the second largest market in the world, with very high quality R & D and standards of production.

Foreign companies in Japan have made innovations and obtained a large number of patents, and usually they have a high degree of autonomy from their headquarters. Also, they have been transferring R & D results and production know-how to their headquarters and other subsidiaries. They have supported the parent company's efforts to achieve global synergy in R & D and production by exchanging production and R & D results with the parent company and other subsidiaries.

MNCs and TNCs generally station expatriates in their Japanese subsidiaries. At the same time, they successfully utilize their highly qualified and talented Japanese staffs' expertise in other subsidiaries worldwide, generating a two-way flow of goods and personnel exchanges.

We advocate that foreign companies' strategy for Asia be based on a strategy for Japan, since Japan comprises over 80% of Asia's GNP. It is not practical for foreign companies to establish their regional headquarters in Southeast Asia and from there cover sales and manufacturing activities in Japan.

9 IMPLICATIONS

The research findings suggest some implications for Japanese and foreign policymakers as well as for overcoming shortcomings in the traditional theories of multinational enterprises.

9.1 INTRODUCTION

We have by now given answers to the basic research questions of this study, covering the strategies and performance of foreign companies in Japan, the features of successful foreign companies in Japan, critical factors for success in Japan, problems foreign companies meet in the Japanese market and their resolution, the relationship between headquarters and the subsidiary in Japan, and the reverse transfer of technology and know-how from a subsidiary to its parent company. We have also provided guidance to potential new entrants and those foreign companies that have been established recently in Japan. In this last chapter, we highlight our study's contribution toward developments in the theory of multinational enterprises and discuss policy issues for Japanese and foreign policymakers with regard to boosting FDI by foreign companies in Japan.

From the beginning, we expected to identify major differences between American and European companies' strategies and performances in Japan and at the same time show the differences among various industrial branches. However, the deeper we investigated these issues, the larger grew the number of similarities among American and European companies and among various branches.

We were not able to highlight the strategy and performance of foreign companies from developing countries in Japan. The major reason is that very little FDI is made by these countries, which could be due to the high cost of doing business, and tough competition. Unfortunately, the sample in our survey is too small to draw any major specific conclusions for foreign companies from developing countries or the Asian NIEs.

In our study a large number of foreign companies classified themselves as successful. Very few failing companies claimed that their failure in the Japanese market was directly attributable to impediments on the market, although these may have lowered their ROI or extended the pay-back period.

We have already seen that most of the 436 foreign companies participating in this study were able to overcome various difficulties in the Japanese market. They were able to find ways to tackle these problems that did not negatively affect their sales or financial performance. Moreover, many of these companies have reversed the flow of technology and know-how, directing it from themselves to their parent companies.

9.2 CONTRIBUTION TO THEORIES OF MULTINATIONAL ENTERPRISES

In Chapter 1 we discussed the three conventional theories of MNEs: the control model (industrial organization approach), the PCM (product cycle model), and the theory of technology transfer.

Some experts claim that control of practically every aspect of the subsidiary by a parent company is one of the essential characteristics of FDI. We mentioned in Chapter 1 that Hymer's theory of multinational enterprises does not leave room for the autonomous management of a foreign subsidiary.[1]

In our study, successful foreign companies in Japan were managed with great autonomy from the parent company. The foreign subsidiary was not regarded as an entity to be controlled by the parent company in its day-to-day operations. The parent company exercised some control in the form of formulating overall strategies, setting up financial objectives and goals for its subsidiary, but left management in many cases entirely in the hands of Japanese personnel (CEOs and other top-ranking executives), who exercised a Japanese management style.

Generally, it has been the case that technology and various other managerial resources flow from the parent company to its foreign subsidiary, with the subsidiary using these as weapons to compete against local companies. Moreover, technology and know-how transfer is realized under the overall guidance of the parent company.

Our study shows that the successful Japanese subsidiary enjoys autonomy, using its own resources to create new technology and know-how, which are then transferred to the parent company. In addition, there are several examples of horizontal technology transfer to other foreign subsidiaries. These reverse technology and know-how transfers and horizontal transfers occur frequently in foreign companies' Japanese subsidiaries. They are not, however, satisfactorily treated in the existing literature on MNEs, PCMs, or technology transfer.

Vernon and Wells' product cycle model has formed one of the theoretical pillars of this study.[2] We have been able to show that the PCM has some shortcomings, since it is unable to take into account the factors mentioned above. Subsidiaries of foreign companies in Japan are also able to develop products (including technology, production techniques, patents, and marketing know-how) that meet the needs not only of the Japanese market but also of their parent company's market globally, and they can therefore reverse the flow of technology and other managerial resources from Japan to their parent company and other foreign subsidiaries. Technology and managerial resource transfer is not a one-way but a two-way transfer.

Furthermore, products/services are developed not only in the parent company in the United States or Europe but also in Japan. The subsidiary could also be the source of new product development and innovation, with the US or European parent company receiving the new product or innovation. We also observed a number of cases where Japanese R & D and production personnel were provided excellent guidance to the parent company or its subsidiary outside Japan.

At present, the existing theories of international trade and multinational enterprises (including the product cycle model) cannot satisfactorily explain entrepreneurship and innovation at foreign subsidiaries, reverse technology transfer, and subsidiary support for the parent company in realizing global synergy effects of R & D and production. Since the existing MNE theories have reached their limits, we suggest that FDI theories be improved and reinforced by taking into consideration the new dimensions identified in our study.

9.3 ISSUES FOR POLICYMAKERS

During the last ten years, Japan's average outward FDI has been 10 to 20 times more than the inward FDI to Japan. Japan's massive trade surplus with most countries in the world is expected to continue for a long time in the future. The appreciation of the yen is not expected to considerably reduce this massive trade imbalance (at least in the short run or in dollar terms) and neither is the imposition of numerical targets in certain sectors. We argue that the most important tool for reducing the trade surplus is increasing FDI, which would also generate increased imports into Japan, as our study has shown. Increased FDI and imports into Japan could be expected to intensify competition and lead to increased benefits for Japanese consumers through a lowering of price levels. Ironically, recession and intensive competition in the Japanese market has made Japanese competitors even more determined not to lose market shares to foreign companies in Japan.

We argue that the Japanese government should minimize excessive government regulations (administrative guidance, oral directives and authorization procedures) and amend business practices that are considered to constrain, to some extent, Japanese market access by foreign companies.

This study has shown that some participating companies find the investment climate in Japan restrictive or the Japanese market closed. However, it is somewhat astonishing that Japanese embassies abroad, JETRO offices, and various other Japanese governmental organizations have been extremely unsuccessful in convincing foreign countries and their mass media that today Japan is not a closed market. Great efforts are required on the part of the Japanese policymakers to change this attitude, and this can be accomplished by further improving the investment climate. However, this will not be an easy task as long as Japanese outward FDI remains disproportionately high, huge trade surpluses continue to exist, and foreign FDI and imports into Japan keep declining. Sector-specific obstacles continue to impede the entry or expansion of foreign companies. Cumbersome bureaucracy prevails, and it is virtually impossible for foreign companies to carry out M & A. The practice of doing business in Japan based on long-term interpersonal relationships makes it difficult for foreign companies to become "insiders." Also, there is suspicion in Japan about goods and services of foreign origin.

Implications for Japanese policymakers

There is still much in Japan's investment climate that needs to be improved so that there is freer competition in the Japanese market. Accelerating the opening of the Japanese market can be achieved by deregulation, elimination of remaining tariffs and quotas, increased clarity of the administrative policy for procedures, liberalizing and abolishing the oligopoly in certain areas (for example, the distribution system), and harmonization of product testing procedures. Through public relations, the Japanese government has to intensify its efforts to remove the global image of Japan as a closed market in the eyes of foreign investors.

Japan should also offer more opportunities for foreign companies to come to Japan, since the soaring trade surplus, in particular with the United States and the EC, is turning increasingly into a political issue, exacerbating anti-Japanese sentiment caused by rising unemployment, particularly in Europe.

We believe that the Japanese government and other concerned organizations are making some positive steps in the right direction, for example, MITI's Import Promotion Program, including FAZ (foreign access zones). Areas that require action by the Japanese government and policymakers are discussed in the next sections.

Japanese business practices. Keiretsu are criticized by some foreign companies for various reasons, as described earlier. The Fair Trade Commission, under the auspices of the EPA (Economic Planning Agency), in its investigation could not find that the Keiretsu are carrying out activities that can be considered a direct breach of antitrust laws. However, we believe that there is a need to closely monitor these groups so that they do not discriminate against foreign companies, carry out exclusionary transactions, or exert monopoly control in the market, particularly due to declining market shares in the wake of the ongoing recession in Japan.

A Study Group on Trade Associations under the auspices of the Fair Trade Commission has criticized the discriminatory conduct of Japan's trade associations against foreign companies, particularly because most of the foreign companies do not qualify to become members of these associations. These trade associations hold valuable industrial trade data and work intimately with government administrative institutions. They guide and provide assistance to their members, and we therefore urge that these associations should become more open and accept foreign companies, irrespective of the size of their foreign equity holding, as members. We would expect this to lead to more open and fair competition in Japan.

The industrial data bases in Japan are comprehensive, however, only a few can be easily accessed without knowledge of the Japanese language or with the membership restrictions imposed by industrial associations on foreign companies in Japan as mentioned above. On the other hand, Japanese business and researchers can easily get access to worldwide data bases. Language convertibility programs are also facilitating this access for Japanese business. At present the swapping appears one sided. Therefore, we argue that there is a need to internationalize the data bases so that foreign companies in Japan and foreign researchers can easily obtain access to them.

FDI restrictions. Despite the fact that recent improvements have been made regarding the Foreign Exchange and Foreign Trade Control Law by the Ministry of Finance (MOF) and the Bank of Japan (BOJ), foreign companies still find that they lack clarity regarding ex post facto notification, or prior notice regarding their investment (for details, see Chapters 1 and 2). The lack of proper administrative guidelines and general criteria have led to arm twisting and excessive bureaucracy on the part of the authorities, and foreign companies are unable to determine into which category their investment falls without lengthy consultations with the authorities.

We believe that there is a need to simplify the procedures required for FDI in Japan, including the requirement of ex post facto notification and prior notice. We argue that there is an urgent need for the Japanese government to make its regulations and administrative guidance so clear that foreign companies can easily grasp them, and, if possible, to publish them in foreign languages simultaneously with Japanese.

Recruitment of Japanese personnel. Despite the recession prevailing in the Japanese market and the fact that the tradition of lifetime employment has been abandoned by several Japanese companies, the labor shortage is expected to continue. Most of the foreign companies, whether they are recent comers or have been in Japan for a long period of time, face difficulties recruiting new graduates, especially from Japan's elite universities. However, this has been partially offset by mid-career recruitment by foreign companies, mainly due to a large number of layoffs and the early retirement policy implemented by many Japanese companies, which have occurred because of difficulties in maintaining traditional Japanese-style management.

We described in Chapter 2 that MITI, together with JETRO, provides support activities through FIND (Foreign Investment in Japan Development, Inc.). It is too early to determine if FIND's activities will facilitate the recruitment of recent graduates by foreign companies in Japan. We recommend that several such agencies similar to FIND be established to assist foreign companies in Japan.

Land prices. Land prices in Japan are considered to be some of the highest in the world, despite the bursting of the economic bubble and subsequent fall in real estate prices. We recommend that government agencies such as MITI and JETRO and prefectural governments provide land at concessional rates to foreign companies in various industrial parks and in the vicinity of ports so that foreign companies are not scared by high land prices, particularly in Tokyo, and the difficulties of locating an office there. Most foreign companies prefer a location in central Tokyo due to such factors as easier recruitment, customer location, and access to key government officials. On the other hand, land prices outside Tokyo have fallen considerably, and it is relatively easy to obtain office space there. Government agencies together with foreign chambers of commerce should try to inform and assist foreign companies in obtaining the cheaper office space outside Tokyo.[3]

Tax incentives. Japan has some of the highest corporate taxes of all the OECD countries. Some tax incentives are offered to importers or manufacturers using imported items (for details, see Chapter 2). It is recommended that these incentives be further expanded. The OECD Model Convention on Taxation regarding the withholding tax rate on dividends paid from a subsidiary to its parent company recommends a 5% tax. Japan, however, with few exceptions, is still charging a 10% withholding tax rate on paid dividends. Similarly, higher taxes are charged on royalties and interest in Japan. We urge that these taxes be lowered as soon as possible.

Loan programs. Low-interest financing to foreign companies is provided to a limited extent by the JDB and the Hokkaido-Tohoku Development Finance Corporation. We hold that there is a need to increase the funds available to these institutions, that the loan ceiling be raised, that foreign equity limits be lowered, that the definition of projects eligible for JDB loans be further broadened, and at the same time that the public relations activities of these institutions be intensified (for more details, see Chapter 4).

There is also a need to expand the Export-Import Bank of Japan's program providing various loans for product import promotion. This also facilitates attracting FDI into Japan. Moreover, in order to increase foreign SMEs' FDI into Japan, other institutions catering to Japanese SMEs with preferential financing ought to be involved. Two such institutions are the Small Business Finance Corporation (SBFC) and the People's Finance Corporation (PFC).

Legal services. Japan has been criticized because the non-manufacturing sector is lagging far behind the manufacturing sector in terms of liberalization. Examples of this are various restrictions in financial and capital markets, insurance and securities, and legal services. Regarding foreign lawyers, we argue that foreign lawyers should be allowed to form partnerships with Japanese lawyers, to hire Japanese lawyers, and to use their own law firm name, since all of these measures would boost FDI into Japan. We recommend that the Ministry of Justice intervene and remove the discriminatory policies.

Implications for foreign policymakers

In the past, Japan was particularly neglected by European countries; however, today it is an integral part of the triad with the United States and Europe. First of all, it is vital that the major trading partners of Japan intensify their research on Japan, with intensive and extensive travel to Japan by members of their business community, trade unions, researchers, and governmental and non-governmental organizations. Efforts should be made to study the Japanese language, business practices, market situation, economy, and culture with the aim of increasing understanding of Japan.

Contract research among Japanese and foreign businesses, universities, and research institutes also needs to be intensified. We suggest the following measures: foreign companies should disregard the short-term objective of profit maximization, they should pay attention to using multiple entry channels, they have to invest heavily in the distribution channels, patience is required for building a positive image, and foreign companies have to adapt to the peculiarities of the Japanese market. Foreign chambers of commerce should advise their business community on how to effectively penetrate the Japanese market based on the results of this study.

A large number of companies possessing competitive products/services in Europe and the United States--in particular SMEs--shy away from making investments in Japan, either due to a lack of information about the Japanese market or the concept that it is a closed market with tremendous barriers. These companies therefore concentrate their activities mainly within the confines of North America or within Europe (in the EC and EFTA). This tendency is found not only in the United States and Europe but also in the Japan's neighboring Asian countries.

Fierce competition for example, makes it difficult for many foreign companies to match the financial, and in particular the human, resources available to their Japanese competitors. Therefore, we recommend that there be public relations efforts to increase information about successful foreign companies in Japan, such as those who have been able to develop new products in Japan and have reversed the flow of technology, thus strengthening the competitiveness of their parent company despite various problems encountered in the Japanese market.

The representatives of foreign countries in Japan should take part in public relations activities, and this may also lead to more cooperation, collaboration, and alliance between foreign and Japanese companies. Foreign government representatives (such as chambers of commerce and trade attaches from the United States, EC, EFTA, etc.) in Japan could jointly form a lobbying group by developing Western alliances, assisting their business communities in meeting the competitive challenge of the Japanese market.

Without doubt, Japan is the costliest market in the world. The currency turmoil in the world market, in particular in the EC and EFTA countries, has made the Japanese market considerably more costly for foreign companies. It is therefore important that foreign governments, through their chambers of commerce, trade and technical commissioners, or representatives in Japan, intensify their efforts to identify business opportunities, particularly for their SMEs. They should furnish market and feasibility studies at preferential rates and provide other assistance (such as preferential loan schemes and insurance against currency fluctuation losses) in conjunction with the Japanese governmental and semi-governmental organizations we have mentioned.

Foreign companies, irrespective of nationality, should also be encouraged to intensify their cooperation within the same industry in Japan. We argue that this kind of industrial cooperation is also potentially a promising instrument for increased FDI in Japan. Foreign chambers of commerce should sponsor more seminars in their countries about Japanese business policies, practices, and customs. They should also encourage more research related to Japanese industry and distribution and retail systems.

Discussions of specific other areas that require action by foreign policy-makers follows.

Japanese business practices. The impression is given in the mass media that entry into Keiretsu dealings is more difficult than entry into the Japanese market; however, we argue that the role of Keiretsu is somewhat exaggerated. Many foreign companies in our study mentioned that once a stable relationship is established with a Keiretsu group of companies, they are very reliably to do business with them. Therefore, we recommend that foreign chambers of commerce continue to monitor Keiretsu activities but at the same time encourage foreign companies to enter into business dealings with these groups.

Moreover, as share prices have plunged on the stock market during the last two years (over 30%) and as various liberalizations as well as strict regulations of the Bank for International Settlements (BIS) have appeared, it has become easier to acquire shares of Japanese companies. Therefore, foreign companies should be encouraged to make stock acquisitions and thus increase M & A by foreign companies in Japan.

Land prices. Since land prices are exorbitant in Japan, it is recommended that foreign chambers of commerce and other foreign countries' representatives in Japan inform foreign companies about the availability of cheaper land and office space outside of Tokyo. The land prices are considerably lower, for example, they are up to three times or more lower compared to Tokyo in Yokohama, Osaka, and Kobe, and these cities offer international schools, excellent housing conditions, and convenient airport and port facilities. Several foreign companies have already moved their headquarters outside of Tokyo, for example, Chase Manhattan Bank, Nihon Digital Equipment, Yokogawa-Hewlett-Packard, Nestlé S.A., Ciba-Geigy, ABB (Asea Brown Boveri), and Proctor & Gamble Far East.

Foreign chambers of commerce can also develop joint office centers, such as the one developed for German companies in Yokohama (German Industry Center), or for Swedish companies in Tokyo by the Commercial Office of the Embassy of Sweden.

Recruitment of Japanese personnel. Foreign companies find that despite the fact that they continuously show long-term commitment to the Japanese market, it is quite difficult to recruit recent university graduates. We recommend that foreign chambers of commerce and government representatives in Japan, together with MITI, JETRO, KEIDANREN, RENGO (Japanese Trade Union Confederation), NIKKEIREN (Japan Federation of Employers' Associations) and Japanese chambers of commerce (including prefectural authorities), among other groups, provide information and hold seminars at universities regarding employment conditions and opportunities at foreign companies in Japan.

Moreover, these foreign chambers of commerce should, along with foreign companies, establish ties with Japanese universities and their staff, offer summer jobs at their companies for Japanese students, and in general intensify public relations activities with Japanese universities. We at Kobe University, one of the elite universities of Japan, have rarely seen public relations activity carried out by foreign companies on our campus.

FAMA (Foreign Affiliated Companies Management Association), which we mentioned in Chapter 5, may also facilitate the recruitment of local personnel. Moreover, other foreign company associations based on industry and nationality provide strong lobbying groups that promote the interests of foreign companies in Japan. It is important that all these organizations join together with their chambers of commerce to, among other things, facilitate the recruitment of university graduates by increasing public relations and strengthening ties with government agencies.

9.4 CONCLUSIONS

The objectives of this present study have been fulfilled in terms of our contribution toward new developments in the theories of MNEs and international trade based on the features of successful foreign companies in Japan. Joint efforts to implement the recommendations made in this book by Japanese and foreign policymakers in conjunction with the business community are expected to boost FDI and imports into Japan. Furthermore, joint efforts are required by the Japanese government and those of foreign countries to stimulate businesses in various countries to export and make FDI into Japan. Otherwise, investment and trade frictions will lead to protectionism and trade wars.

NOTES

1. See Hymer, S. H., 1976.
2. Vernon, R., and Wells, L. T., Jr., 1991, pp. 82-86; Vernon, R., 1971, pp. 65-77.
3. See Brull, S., 1992.

APPENDIX A

Project title:
STRATEGY AND PERFORMANCE OF
FOREIGN COMPANIES IN JAPAN

Note:
- *Throughout the questionnaire "parent company" of a Japanese subsidiary (including joint ventures) and "headquarters" refer only to the foreign partner's parent company outside Japan*
- *Figures have been rounded up and therefore percentage figures may not always add up to 100%*
- *The base consists of 436 foreign companies that returned the filled-in questionnaire*
- *n = the total number of companies that responded per question*

A.   BASIC DATA

CHARACTERISTICS OF RESPONDING COMPANIES

Line of Business

Manufacturers * and Non-Manufacturers
n = 436

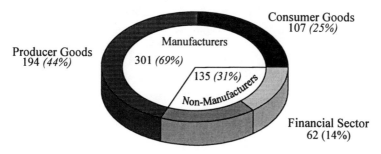

Producer Goods
194 *(44%)*

Manufacturers
301 *(69%)*

135 *(31%)*
Non-Manufacturers

Consumer Goods
107 *(25%)*

Financial Sector
62 (14%)

Services 73 (17%)

Number of Companies

*Note: * "Manufacturer" refers to the parent company (of a foreign partner) who is manufacturing and exporting goods to its subsidiary for sales in Japan. In addition, the subsidiary may also be manufacturing goods in Japan.*

Characteristics of Respondent
n = 436

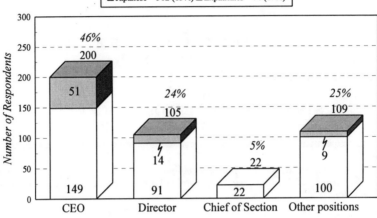

☐ Japanese = 362 (83%) ☐ Expatriates = 74 (17%)

Position of Respondent

Location of Headquarters of Parent Company
n = 435

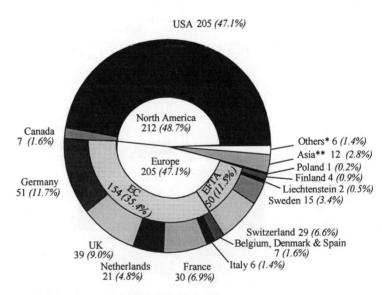

Number of Companies

Note: *Others = South America (Brazil) 1 (0.4%) and Australia & New Zealand 5 (1%)
   **Asia = S. Korea, Hong Kong, Taiwan, P.R.China, India & Singapore

B.   SPECIFIC QUESTIONS

I.   INVESTMENT STRATEGIES

1. Purpose of your company's doing business in Japan. Kindly indicate major purposes (past [indicate the year] and present)! Please choose the appropriate number/s and place a tick (√) in the relevant box (multiple answers are possible).
For details see Figure 4.1

2. Which of the following entry channels have been used by your company in Japan? Please circle the appropriate number/s and indicate the starting and terminating year (where applicable) of the channels in the relevant box (multiple answers are possible).
For details see Figure 4.2

II.   MANAGEMENT STYLE

3. What type of management style is your company using in Japan? Please circle the appropriate number.
For details see Figure 4.5

4. Indicate the extent of control exercised by the headquarters (if applicable) in the affairs of the Japanese subsidiary. Please circle the appropriate number/s (multiple answers are possible).
For details see Figure 4.7

5. In case of a joint venture, which partner has the management responsibility? Please circle the appropriate number.
For details see Figure 4.8

6. Have the headquarters given any special responsibility to your company outside Japan (e.g. Japanese subsidiary's strategic position in the global corporate system)? Please circle the appropriate number.
For details see Figure 4.9

III.   HUMAN RESOURCE MANAGEMENT

7. How many foreign expatriates are there in your company?
For details see Figure 5.1

8. Are the heads of departments Japanese or expatriates?
For details see Figure 5.2

9. What types of training programs do you offer to your employees? Please circle the appropriate number/s (multiple answers are possible).
For details see Figure 5.3

10. Indicate which criteria are important for selecting the local personnel (white collar). Please mark the appropriate number/s (multiple answers are possible).
For details see Figure 5.4

11. From the total yearly recruitment for white collar positions this year, what is the percentage of new graduates?

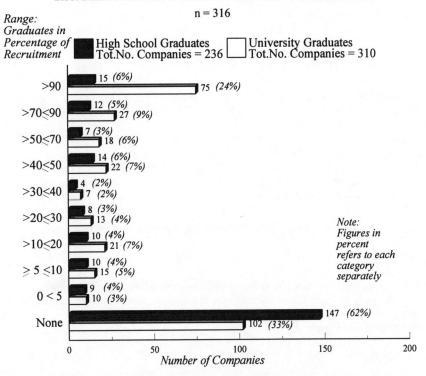

Recruitment of New Graduates for White Collar Positions

n = 316

Range:
Graduates in
Percentage of   ■ High School Graduates   □ University Graduates
Recruitment   Tot.No. Companies = 236   Tot.No. Companies = 310

Note:
Figures in percent refers to each category separately

Number of Companies

12. In your opinion, which are the main factors given importance by the local managerial employees in choosing your company as their employer? Please circle the appropriate number/s (multiple answers are possible).
For details see Figure 5.7

13. In your opinion, what types of common difficulties are encountered by the local employees while interacting with the expatriates? Please circle the appropriate number/s (multiple answers are possible).
For details see Figure 5.9

14. The recruitment strategy of your company regarding local managerial employees consists of: Please circle the appropriate number/s (multiple answers are possible).
For details see Figure 5.6

15. What types of problems is your company facing regarding the Japanese personnel? Please circle the appropriate number/s (multiple answers are possible).
For details see Figure 5.8

16. Regarding the seniormost expatriate (CEO or similar level), please provide background information on him/her according to the questions below.

n = 208

1 = Current Function and Status of the Seniormost Expatriate

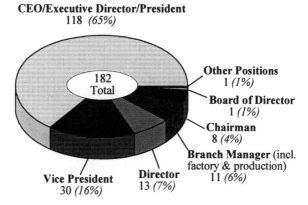

Number of Companies

2 = Status in the Headquarters of the Seniormost Expatriate

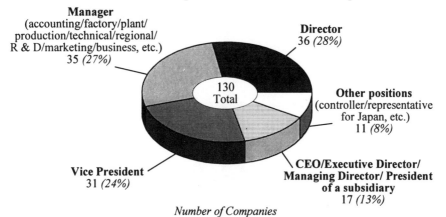

Number of Companies

**3 = Working Experience in a Foreign Country (excluding headquarters)
Before Being Transferred to Japan of the Seniormost Expatriate**

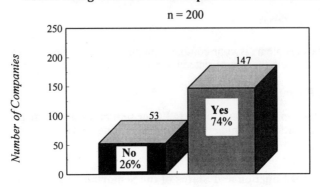

4 = Number of Years Stationed in Japan of the Seniormost Expatriate

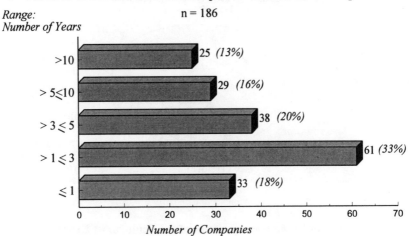

5 = Education in Japan of the Seniormost Expatriate

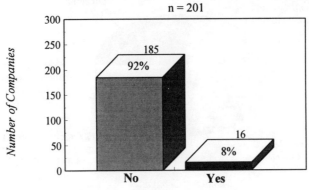

6 = Language Abilities of the Seniormost Expatriate

(circle the number if the ability is good to excellent):

1. English
141 *(71%)*

3. English & Japanese
46 *(23%)*

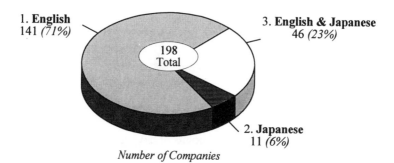

198
Total

2. Japanese
11 *(6%)*

Number of Companies

7 = Total Planned Period of Stay in Japan of the Seniormost Expatriate

Range: Number of Years   n = 126

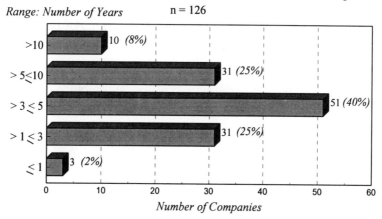

Number of Companies

17. From which types of companies were the mid-career local managers recruited this year? Indicate only main sources (multiple answers are possible). *For details see Figure 5.5*

18. Are any of the Japanese executives on your parent company's board?

Japanese Executives on Parent Company's Board

n = 419

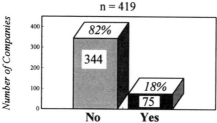

19. Does your company have a trade union/s?

Existence of Trade Unions in the Companies

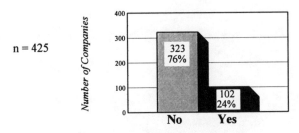

n = 425

If "Yes", what are the good points of having a trade union? Please circle the appropriate number/s (multiple answers are possible). *For details see Figure 5.10*

IV. *COMMUNICATION BETWEEN HEADQUARTERS AND SUBSIDIARY*

20. Has your company encountered any communication problems with the headquarters? If so, please circle the relevant number/s (multiple answers are possible).
For details see Figure 4.10

V. *FINANCING*

21. How is the capital investment for the Japanese subsidiary obtained? Please circle the appropriate number/s (multiple answers are possible).
For details see Figure 4.10

VI. *RELATIONSHIP WITH THE JAPANESE GOVERN-MENT AND PROBLEMS ENCOUNTERED IN THE JAPANESE MARKET*

22. What are the problems your company is encountering with respect to the Japanese Government's behaviour? Please circle the appropriate number/s (multiple answers are possible).
For details see Figure 2.5

QUESTION ONLY FOR FINANCIAL INSTITUTIONS

23. Describe in brief your activities in Japan:

n = 66

Note: Question was meant only for financial institutions (62 institutions were taking part in the survey), however 12 companies in the manufacturing and service sectors also provided some minor comments.

1. Type of services provided to your customers: **n = 62**
2. Type and degree of competition you face in Japan: **n = 53**
3. On what strengths do you compete with Japanese competitors? **n = 61**
4. Have you ever experienced any kind of discrimination as a foreign financial institution on the Japanese market? **n = 55**
     1 = No: **36**; 2 = Yes: **18**; If "Yes", specify: **18**
5. Other factors (specify and use extra sheet if necessary): **n = 6**
For discussion of the different responses see Chapter 6.

Companies involved in the financial sector should also try to answer the questions in Section VII (Marketing) which are relevant and applicable to their companies.

VII.   MARKETING

In order to answer the questions related to the marketing activities of your company, please refer to your major product or service group.

24. How would you characterise the business environment for your company? Please circle the appropriate number on the 3 point scale which best represents your judgement.
For details see Figure 6.1

25. What are the marketing problems your company is encountering in Japan? Please circle the number/s that best represent(s) your judgement (multiple answers are possible).
For details see Figure 6.2

26. Kindly describe your company's marketing/sales strategies. Please circle the appropriate number/s (multiple answers are possible).
For details see Figure 6.3

27. Please evaluate your company's market position in Japan. Kindly circle the appropriate number/s (multiple answers are possible).
For details see Figure 6.4

28. Please provide the yearly expenditure on marketing as a percentage of total sales. Marketing expenditure includes: sales and marketing staff related costs/market research/sales promotion material/advertising and sales training, etc. Please circle the appropriate number.
For details see Figure 6.5

29. Is your company following global standardization of the product/service (e.g. similar product/service concept all over the world including advertising and promotional material)?

Global Standardization of Product/Service

n = 389

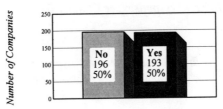

30. Is there a time lag between introducing the new major product models or service concept(s) in the parent company's home market and in Japan?

Time Lag between Marketing in the Parent Company's Home Market and in Japan

n = 365

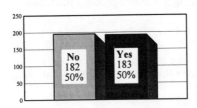

31. How is your company carrying out market intelligence in Japan? Please circle the appropriate number/s (multiple answers are possible).
For details see Figure 6.6

32. Is your company using the profit centres approach for each product/ service group?

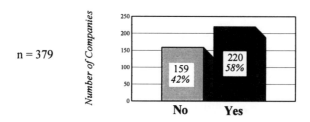

n = 379

if "No", is your company following a policy of cross-subsidization, (i.e. profitability of each product/service group is not of paramount importance, but the total profitability of the entire Japanese company).

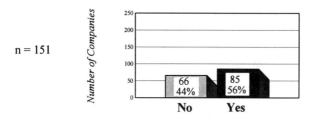

n = 151

33. Has your company developed and introduced a unique marketing program/strategy (especially tailored for Japanese consumers/buyers) for your product or service that has led to success in the Japanese market?
For details see Figure 6.7

34. Has your company transferred the successful marketing program or strategy to the headquarters or any other subsidiary outside Japan?
For details see Figure 6.8

VIII. PRODUCTION

Note: M1 = Consumer goods; M2 = Producer goods;
*   N1 = Services sector;   N2 = Financial sector*

35. Why do you have production facilities in Japan? Please circle the appropriate number/s (multiple answers are possible).
For details see Figure 7.1

36. How is the performance (with respect to productivity, cost, quality, delivery time, etc.) of your factory/ies as compared to the factories of your parent company outside Japan? Please circle the appropriate number.
For details see Figure 7.2

37. Have any of the Japanese production techniques (production equipment, production management, etc.) been transferred to the parent company or its subsidiaries outside Japan?
For details see Figure 7.3

38. Does your company have any difficulties while performing production activities in Japan? Please circle the appropriate number/s (multiple answers are possible).
For details see Figure 7.4

IX. RESEARCH AND DEVELOPMENT (R & D)

For number of manufacturing companies conducting R & D in Japan see Figure 7.6 (Figure based on responses to question 39).

39. When did the R & D activities start in Japan?
For details see Figure 7.5

40. **Number of Researchers and Technicians carrying out R & D activities in Japan:**

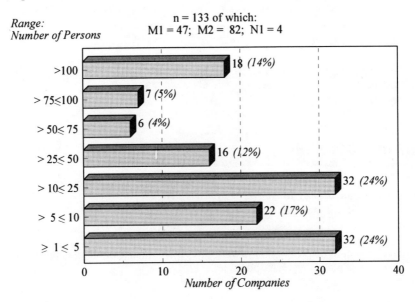

Range:
Number of Persons

n = 133 of which:
M1 = 47; M2 = 82; N1 = 4

>100 — 18 *(14%)*
> 75≤100 — 7 *(5%)*
> 50≤ 75 — 6 *(4%)*
> 25≤ 50 — 16 *(12%)*
> 10≤ 25 — 32 *(24%)*
> 5 ≤ 10 — 22 *(17%)*
≥ 1 ≤ 5 — 32 *(24%)*

0   10   20   30   40
Number of Companies

... of which are Expatriates:

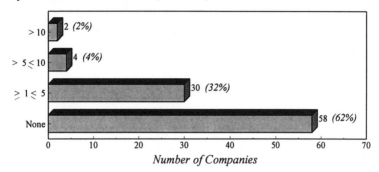

Range: n = 94 of which:
Number of Persons   M1 = 36; M2 = 56; N1 = 2

41. Indicate average expenditure on R & D as percentage of total sales: (R & D expenditure includes staff cost, equipment, laboratory, etc.).
For details see Figure 7.8

42. Please provide the percentage figures regarding the R & D fund allocations. In case you do not have the detailed figures, please mark each activity column with "Yes", if you are conducting the activity, or "No" if not.

Percentage Figures of R & D Fund Allocations

n = 129 of which:
M1 = 44; M2 = 83; N1 = 2

■Allocation□No Allocation

* Fund allocation in basic research (% of total R & D expenditure)
  41 — 32% | 88 — 68% | 129 — 100%

* Fund allocation in applied research (% of total R & D expenditure)
  98 — 76% | 31 — 24% | 129 — 100% | 1 — 0%

* Fund allocation in development research (% of total R & D expenditure):
  128 — 100% | 129 — 100%

Number of Companies

43. Indicate the number of patents your company (only Japanese subsidiary/ies) has obtained up till now in Japan. Please circle the appropriate number.
For details see Figure 7.9

44. How autonomous are your R & D activities in Japan (integrated and controlled by the headquarters or fully decentralised in terms of funding, R & D objectives, activities, etc.)? Please circle the appropriate number.
For details see Figure 7.10

45. Have any of your R & D results (including patents, licences, product development/innovation, etc.) been transferred to the parent company or to other subsidiaries?
For details see Figure 7.11

46. What difficulties are you confronted with while conducting R & D in Japan? Please circle the appropriate number/s (multiple answers are possible).
For details see Figure 7.12

47. Why are you conducting/or do you intend to conduct R & D in Japan? Please circle the appropriate number/s (multiple answers are possible).
For details see Figure 7.5

X.   PERFORMANCE

Please evaluate your company's total performance in Japan by taking into consideration the financial and non-financial criteria.

Do you consider that your company has been successful or has failed in the Japanese market?

48. Success or failure based on financial criteria, please circle the appropriate number:
For details see Figure 3.1

Criteria used for measuring your company's financial performance. Please circle the appropriate number/s (multiple answers are possible).

Criteria Used for Measuring Financial Performance
n = 403

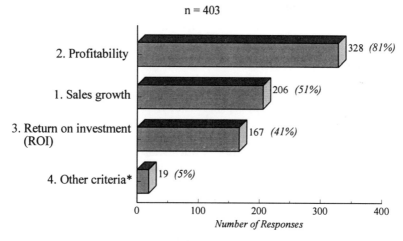

Number of Responses

* Other criteria specified - List in order of importance:

1. ROCE/ROTC - Return on capital employed/return on total capital
2. ORAD - Operational results after depreciation
3. Profits for parent company through transfer pricing
4. ROE - Return on equity
5. Cash flow
6. Asset growth
7. Efficiency of investment

49. Success or failure based on non-financial criteria, please circle the
appropriate number.

Evaluation of Performance
Success or Failure Based on Non-Financial Criteria

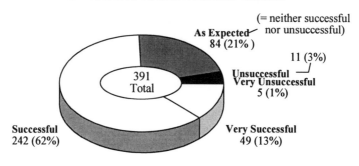

Number of Companies

Criteria used for measuring your company's non-financial performance.
Please provide one or more of your company's non-financial criteria by listing
them below.

n = 264

List in order of importance:

1. Won or obtained market share/market penetration/industry penetration/
   obtained foothold in the Japanese market
2. Developed new products
3. Customer satisfaction/trust/increase in number of customers/high pre-
   and post-sales services/customer orientation
4. Brand image or brand name including image of parent company/our
   reputation/recognition of brand name/corporate image/popularity in
   the Japanese market
5. Quick delivery or delivery on time/high quality/appreciation of our
   product quality
6. Employee satisfaction/improvement in employees morale/stable labor
   force/staff retention/increase in number of Japanese employees
7. Reverse flow of technology and know-how to parent company/learning
   from the Japanese market/improvement in R & D and productivity/
   production efficiency/contributed to parent company's successes
   through reverse flow of technology
8. Acknowledged as a technology leader in certain segments
9. Close and friendly relationship among the joint venture partners/
   contributed toward internationalization of the Japanese partner
10. Increased the number of stores/franchise/growth in amount of orders/
    attainment of goals
11. Overtook competitors
12. Market intelligence efficiency
13. Contributed to the Japanese society

50. Key success and failure factors in the Japanese market. Why do you consider
your company has been successful or unsuccessful? Please circle the appropriate
number/s (multiple answers are possible).
For details see Figure 8.1

C. GENERAL QUESTIONS

51. Indicate the future plans of your company in Japan. Please circle the appropriate number/s and specify where required (multiple answers are possible).

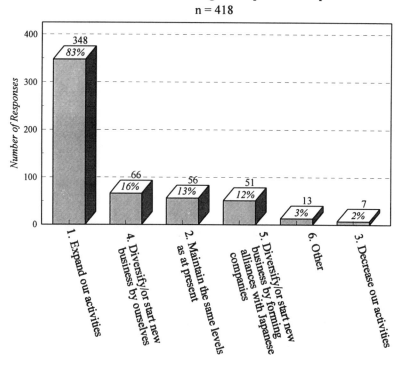

Future Plans of Foreign Companies in Japan

n = 418

52. **Please provide practical advice to foreign companies that plan to invest in Japan.**

    1. Foreign prospective companies should do the following:

    n = 225 responses

    2. Foreign prospective companies should not do the following:

    n = 167 responses

For discussion of the responses see Chapter 8.

53. Please provide the following information (as is applicable to your company):
[Note: mil = million; B = Billion; All figures refer to Fiscal/Calender Year 1990.]

n = 395

Total Assets, Paid Capital and Sales

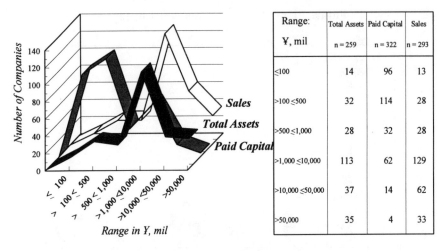

Range: ¥, mil	Total Assets n = 259	Paid Capital n = 322	Sales n = 293
≤100	14	96	13
>100 ≤500	32	114	28
>500 ≤1,000	28	32	28
>1,000 ≤10,000	113	62	129
>10,000 ≤50,000	37	14	62
>50,000	35	4	33

Ordinary Profits

n = 265

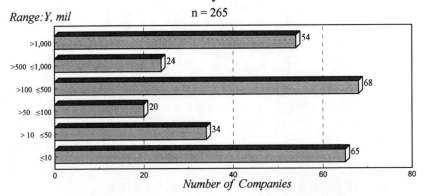

Accumulated Profit or Loss

n = 291

Dividends Paid

n = 295

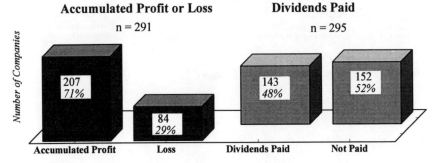

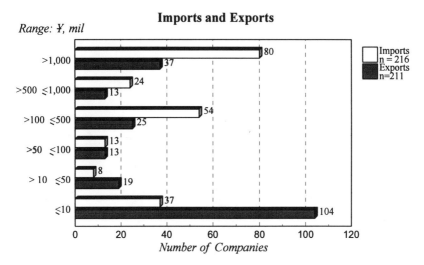

Imports and Exports

Range: ¥, mil

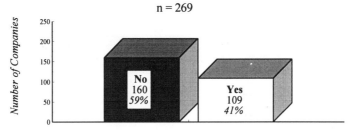

Exports to Parent Company

n = 269

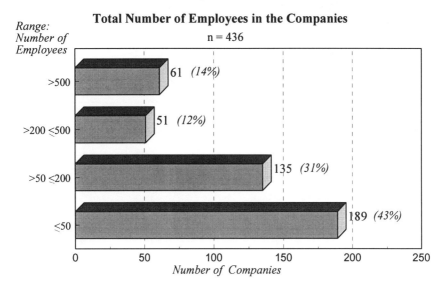

Total Number of Employees in the Companies

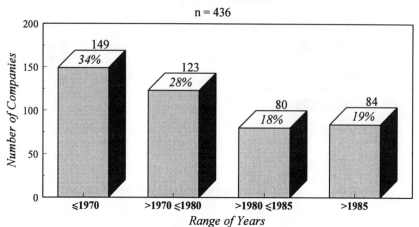

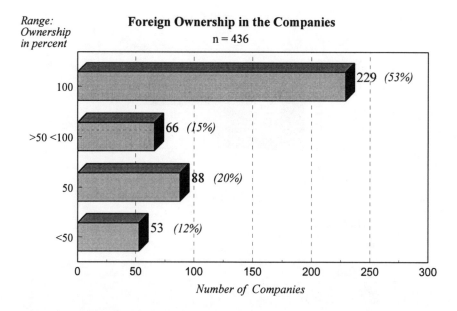

Note: 72 companies provided their annual reports, product information, and various other published materials.

APPENDIX B

Statistical Tables

Table B1.1 Location of participating foreign companies in Japan

Prefectures	Number of foreign companies	In percent
Kanto area		
Tokyo Metropolis	348	80
Kanagawa	23	5
Saitama	3	1
Ibaraki	2	
Chiba	1	1
Tochigi	1	
Total	78	87
Kansai area		
Osaka	27	6
Hyogo	11	2
Kyoto	3	1
Shiga	3	1
Total	44	10
Others		
Shizuoka	4	1
Aichi	5	1
Hokkaido	1	
Fukui	1	
Iwate	1	1
Niigata	1	
Yamaguchi	1	
Total	14	3
Total	436	100

**Table B3.1   Distribution of American and European companies based on
year established and number of employees in Japan**

YEAR ESTABLISHED IN JAPAN	American companies (Number)	In %	European companies (Number)	In %	Total Number of companies
< 1971	72	36	70	35	142
> 1970 < 1981	60	29	57	28	117
> 1980 < 1986	34	17	30	15	64
> 1985	35	18	44	22	79
TOTAL	201	100	201	100	402

NUMBER OF EMPLOYEES	American companies (Number)	In %	European companies (Number)	In %	Total Number of companies
< 51	75	37	94	47	169
> 50 < 201	64	32	59	29	123
> 200 < 501	23	12	26	13	49
> 500	39	19	22	11	61
TOTAL	201	100	201	100	402

Table B3.2   Actual profitability and performance
Entire sample (Number of companies)   (Q 48)

Profitability in %	Sample 1	Sample 2	Sample 3	Total
< 0	9	20	9	38
≥ 0 < 5	74	21	3	98
≥ 5 < 10	50	3	1	54
≥ 10 < 15	19	3		22
≥ 15 < 20	12	1		13
≥ 20	11	2		13
Total	175	50	13	238

(continued)

Table B3.2 (continued)

USA

Profitability in %	Sample 1	Sample 2	Sample 3	Total
< 0	1	8	3	12
⩾ 0 < 5	36	5	1	42
⩾ 5 < 10	23	3		26
⩾ 10 < 15	12	3		15
⩾ 15 < 20	7	1		8
⩾ 20	6	2		8
Total	85	22	4	111

European Countries

Profitability in %	Sample 1	Sample 2	Sample 3	Total
< 0	8	12	4	24
⩾ 0 < 5	32	16	2	50
⩾ 5 < 10	24			24
⩾ 10 < 15	7			7
⩾ 15 < 20	4			4
⩾ 20	5			5
Total	80	28	6	114

Other Countries

Profitability in %	Sample 1	Sample 2	Sample 3	Total
< 0			2	2
⩾ 0 < 5	6			6
⩾ 5 < 10	3		1	4
⩾ 15 < 20	1			1
Total	10		3	13

Legend
Sample 1 = Very successful and successful; Sample 2 = As expected;
Sample 3 = Very unsuccessful and unsuccessful.

Table B3.3   Profitability based on ownership groups
Entire sample (Number of companies)

Profitability in %	Ownership 25 - 49%	50%	51 - 99%	100%	Total
< 0	3	6	8	23	40
≥ 0 < 5	17	23	13	49	102
≥ 5 < 10	7	12	15	21	55
≥ 10 < 15	1	14	5	2	22
≥ 15 < 20	1	1	4	7	13
≥ 20	4	1	1	7	13
Total	33	57	46	109	245

American companies Profitability in %	Ownership 25 - 49%	50%	51 - 99%	100%	Total
< 0	2	4	3	3	12
≥ 0 < 5	10	13	4	17	44
≥ 5 < 10	6	8	7	5	26
≥ 10 < 15	1	11	2	1	15
≥ 15 < 20	1		2	5	8
≥ 20	3	1	1	3	8
Total	23	37	19	34	113

European Companies Profitability in %	Ownership 25 - 49%	50%	51 - 99%	100%	Total
< 0		2	4	19	25
≥ 0 < 5	6	9	7	29	51
≥ 5 < 10	1	4	6	14	25
≥ 10 < 15		3	3	1	7
≥ 15 < 20		1	2	1	4
≥ 20	1			4	5
Total	8	19	22	68	117

Other Countries (companies) Profitability in %	Ownership 25 - 49%	50%	51 - 99%	100%	Total
< 0	1		1	1	3
≥ 0 < 5	1	1	2	3	7
≥ 5 < 10			2	2	4
≥ 15 < 20				1	1
Total	2	1	5	7	15

Note: Profitability (FY/CY 1990) = Ordinary profits divided by sales.

Table B3.4 Cross-tabulation based on profitability and business line

Profitability Range in %	Code Manufacturing (number of companies)											Services						Grand total
	1	2	3	4	5	6	7	8	9	10	Total	11	12	13	14	15	Total	
< 0	1	1		8	2		9	5	3	3	32	2	2		1	3	8	40
⩾ 0 < 5	4	4	2	12	5	9	18	12	5	3	74	11	1	2	2	12	28	102
⩾ 5 < 10				16	1	1	13	8		4	43	3	2		2	5	12	55
⩾ 10 < 15				7	1	1	6	3		2	20					2	2	22
⩾ 15 < 20	1			2			5	2			10	1	1			1	3	13
⩾ 20				2			4			1	7	2		1		3	6	13
Total	6	5	2	45	11	11	55	30	8	13	186	19	6	3	5	26	59	245

Legend   Code
1. Food (Processed & Non-processed)   7. Machinery (commercial and   11. Wholesale & retail
2. Textiles   industrial)   trade
3. Petroleum   8. Electronic/electrical   12. Banks and credit
4. Chemicals   equipment   institutes
5. Pharmaceuticals   9. Cars & car parts   13. Securities
6. Metals   10. Other manufacturing   14. Insurance
                                                                                                               15. Other services

Table B3.5 Accumulated profit and loss and performance

Accumulated profit (Q 53)	Performance (Q 48)						Total Number of companies	In %
	Sample 1	In %	Sample 2	In %	Sample 3	In %		
Profit	178	86	21	36	4	24	203	72
Loss	29	14	38	64	13	76	80	28
Total	207	100	59	100	17	100	283	100

Legend   Sample 1 = Very successful and successful; Sample 2 = As expected;
             Sample 3 = Very unsuccessful and unsuccessful.

Table B3.6 Dividends paid and performance

Dividends paid (Q 53)	Performance (Q 48)						Total Number	In %
	Sample 1	In %	Sample 2	In %	Sample 3	In %		
Yes	126	62	10	16	3	18	139	49
No	78	38	54	84	14	82	146	51
Total	204	100	64	100	17	100	285	100

Legend   Sample 1 = Very successful and successful; Sample 2 = As expected;
             Sample 3 = Very unsuccessful and unsuccessful.

**Table B3.7   Future plans of foreign companies in Japan based on
nationality**   (Q 51)

Nationality of parent company	1	Alternative 2	3	4	5	6	Total (number)
I North America							
Canada	5	1	1				7
USA	157	25	2	30	18	7	239
Total	162	26	3	30	18	7	246
II Europe							
EC							
Germany	36	6	3	8	6	1	60
UK	32	3		6	4	2	47
Netherlands	23	4		2	3		32
France	22	4		5	6		37
Italy	3	2		1	3		9
Belgium	2						2
Denmark	4			1			5
Spain	2						2
Total	124	19	3	23	22	3	194
EFTA							
Switzerland	22	1		5	2		30
Sweden	16	2	1	3	3	2	27
Liechtenstein	2						2
Finland	3			2	2		7
Total	43	3	1	10	7	2	66
OTHERS							
Poland	1						1
Total (Europe)	168	22	4	33	29	5	261
III Asia							
S. Korea	3	3					6
Hong Kong	3	1					4
Taiwan	1						1
China	1	1		1	1	1	5
India		1					1
Singapore	1						1
Total	9	6		1	1	1	18

(continued)

Table B3.7 (continued)

Nationality of parent company	Alternative					Total
	1	2	3	4	5	6 (number)
IV Others						
Australia	2	1				3
New Zealand	2			1		3
Panama	3				2	5
Bermuda	1					1
Brazil		1				1
Total	8	2		1	2	13

Legend   Alternative
1 = Expand our activities   4 = Diversify/ or start new business by ourselves
2 = Maintain the same levels as at present   5 = Diversify/ or start new business by forming
3 = Decrease our activities   alliances with Japanese companies
                           6 = Other

Table B4.1 Entry channels and nationality of parent company

Nationality of parent company	Alternative (entry channels, Q 2) (multiple answers)											Total Number of responses
	1	2	3	4	5	6	7	8	9	10	11	
I North America												
Canada	1	4	2	2	1		3					13
USA	58	30	48	74	72	12	43	22	15	40	11	425
Total	59	34	50	76	73	12	46	22	15	40	11	438
II Europe												
EC												
Germany	15	6	10	16	9	3	12	2	3	8	2	86
UK	7	4	19	8	3		4	2	4	3	6	60
Netherlands	8	8	7	6	9	1	6		1	3	1	50
France	8		10	7	6	1	5	3	3	4	2	49
Italy	2		1	3	3		3	1	1	3	1	18
Belgium	1	2	1	2	1		1			1		9
Denmark	2	1		2				1	1		1	8
Spain			1	1	1							3
Total	43	22	49	45	31	5	31	9	13	22	13	283
EFTA												
Switzerland	7		10	5	5	1	9	3	3	5	3	51
Sweden	10	4	5	7	5	2	10	4	4	7	4	62
Liechtenstein	2	2	2	1	1		1	1		1		11
Finland	1	1	1		1			1				5
Total	20	7	17	14	11	4	20	8	8	13	7	129

(countinued)

Table B4.1   (continued)

Nationality of parent company	Alternative (entry channels, Q 2) (multiple answers)											Total Number of responses
	1	2	3	4	5	6	7	8	9	10	11	
OTHERS												
Poland					1							1
Total (Europe)	63	29	66	60	42	9	51	17	21	35	20	413
III Asia												
S. Korea			5	1								6
Hong Kong			3				1					4
Taiwan	1			1			1					3
China		1		2								3
India			1									1
Singapore			1									1
Total	1	1	10	4			2					18
IV Others												
Australia			2			1						3
New Zealand		1	1	1			1					4
Panama		1	1				2	1	2		1	8
Bermuda	1			1								2
Brazil			1									1
Total	1	2	5	2		1	3	1	2		1	18

Legend   Alt. = Alternative   n = 403 companies

Alt. 1 = Through a Japanese agent/distributor   Alt. 7 = Wholly owned sales subsidiary

Alt. 2 = Through a Japanese trading company   Alt. 8 = Wholly owned manufacturing subsidiary

Alt. 3 = Through our own branch office   Alt. 9 = R & D laboratory

Alt. 4 = A joint venture for marketing/sales purposes   Alt. 10 = Licensing/franchising rights/ technology agreement

Alt. 5 = A joint venture for production purposes   Alt. 11 = Other channels

Alt. 6 = Acquisition of a Japanese company

Table B4.2 Entry channels according to industrial branches

Branch	Alternative (entry channels, Q 2) (Multiple answers)											Total Number of responses
	1	2	3	4	5	6	7	8	9	10	11	
Foods	5	4	4	5	4	1	3		1	4		31
Textiles	3	1		3		1	1			1	1	11
Petroleum											1	1
Chemicals	28	17	14	25	38	4	22	9	19	21	3	200
Pharmaceuticals	10		7	12	7	4	7	6	6	7		66
Metals	4	3	4	6	6		3	3		6	1	36
Machinery	18	18	18	20	23	4	29	10	3	11	5	159
Electronic/electric	21	8	9	18	16	3	15	6	6	10	4	116
Cars & car parts	3	1		4	5	1	4	1		1	1	21
Other Manufacturing	11	5	4	12	12	3	3	4	4	4	1	63
Total Manufacturing	103	57	60	105	111	21	87	39	39	65	17	704 (a)
Wholesale, retail trade and other services	16	10	24	32	3	2	16	1		8	4	116
Banks, credit institutes securities and insurance	6		48	6	2			1		2	11	76
Total Services	22	10	72	38	5	2	16	2		10	15	192 (b)
Grand Total	125	67	132	143	116	23	103	41	39	75	32	896 (c)

Legend
(a) n = 275; (b) n = 128; (c) n = 403.

Alt. = Alternative

Alt. 1 = Through a Japanese agent/distributor
Alt. 2 = Through a Japanese trading company

Alt. 3 = Through our own branch office
Alt. 4 = A joint venture for marketing/sales purposes
Alt. 5 = A joint venture for production purposes
Alt. 6 = Acquisition of a Japanese company

Alt. 7 = Wholly owned sales subsidiary
Alt. 8 = Wholly owned manufacturing subsidiary
Alt. 9 = R & D laboratory
Alt. 10 = Licensing/franchising rights/ technology agreement
Alt. 11 = Other channels

Table B4.3 Cross-tabulation based on management style and ownership
Entire sample (Q 3; number of companies)

Management Style	Ownership				Total
	25 - 49%	50%	51-99%	100%	
1 = Parent company's style/(Western)			2	11	13
2 = Partly Japanese style, but basically parent company's style	3	2	7	52	64
3 = Mixture of parent company's style and Japanese style (50/50 mix)	2	13	16	68	99
4 = Partly parent company's style, but basically Japanese style	20	34	30	73	157
5 = Japanese style	28	37	11	19	95
Total	53	86	66	223	428

American companies

Management Style	Ownership				Total
	25 - 49%	50%	51-99%	100%	
1 = Parent company's style/(Western)			1	2	3
2 = Partly Japanese style, but basically parent company's style	2	1	5	17	25
3 = Mixture of parent company's style and Japanese style (50/50 mix)	1	6	6	23	36
4 = Partly parent company's style, but basically Japanese style	13	24	14	33	84
5 = Japanese style	19	21	3	7	50
Total	35	52	29	82	198

European Companies

Management Style	Ownership				Total
	25 - 49%	50%	51-99%	100%	
1 = Parent company's style/(Western)				5	5
2 = Partly Japanese style, but basically parent company's style	1	1	2	27	31
3 = Mixture of parent company's style and Japanese style (50/50 mix)	1	7	10	40	58
4 = Partly parent company's style, but basically Japanese style	6	10	13	33	62
5 = Japanese style	7	15	7	11	40
Total	15	33	32	116	196

(continued)

Table B4.3 (continued)

Other Countries

Management Style	Ownership 25 - 49%	50%	51-99%	100%	Total
1 = Parent company's style/(Western)			1	4	5
2 = Partly Japanese style, but basically parent company's style				8	8
3 = Mixture of parent company's style and Japanese style (50/50 mix)				5	5
4 = Partly parent company's style, but basically Japanese style			3	7	10
5 = Japanese style	2	1	1	1	5
Total	2	1	5	25	33

Table B4.4 Cross-tabulation based on management style and CEO

Management style (Q 3)	Expatriate (E)	CEO (Q 8) Japanese (J)	Both J & E	Total (number)
USA				
Alt. 1	2	1		3
Alt. 2	9	14	1	24
Alt. 3	10	22	1	33
Alt. 4	16	64	4	84
Alt. 5		45	4	49
Subtotal	37	146	10	193
EC				
Alt. 1	5			5
Alt. 2	12	7	3	22
Alt. 3	19	15	3	37
Alt. 4	12	27	1	40
Alt. 5	2	31	2	35
Subtotal	50	80	9	139
EFTA				
Alt. 2	5	1		6
Alt. 3	15	4		19
Alt. 4	6	11	2	19
Alt. 5		4	1	5
Subtotal	26	20	3	49
Other Europe				
Alt. 3	1			1
Subtotal	1			1

(continued)

Table B4.4   (continued)

Management style (Q 3)	Expatriate (E)	CEO (Q 8) Japanese (J)	Both J & E	Total (number)
Asia				
Alt. 1	4			4
Alt. 2	2	2		4
Alt. 3	2			2
Alt. 4	2	1		3
Alt. 5	1	1	1	3
Subtotal	11	4	1	16
Others				
Alt. 2	3	1		4
Alt. 3		1	1	2
Alt. 4	2	5		7
Alt. 5	1	1		2
Subtotal	6	8	1	15
Grand Total	131	258	24	413

Legend   Alt. = Alternative   Alt. 1 = Parent company's style/(Western);
Alt. 2 = Partly Japanese style, but basically   Alt. 3 = Mixture of parent company's style and
            parent company's style;   Japanese style (50/50 mix);
Alt. 4 = Partly parent company's style, but basically Japanese style;   Alt. 5 = Japanese style.

Table B4.5   Management style and performance groups

Management style (Q 3)	Sample 1 Number	Sample 1 %	Sample 2 Number	Sample 2 %	Sample 3 Number	Sample 3 %
1 = Parent company's style/ (Western)	8	3	1	1	2	8
2 = Partly Japanese style, but basically parent company's style	43	14	17	19	3	12
3 = Mixture of parent company's style and Japanese style (50/50 mix)	71	24	17	19	6	25
4 = Partly parent company's style, but basically Japanese style	108	37	31	34	9	38
5 = Japanese style	64	22	25	27	4	17
Total	294	100	91	100	24	100

Legend
Sample 1 = Very successful and successful; Sample 2 = As expected;
Sample 3 = Very unsuccessful and unsuccessful; see Appendix A for details.

Table B4.6 Cross-tabulation based on CEO and management style according to performance groups

Sample 1 = Very successful and successful companies

CEO	Management Style (Q 3)					Total
	Alt. 1	Alt. 2	Alt. 3	Alt. 4	Alt. 5	
	Entire sample (number of companies)					
E	7	21	36	24	3	91
J	1	16	29	80	58	184
J/E		4	2	3	3	12
	USA					
E	1	7	9	12		29
J	1	10	17	48	31	107
J/E		1	1	3	1	6
	EUROPE					
E	3	11	25	10	2	51
J		5	12	28	25	70
J/E		3	1		1	5
	OTHERS					
E	3	3	2	2	1	11
J		1		4	2	7
J/E					1	1
Total	8	41	67	107	64	287

Sample 2 = As expected companies

CEO	Management Style (Q 3)					Total
	Alt. 1	Alt. 2	Alt. 3	Alt. 4	Alt. 5	
	Entire sample (number of companies)					
E	1	9	5	8		23
J		7	10	19	20	56
J/E			2	3	5	10
	USA					
E		2	1	3		6
J		3	4	11	10	28
J/E				1	3	4
	EUROPE					
E	1	5	4	5		15
J		3	5	8	10	26
J/E			1	2	2	5

(continued)

Table B4.6 (continued)

CEO	Management Style (Q 3)					Total
	Alt. 1	Alt. 2	Alt. 3	Alt. 4	Alt. 5	
OTHERS						
E		2				2
J		1	1			2
J/E			1			1
Total	1	16	17	30	25	89

Sample 3 = Very unsuccessful and unsuccessful companies

CEO	Management Style (Q 3)					Total
	Alt. 1	Alt. 2	Alt. 3	Alt. 4	Alt. 5	
Entire sample (number of companies)						
E	2	1	4	4	1	12
J		2	2	5	3	12
USA						
E	1			1		2
J		1	1	3	3	8
EUROPE						
E	1	1	4	3		9
J			1	1		2
OTHERS						
E					1	1
J		1		1		2
Total	2	3	6	9	4	24

Legend   Alt. = Alternative;   E = Expatriate;   J = Japanese.
Alt. 1 = Parent company's style/(Western)
Alt. 2 = Partly Japanese style, but basically parent company's style
Alt. 3 = Mixture of parent company's style and Japanese style (50/50 mix)
Alt. 4 = Partly parent company's style, but basically Japanese style
Alt. 5 = Japanese style

Table B4.7 Cross-tabulation based on control and performance

Control exercised by the headquarters (Q 4)	Sample 1 n = 292		Sample 2 n = 89		Sample 3 n = 25	
	Number	%	Number	%	Number	%
1 = Involved in recruitment/ personnel management of local personnel	51	17	12	13	6	24
2 = Involved in financial matters of the company	160	55	55	62	17	68
3 = Involved in product development	77	26	22	25	11	44
4 = Involved in R&D	53	18	21	24	8	32
5 = Involved in marketing/ advertising	35	12	12	13	7	28
6 = Parent company provides overall corporate policies and strategy, leaving concrete operation to us	199	68	56	63	19	76
7 = Other	28	10	6	7	2	8

Legend   n = Number of responding companies (multiple answers)
Sample 1 = Very successful and successful; Sample 2 = As expected;
Sample 3 = Very unsuccessful and unsuccessful.

Table B4.8 Cross-tabulation based on control of subsidiary and ownership

Ownership in percent	Control exercised by the headquarters (Q 4)							Total
	Alt. 1	Alt. 2	Alt. 3	Alt. 4	Alt. 5	Alt. 6	Alt. 7	
25 - 49%	4	20	15	8	6	31	7	91
50%	14	36	25	19	10	48	12	164
51 - 99%	10	37	17	12	8	48	4	136
100%	44	152	58	50	34	157	13	508
Total	72	245	115	89	58	284	36	899

Legend   Alt. = Alternative   n = 423 responding companies (multiple answers)
1 = Involved in recruitment /personnel management of local personnel
2 = Involved in financial matters of the company
3 = Involved in product development
4 = Involved in R & D
5 = Involved in marketing/advertising
6 = Parent company provides overall corporate policies and strategy,
    leaving concrete operation to us
7 = Other

Table B4.9   Cross-tabulation based on control of a joint venture and ownership

Ownership in percent	Management responsibility in a joint venture (Q 5)					Total (number)
	Alt. 1	Alt. 2	Alt. 3	Alt. 4	Alt. 5	
25 - 49%	12	9	27	1		49
50%	7	53	26	1		87
51 - 99%	17	8	14	11		50
100%*	11	6	5	3	1	26
Total	47	76	72	16	1	212

Legend   Alt. = Alternative
1 = According to the partner's (percentage) ownership in the joint venture
2 = 50/50% among the foreign and Japanese partner/s
3 = Japanese partner/s
4 = Foreign partner/s
5 = Other
*All the 26 companies answering this question previously had a joint venture or have at present also a joint venture.

Table B5.1   Cross-tabulation based on owner-ship and presence of expatriates
(Q 7)

Ownership	Number of Companies	In %
25 - 49%	12	5
50%	27	13
51 - 99%	34	16
100%	142	66
Total	215	100

Table B5.2   Cross-tabulation based on region/
country and presence of expatriates (Q 7)

Region/ country	Number of Companies	In %
USA	81	38
Europe	111	52
Asia	12	5
Other	11	5
Total	215	100

Table B5.3   Cross-tabulation based on CEO and performance

CEO (Q 8)	Sample 1 Number	%	Sample 2 Number	%	Sample 3 Number	%
Expatriate	92	32	23	25	12	48
Japanese	188	64	58	64	13	52
J/E	12	4	10	11		
Total	292	100	91	100	25	100

Legend
CEO: J/E = Japanese and expatriate combined
Sample 1 = Very successful and successful; Sample 2 = As expected;
Sample 3 = Very unsuccessful and unsuccessful.

Table B5.4   Cross-tabulation based on CEO and ownership
according to performance groups
Sample 1 = Very successful and successful companies

CEO (Q 8)	25 - 49%	50%	Ownership 51 - 99%	100%	Total (number)
			Entire sample		
Expatriate		3	16	73	92
Japanese	36	49	30	73	188
J/E	2	3		7	12
			USA		
Expatriate		1	8	20	29
Japanese	27	32	11	39	109
J/E	1	2		3	6

(continued)

Table B5.4 (continued)

CEO (Q 8)	25 - 49%	50%	Ownership 51 - 99%	100%	Total (number)
			Europe		
Expatriate		2	7	43	52
Japanese	9	16	16	31	72
J/E		1		4	5
			Other countries (companies)		
Expatriate			1	10	11
Japanese		1	3	3	7
J/E	1				1
Total	38	55	46	153	292

Sample 2 = As expected companies

	25 - 49%	50%	51 - 99%	100%	Total
			Entire sample		
Expatriate	1	1	4	17	23
Japanese	9	18	8	23	58
J/E	1	8		1	10
			USA		
Expatriate			2	4	6
Japanese	4	11	4	10	29
J/E	1	3			4
			Europe		
Expatriate	1	1	2	11	15
Japanese	5	7	4	11	27
J/E		5			5
			Other countries (companies)		
Expatriate				2	2
Japanese				2	2
J/E				1	1
Total	11	27	12	41	91

(continued)

Table B5.4 (continued)

Sample 3 = Very unsuccessful and unsuccessful companies

CEO (Q 8)	25 - 49%	50%	Ownership 51 - 99%	100%	Total (number)
			Entire sample		
Expatriate	1		1	10	12
Japanese		5	4	4	13
			USA		
Expatriate				2	2
Japanese		5	3		8
			Europe		
Expatriate			1	8	9
Japanese				3	3
			Other countries (companies)		
Expatriate	1				1
Japanese			1	1	2
Total	1	5	5	14	25

Legend	J/E Japanese and expatriate

Table B5.5 Cross-tabulation based on CEO and ownership according to nationality

CEO (Q 8)	25 - 49%	50%	Ownership 51 - 99%	100%	Total (number)
			Entire sample		
Expatriate	2	4	21	105	132
Japanese	47	72	43	103	265
J/E	3	12		9	24
Total	52	88	64	217	421
			USA		
Expatriate		1	10	26	37
Japanese	33	48	18	50	149
J/E	2	5		3	10
Total	35	54	28	79	196

Table B5.5   (continued)

CEO	Ownership				Total
(Q 8)	25 - 49%	50%	51 - 99%	100%	(number)
			Europe*		
Expatriate	1	3	10	64	78
Japanese	14	23	21	46	104
J/E		7		5	12
Total	15	33	31	115	194
			Other countries (companies)**		
Expatriate	1		1	15	17
Japanese		1	4	7	12
J/E	1			1	2
Total	2	1	5	23	31

Legend
  J/E Japanese and expatriate
  *   Europe includes: Germany, UK, Holland, France, Switzerland, Sweden, Italy, Belgium,
       Denmark, Finland, Liechtenstein, Poland and Spain.
  **   Other countries includes Australia, Bermuda, Brazil, Canada, New Zealand, Panama, and
       Asian countries.

**Table B6.1   Cross-tabulation based on year of establishment
            and transfer of marketing program/strategy to
            headquarters   (Q 34)**

Year of establishment	No	Yes	Total (number)
< 1971	80	54	134
1971-1980	83	25	108
1981-1985	52	11	63
> 1985	60	9	69
Total	275	99	374

Table B6.2 Cross-tabulation based on nationality of parent company and transfer of marketing program/strategy to headquarters (Q 34)

Nationality of parent company	No	Yes	Total (number)
Australia	2		2
Belgium		1	1
Bermuda	1		1
Canada	4		4
China	2		2
Denmark	2	1	3
Finland	3		3
France	13	8	21
Germany	27	13	40
Hong Kong	3		3
India	1		1
Italy	3	1	4
Korea	3		3
Liechtenstein	2	1	3
Netherlands	14	12	26
New Zealand	2		2
Panama	2	1	3
Poland		1	1
Singapore	1		1
Spain	1	1	2
Sweden	10	7	17
Switzerland	22	2	24
Taiwan	2		2
UK	20	5	25
USA	134	45	179
Total	274	99	373

Table B6.3 Cross-tabulation based on industrial branches and transfer of marketing program/strategy to headquarters (Q 34)

Branch	No	Yes	Total
1. Food (Processed & Non-processed)	14	1	15
2. Textiles	3	3	6
3. Petroleum	1		1
4. Chemicals	42	31	73
5. Pharmaceuticals	14	5	19
6. Metals	11	2	13
7. Machinery (commercial/industrial)	48	18	66
8. Electronic/electrical equipment	33	13	46
9. Cars & car parts	6	2	8
10. Other manufacturing	17	5	22

Table B6.3 (continued)

Branch	No	Yes	Total
11. Wholesale & retail trade	22	5	27
12. Banks & credit institutes	19	3	22
13. Securities	5	2	7
14. Insurance	6	3	9
15. Other services	34	6	40
Total	275	99	374

Table B7.1 Cross-tabulation based on transfer of production techniques and year of establishment (Q 37)

Year of establishment	No	Yes	Total (number)
< 1971	48	39	87
1971-1980	46	19	65
1981-1985	15	7	22
> 1985	24	6	30
Total	133	71	204

Table B7.2 Cross-tabulation based on transfer of production techniques and industrial branches (Q 37)

Branch	No	Yes	Total
1. Food (Processed & Non-processed)	8	2	10
2. Textiles	1		1
3. Petroleum	2		2
4. Chemicals	37	29	66
5. Pharmaceuticals	13	6	19
6. Metals	6	4	10
7. Machinery (commercial/industrial)	31	7	38
8. Electronic/electrical equipment	18	13	31
9. Cars & car parts	2	2	4
10. Other manufacturing	13	6	19
11. Banks & credit institutes	1	1	2
12. Other services	1	1	2
Total	133	71	204

Table B7.3 Cross-tabulation based on transfer of production techniques and nationality of parent company (Q 37)

Nationality of parent company	No	Yes	Total (number)
Belgium	1		1
Canada	2		2
Denmark	2		2
Finland	2		2
France	9	2	11
Germany	16	8	24
Italy	2	1	3
Liechtenstein	1		1
Netherlands	7	7	14
Panama		1	1
Singapore	1		1
Sweden	8	3	11
Switzerland	10	4	14
Taiwan	1		1
UK	3	3	6
USA	68	41	109
Total	133	70	203

Table B7.4 Cross-tabulation based on number of patents obtained and performance

Number of patents obtained (Q 43)	Sample 1 Number	%	Sample 2 Number	%	Sample 3 Number	%
Zero	21	22	14	52	4	57
1 to 5	28	29	6	22	1	14
6 to 10	13	14	4	15	2	29
> 10	33	35	3	11		
Total	95	100	27	100	7	100

Legend
Sample 1 = Very successful and successful; Sample 2 = As expected;
Sample 3 = Very unsuccessful and unsuccessful.

**Table B7.5   Cross-tabulation based on transfer of R & D results
to parent company and year of establishment**   (Q 45)

Year of establishment	No	Yes	Total (number)
< 1971	23	53	76
1971-1980	14	25	39
1981-1985	6	11	17
> 1985	11	7	18
Total	54	96	150

**Table B7.6   Cross-tabulation based on transfer of R & D results to
parent company and industrial branches**   (Q 45)

Branch	No	Yes	Total
1. Food (Processed & Non-processed)	4	2	6
2. Textiles	1		1
3. Petroleum	1	1	2
4. Chemicals	16	33	49
5. Pharmaceuticals	12	7	19
6. Metals	1	3	4
7. Machinery (commercial/industrial)	6	17	23
8. Electronic/electrical equipment	2	19	21
9. Cars & car parts	1	2	3
10. Other manufacturing	6	10	16
11. Wholesale & retail trade	1		1
12. Banks & credit institutes	2		2
13. Other services	1	2	3
Total	54	96	150

**Table B7.7   Cross-tabulation based on transfer of R & D
results and nationality of parent company** (Q 45)

Nationality of parent company	No	Yes	Total (number)
Canada	1		1
Denmark		1	1
Finland	1		1
France	5	4	9
Germany	8	12	20
Italy		3	3
Liechtenstein	1		1
Netherlands	2	7	9

(continued)

Table B7.7 (continued)

Nationality of parent company	No	Yes	Total (number)
Panama	1	1	2
Singapore	1		1
Sweden	2	4	6
Switzerland	6	4	10
UK	3	5	8
USA	23	54	77
Total	54	95	149

Table B8.1 Success factors by region and country   (Q 50)

REGION/ COUNTRY	AL 1	AL 2	AL 3	AL 4	AL 5	AL 6	AL 7	AL 8	AL 9	AL 10	AL 11	AL 12	AL 13	AL 14	AL 15	AL 16
USA (N=180)	127	69	56	29	88	24	84	17	70	74	41	35	67	21	40	1
EUROPE																
EC (n =133)																
GERMANY	28	15	6	4	20	3	14	1	10	10	6	8	17	6	9	
UK	16	15	9		13	2	12	4	5	9	4	8	13	6	11	1
NETHERLANDS	16	14	7	4	6	3	12	5	10	11	2	6	10	3	11	
FRANCE	11	8	6	4	6	3	7	3	5	5	3	5	11		7	
ITALY	2	3	1		2	1	2		1	1			1			
BELGIUM	2		1	1	1		1		1	1	1		1		1	
DENMARK	3	1			1		1	1	3	1			2	1	1	1
SPAIN	2		1				1	1	1	1	1		1	1		
TOTAL	80	56	31	13	49	12	50	15	36	39	17	27	56	17	40	2
EFTA (n = 43)																
SWITZERLAND	18	9	6	1	8		7	4	2	6	2	2	8	2	8	
SWEDEN	16	7	4	1	10		8	2	2	8	6	5	6	2	8	2
LIECHTENSTEIN	2				1			1		1	1				1	
FINLAND	2	1	1		2		1		1				1		1	
TOTAL	38	17	11	2	21		16	7	5	15	9	7	15	4	18	2
OTHERS																
POLAND									1	1		1			1	
TOTAL: EUROPE	118	73	42	15	70	12	66	22	42	55	26	35	71	21	59	4
OTHERS																
AUSTRALIA	1						1			1		1	1		2	1
BERMUDA																
BRAZIL							1									
CANADA	4	1	1		1		5			2		2	2	1	1	
CHINA			1				1			1		1	1			
HONG KONG	2				1								2			

(continued)

Table B8.1 (continued)

REGION/ COUNTRY	AL 1	AL 2	AL 3	AL 4	AL 5	AL 6	AL 7	AL 8	AL 9	AL 10	AL 11	AL 12	AL 13	AL 14	AL 15	AL 16
INDIA								1		1		1	1	1	1	1
S. KOREA							1		1	1		1	2	1		1
NEW ZEALAND	2	2	1		1		1		1	1			1		1	
PANAMA	1	1	1	1			1			1			1		1	
SINGAPORE													1			
TAIWAN	1	1	1							1						
TOTAL	11	5	5	1	3		11	1	2	9		6	12	3	6	3
GRAND TOTAL	256	147	103	45	161	36	161	40	114	138	67	76	150	45	105	8

Legend

AL = Alternative (multiple answers).   n = 381 responding companies

SUCCESS FACTORS

1 = Excellent in products/services
2 = Company and brand name have been well-known
3 = Excellent marketing capabilities
4 = Introduced Japanese production techniques
5 = Excellent technology and know-how
6 = Acquired new technology and know-how on the Japanese market
7 = Highly qualified and talented Japanese personnel
8 = Plenty of funds
9 = Japanese joint venture partner has been excellent
10 = Timing was right for investment in Japan

11 = No/or few competitors
12 = Not controlled by the parent company
13 = Our parent company provided a lot of support
14 = Reached satisfactory corporate profit (ROI) levels in a short time period
15 = Had an overall commitment towards the Japanese market
16 = Other factors

Table B8.2   Failure factors by region and country   (Q 50)

REGION/ COUNTRY	AL 1	AL 2	AL 3	AL 4	AL 5	AL 6	AL 7	AL 8	AL 9	AL 10	AL 11	AL 12	AL 13	AL 14	AL 15	AL 16
USA (N= 47)	7	13	9	2	3	4	10	9	4	9	22	10	7	18	13	1
EUROPE EC (n = 44)																
GERMANY	4	5	4	1		1	7				11	2	3	4	1	
UK		1	2			1		3		1	5			2		1
NETHERLANDS	1	1	3			1	1	3	2		3	1	1	3	2	1
FRANCE		1	3		1		1	1	1	1	2		1	4	2	1
ITALY	1	1					1								1	
BELGIUM																
DENMARK		1														
SPAIN																
TOTAL	6	10	12	1	1	2	11	7	3	2	21	3	5	13	6	3

(continued)

Table B8.2 (continued)

REGION/ COUNTRY	AL 1	AL 2	AL 3	AL 4	AL 5	AL 6	AL 7	AL 8	AL 9	AL 10	AL 11	AL 12	AL 13	AL 14	AL 15	AL 16
EFTA (n = 16)																
SWITZERLAND		1	1				1				1			1		
SWEDEN		3	2	3		2	3				6		1		2	1
LIECHTENSTEIN																
FINLAND				1		1		1	1		2					
TOTAL		4	3	4		3	4	1	1		9		1	1	2	1
OTHERS																
POLAND			1													
TOTAL: EUROPE	6	14	16	5	1	5	15	8	4	2	30	3	6	14	8	4
OTHERS																
AUSTRALIA		2		1		1				1	2					
BERMUDA																1
BRAZIL																
CANADA	1			1						1						
CHINA	1			1				1	1	1			1			
HONG KONG																
INDIA																
S. KOREA								1								
NEW ZEALAND																
PANAMA			2											1		
SINGAPORE											1					1
TAIWAN																
TOTAL	2	2	2	3		1		2	1	3	3		1	1		2
GRAND TOTAL	15	29	27	7	7	9	26	19	9	14	55	13	14	33	21	7

Legend

AL = Alternative (multiple answers);   n = 118 responding companies

FAILURE FACTORS

1 = Not excellent in products/services

2 = Our company and brand name have not been well-known

3 = Not excellent in marketing capabilities

4 = Did not introduce Japanese production techniques

5 = Did not possess excellent technology and know-how

6 = Did not acquire new technology and know-how on the Japanese market

7 = Did not have highly qualified and talented Japanese personnel

8 = Lacked funds

9 = Japanese joint venture partner has been inexperienced (or weak)

10 = Timing was not right for investment in Japan

11 = Too many competitors

12 = Tightly controlled by the parent company

13 = Our parent company did not provide sufficient support

14 = Difficult to reach satisfactory corporate profit {ROI} levels in a short time period

15 = Did not have an overall commitment towards the Japanese market

16 = Other factors

APPENDIX C

Acknowledgments to Participating Foreign Companies, Ministries, Banks, and Industrial Associations

1. A. G. International Chemical Co., Inc.
2. ABB Gadelius Industry K.K.
3. Acheson (Japan) Ltd.
4. Admiral Equipment Japan Ltd.
5. AEG Japan Ltd.
6. Agfa Copal Co., Ltd.
7. Agfa-Gevaert Japan Ltd.
8. Agropol Ltd.
9. Ahlstrom Daiichi Co., Ltd.
10. Air Liquide Laboratories, (K.K.)
11. AIU Insurance Co. (headquarters)
12. AIU Insurance Co. (subsidiary)
13. Ajinomoto General Foods Inc.
14. Akzo Coatings (Japan) Ltd.
15. Akzo Japan Ltd.
16. Akzo Kashima Ltd.
17. Alcon Japan Ltd.
18. Allstate Automobile & Fire Insurance Co., Ltd.
19. AMD Japan Ltd.
20. American Family Life Assurance Co.
21. American Life Insurance Co.
22. AMF Bowling Inc.
23. Aqua-lung (Nihon) K.K.
24. Arbor Acres Japan Co., Ltd.
25. Atlas Copco K.K.
26. Australia & New Zealand Banking Group Ltd.
27. Avdel K.K.
28. B-R31 Ice Cream Co., Ltd.
29. Bailey Japan Co., Ltd.
30. Banco do Estado de Sao Paulo S.A.
31. Banco Hispano Americano
32. Bang & Olufsen of Japan Ltd.
33. Bank of Nova Scotia
34. Banque Indosuez
35. Barcleys Bank plc
36. Barcleys de Zoete Wedd Investment Management
37. Barcleys de Zoete Wedd Securities (Japan) Ltd.
38. Baring Securities (Japan) Ltd.
39. Baxter Ltd.
40. Bayer Yakuhin, Ltd.
41. Beiersdolf Japan K.K.
42. Belcos Ltd.
43. Berliner Handels-und Frankfurter Bank
44. Beverly Japan Corp.
45. BMW Tokyo Corp.
46. BNP Securities (Japan) Ltd.
47. Borden Japan Inc.
48. Bosch K.K.
49. Braun Japan K.K.
50. Brooks Brothers (Japan), Ltd.
51. Brown & Williamson (Japan) Inc.
52. BSB Japan Ltd.
53. BT Asia Securities Ltd.
54. Bueltel International (Japan) Ltd.
55. Bush Boake Allen Morimura Ltd.
56. Bussan Lladro Co., Ltd.
57. BW Mechanical Seals K.K.
58. Cadam Systems Co. Inc.
59. Calsonic Harrison Co., Ltd.
60. Canadian Imperial Bank of Commerce
61. Cargill North Asia Ltd.
62. Carrier Transicold (Japan) Ltd.
63. Catalysts & Chemicals Inc., Far East
64. Cazenove & Co. (Japan) Ltd.
65. CEZUS Japon
66. Chanel K.K.

67. Charles River Japan Inc.
68. Chase Manhattan Bank, N.A.
69. CHBS Chemicals Ltd.
70. Chemical Data Systems, Inc.
71. Chemical Trust & Banking Co., Ltd.
72. Chiyoda Dames & Moore Co., Ltd.
73. Cho Hung Bank
74. Ciba Corning Diagnostics K.K.
75. CIBA-GEIGY (Japan) Ltd.
76. Cigna Insurance Co.
77. Cincinnati Milacron International Marketing Co.
78. Cititrust & Banking Corp.
79. Coca-Cola (Japan) Co., Ltd.
80. Commercial Bank of Korea Ltd.
81. Commerzbank AG
82. Conair Japan Corp.
83. Concurrent Nippon Corp.
84. Consew International Ltd.
85. Cray Research Japan Ltd.
86. Daido Permawick Co., Ltd.
87. Dainabot Co., Ltd.
88. Damart K.K.
89. Dana Japan, Ltd.
90. Danzas K.K.
91. Data Card Japan Ltd.
92. Daya International Industry Co., Ltd.
93. DB Capital Management (Asia) Ltd.
94. DB Morgan Grenfell Asset Management Co., Ltd.
95. Denak Co. Ltd.
96. Denal Silane Co., Ltd.
97. Denshi Media Services Co., Ltd.
98. Dentsu, Young & Rubicam Inc.
99. Desco (Japan) Ltd.

100. DG Securities
101. DHL Japan Inc.
102. Digital Equipment Corp. Japan
103. Dover Japan Inc.
104. Dow Corning Japan Ltd.
105. Dow Kakoh K.K.
106. Dow Elanco Japan Ltd.
107. Dragoco Japan Ltd.
108. Dresser Japan Ltd.
109. DSM Idemitsu Co. Ltd.
110. Du Pont-Idemitsu Co., Ltd.
111. Eastman Kodak (Japan) Ltd.
112. Ebara Carrier Co., Ltd.
113. Egon Zehnder International Co., Ltd.
114. Electrolux (Japan) Ltd.
115. Eli Lilly Japan K.K.
116. Emerson Japan Ltd.
117. EMS Datalogic Ltd.
118. ENIMONT JAPAN Ltd.
119. Esso Sekiyu K.K.
120. ESTECH Corp.
121. Evergreen International (Japan) Corp.
122. Falconbridge (Japan) Ltd.
123. Far East Westfalia Separator K.K.
124. Federal Express Japan K.K.
125. Feintool Engineering Co., Ltd.
126. Festo K.K.
127. Fidelity Investment (Japan) Ltd.
128. France Telecom Japan Co., Ltd.
129. Fresenius-Kawasaki Co., Ltd.
130. Fuji Xerox Co., Ltd.
131. Fuji-Hunt Electronics Technology Co., Ltd.
132. Fujikokusai Kogyo., Ltd.
133. Fujisawa-Astra Ltd.
134. Fujisawa Synthelabo Co., Ltd.
135. G.T.Management (Japan) Ltd.
136. Gadelius Fudosan K.K.

137. Gadelius Marine K.K.
138. General Electric Japan Ltd.
139. GE Plastics Japan Ltd.
140. Gelman Sciences Japan, Ltd.
141. GEM Polymers Ltd.
142. General Petrochemical Industries Ltd.
143. General Sekiyu K.K.
144. General Warranty Corp. of Japan
145. Geo Wehry International Ltd.
146. Getz Bros. Co., Ltd.
147. Goldman Sachs (Japan) Corp.
148. Grace Japan K.K.
149. Grundfos-Gadelius Pumps K.K.
150. GS-SAFT Ltd.
151. Hagemeyer Export & Import Co., Ltd.
152. Hagglunds Japan Inc.
153. Halifax Associates., (K.K.)
154. Happy Foods K.K.
155. Harcourt Brace Jovanovich Japan Inc.
156. Harris K.K.
157. Heidelberg-PMT Co., Ltd.
158. Heidenhain K.K.
159. Heineken Japan K.K.
160. Heishin Netzsch Co., Ltd.
161. Hengstler Japan Corp.
162. Hercules Japan Ltd.
163. Hilti (Japan), Ltd.
164. Hirose Cherry Precision Co., Ltd.
165. Hoechst Mitsubishi Kasei Co., Ltd.
166. Hoganas Gadelius K.K.
167. Hugo Boss Japan K.K.
168. Hukla Japan Inc.
169. Hunter Douglas Window Fashions Corp.
170. Hyundai Japan Co., Ltd.
171. IHI Trumpf Technologies,Ltd.
172. Ina-Ifo Co., Ltd.
173. Information Services

International-Dentsu, Ltd.
174. Instron Japan Co., Ltd.
175. INVESCO MIM Asset Management (Japan) Ltd.
176. IPI Corp.
177. Jaguar Japan Ltd.
178. James Capel Pacific Ltd.
179. Janssen-Kyowa Co., Ltd.
180. Japan Acrylic Chemical Co., Ltd.
181. Japan Alumoweld Co., Ltd.
182. Japan Communications Satellite Co., Inc.
183. Japan Encore Computer Inc.
184. Japan Lutravil Co., Ltd.
185. Japan NUS Co., Ltd.
186. Japan Power Brake Inc.
187. Japan Schenker Co., Ltd.
188. Japan Speed Shore Co., Ltd.
189. Jardine Wines & Spirits K.K.
190. Jecc Corp.
191. John Crane Japan, Inc.
192. Johnson & Johnson Medical K.K.
193. Johnson Co., Ltd.
194. JPN Chemical Co., Ltd.
195. Junkosha Co., Ltd.
196. Kanematsu Lex Electronics Inc.
197. Kanthal-Gadelius K.K.
198. Kasei Synthelabo Co., Ltd.
199. Kasei Verbatim Corp.
200. Kemira Ube Ltd.
201. Kentucky Fried Chicken Japan, Ltd.
202. Kirin-Tropicana, Inc.
203. Kiwi Japan Ltd.
204. Klockner-Moeller, Ltd.
205. Klockner Nippon Ltd.
206. Kodak Information Systems, K.K.
207. Komatsu-Howmet, Ltd.
208. Kontron Instruments K.K.

209. Korea First Bank
210. Kubota George Fischer Ltd.
211. Kuehne & Nagel (Japan) Ltd.
212. Kyokuto Petroleum Industries, Ltd.
213. Kyoto Machinery Co., Ltd.
214. Labsystems Japan K.K.
215. Lectra Systems Japan Ltd.
216. Leica K.K.
217. Letraset Japan Ltd.
218. LINZ Co., Ltd.
219. Lion Henkel Corp.
220. Lloyds Bank plc
221. Loctite (Japan) Corp.
222. Lonrho Pacific Ltd.
223. LTI/Graco K.K.
224. Lucas K.K.
225. Lurgi AG.
226. M.K. Struers Corp.
227. Mansson K.K.
228. Mario Valentino Japan K.K.
229. Marion Merrell Dow K.K.
230. Marposs K.K.
231. Matsushita Electronics Corp.
232. McCann-Erickson Hakuhodo Inc.
233. McDonald's Co. (Japan) Ltd.
234. McGraw-Hill Publising Co., Japan Ltd.
235. Measurex Japan Ltd.
236. Meggle Japan Co., Ltd.
237. Meiji Borden Co., Ltd.
238. Memorex Telex Japan Ltd.
239. Merck Japan Ltd.
240. Merrill Lynch Futures Japan Inc.
241. Midland Bank plc
242. Mister Minit Japan Co., Ltd.
243. Mitsui Badische Dyes Ltd.
244. Mitsui-Cyanamid Ltd.
245. Mitsui Deutz Diesel Engine Co., Ltd.
246. Mobil Sekiyu K.K.

247. Morgan Stanley Japan Ltd.
248. MSAS Cargo International K.K.
249. Nalken Corp.
250. National Bank of Canada
251. National Machinary Asia Co., Ltd.
252. Nationale Nederlanden Life Insurance Co., N.V.
253. NBD Bank, N.A.
254. NCR Japan, Ltd.
255. Neles-Jamesbury K.K.
256. Nestle Mackintosh K.K.
257. New Zealand Milk Products Japan Ltd.
258. NHK Morse Co., Ltd.
259. NI+C International Corp.
260. Nihon Balluff Co., Ltd.
261. Nihon Mediphisics Co., Ltd.
262. Nihon Millipore Ltd.
263. Nihon Mistron Co., Ltd.
264. Nihon Olivier K.K.
265. Nihon Redken K.K.
266. Nihon Schering K.K.
267. Nihon Sun Microsystems K.K.
268. Nihon Tetra Pak K.K.
269. Nihon Weidmuller Co., Ltd.
270. Niigata Masoneilan Co., Ltd.
271. Niigata MTI Co., Ltd.
272. Nippon Alkyl Phenol Co., Ltd.
273. Nippon Aluminum Alkyls, Ltd.
274. Nippon Amorphous Metals co., Ltd.
275. Nippon Becton Dickinson Co., Ltd.
276. Nippon D.P.C. Corp.
277. Nippon Eirich Co., Ltd.
278. Nippon Enviro Systems Corp.
279. Nippon GATX Co., Ltd.
280. Nippon Giant Tire Co., Ltd.
281. Nippon Lever K.K.
282. Nippon Liton & Silitek

Co., Ltd.
283. Nippon Mayer Co., Ltd.
284. Nippon Peroxide Co.,
    Ltd.
285. Nippon Petroleum
    Detergent Co., Ltd.
286. Nippon Polaroid K.K.
287. Nippon Proteins Co.,
    Ltd.
288. Nippon Rare Earths
    Co., Ltd.
289. Nippon Roche K.K.
290. Nippon Roussel K.K.
291. Nippon Selas Co., Ltd.
292. Nippon Sherwood
    MedicalIndustries Ltd.
293. NNBC Ltd.
294. Nobelpharma Japan
    Inc.
295. NOK EG&G
    Optoelectronics Co.,
    Ltd.
296. Nordica Japan Co., Ltd.
297. Nordson Engneering
    K.K.
298. Nordson K.K.
299. Norton K.K.
300. Novo Nordisk
    Bioindustry Ltd.
301. Occidental Chemical
    Asia, Ltd.
302. ORIX Omaha Life
    Insurance Corp.
303. Oronite Japan Ltd.
304. Overseas Union Bank
    Ltd.
305. Oxford University Press
306. Paine Webber
    International (Japan)
    Inc.
307. Pana Heraeuse Dental
    Co., Ltd.
308. Parfums Christian Dior
    (Japon) S.A.
309. Parfums Christian
    Lacroix K.K.
310. Paribas Asset
    Management Japan,
    Ltd.
311. Peat Marwick
    Consulting Co., Ltd.
312. Pegasus, Inc.
313. Perkin-Elmer Citizen
    Co., Ltd.

314. Perkin-Elmer Japan
    Co., Ltd.
315. Pfizer Pharmaceuticals
    Inc.
316. Pharmacia K.K.
317. Phillips Medical
    Systems Corp.
318. Phillips Petroleum
    Toray Inc.
319. Phizer K.K.
320. Pictet (Japan) Ltd.
321. PNN Corp.
322. Polychrome Japan Co.,
    Ltd.
323. Polyplastics Co., Ltd.
324. Portescap Japan Ltd.
325. PPG-CI Co., Ltd.
326. Princess Marcella
    Borghese Co., Ltd.
327. Pyro Safety Device Co.,
    Ltd.
328. R.P.Scherer K.K.
329. Raychem, (K.K.)
330. RCI Engineering Co.,
    Ltd.
331. Reebok Japan Inc.
332. Remy Japon K.K.
333. Revlon K.K.
334. Rheometrics Far East,
    Ltd.
335. Ric-Wil Japan Ltd.
336. Rockwell International
    Japan Co., Ltd.
337. Rodel Nitta Corp.
338. Rodic Co., Ltd.
339. Rover Japan Ltd.
340. Royal Insurance PLC
341. Royal Marriott & SC
    Corp.
342. RSV Corp.
343. Rudolf Shokai Co., Ltd.
344. Rudolf Wolff K.K.
345. S&I Co., Ltd.
346. S.G. Warburg Securities
    (Japan) Inc.
347. Saison Life Insurance
    Co., Ltd.
348. San Nopco Ltd.
349. Sandoz K.K.
350. Sandoz
    Pharmaceuticals, Ltd.
351. Sandvik K.K.
352. Sanseki-Texaco
    ChemicalsCo., Ltd.

353. Sansui Shoji Co., Ltd.
354. SBC Portfolio
    Management
    International K.K.
355. SBCI Securities (Asia)
    Ltd.
356. Schering-Plough K.K.
357. Schlegel Engineering
    K.K.
358. Schlumberger K.K.
359. Schroder Securities
    (Japan) Ltd.
360. Scovill Japan Ltd.
361. Seishin Tetra Pak K.K.
362. SGS Inc.
363. Shell Kosan K.K.
364. Shin Caterpillar
    Mitsubishi Ltd.
365. Shinhan Bank
366. Showa Cabot
    Supermetals K.K.
367. Showa Products Co.,
    Ltd.
368. Siemens-Asahi Medical
    Technologies Ltd.
369. Sight & Sound
    Education (Japan) Ltd.
370. SKF Japan Ltd.
371. Slendertone Japan K.K.
372. SM Catalyst Co., Ltd.
373. SmithKline Beckman
    Japan Ltd.
374. Societe Generale
375. Sogelease (Japan) Co.,
    Ltd.
376. Solidur Japan Ltd.
377. Sony Life Insurance
    Co., Ltd.
378. Sony/Tektoronix Corp.
379. Spectra Physics K.K.
380. Spom Japan Co., Ltd.
381. Spraying Systems Co.
382. SPS/UNBRAKO K.K.
383. Staedtler Nippon K.K.
384. State Bank of India
385. Sterling Winthrop Inc.
386. Stratus Computer
    Japan Co., Ltd.
387. Sulzer Brothers (Japan)
    Ltd.
388. Sumika Hercules Co.,
    Ltd.
389. Sumitomo 3M Ltd.
390. Sun Elite Corp.

391. Sunflex K.K.
392. Swarovski Japan Ltd.
393. Swire Transtech Ltd.
394. Takeda Badische
    Urethane Industries,
    Ltd.
395. Teisan K.K.
396. Teledyne Japan K.K.
397. Thomas & Betts Japan,
    Ltd.
398. Tiresplus Co., Ltd.
399. TNT Skypak Japan Inc.
400. Toho Badishe
    Structural Materials
    Co., Ltd.
401. Tonex Co., Ltd.
402. Toney Penna Japan Co.,
    Ltd.
403. Toshiba-Ballotini Co.,
    Ltd.
404. Toyo Carrier
    Engineering Co., Ltd.
405. Toyo Hydraulic
    Equipment Co., Ltd.
406. Toyo Morton Ltd.
407. Toyoda Van Moppes
    Ltd.
408. Triple "F" Japan Ltd.
409. Triumph International
    Japan Ltd.
410. TRW Steering &
    Industrial Products
    (Japan) Co., Ltd.
411. Tsubakimoto Emerson
    Co.
412. Tsubakimoto Mayfran
    Inc.
413. Tyton Co. of Japan,
    Ltd.
414. UDJ International
    Liquor Marketing Ltd.

415. Ulvac Cryogenics Inc.
416. Union Showa K.K.
417. Upjohn
    Pharmaceuticals Ltd.
418. Virgin Mega Stores
    Japan Ltd.
419. Viscodrive Japan Ltd.
420. Vitel Japan Ltd.
421. Volkswagen Audi
    Nippon K.K.
422. Volvo Cars Japan Corp.
423. Vorwerk Nippon K.K.
424. W.I. Carr (Overseas)
    Ltd.
425. Warburg Investment
    Trust Management
426. Westpac Banking Corp.
427. Williams Sonoma Japan
    Co., Ltd.
428. Wyatt Company K.K.
429. Xidex Japan Co., Ltd.
430. Yamaha-Olin Metal
    Corp.
431. Yokogawa Cray ELS
    Ltd.
432. Yokogawa-Hewlett-
    Packard, Ltd.
433. Yours Japan, Inc.
434. Yuasa-Ionics Co., Ltd.
435. Zellweger Uster K.K.
436. Not permitted to
    disclose the name

OTHER ORGANIZATIONS

American Chamber of
    Commerce in Japan
A. T. Kearney, Inc.
Electronic Industries
    Association of Japan

Embassy of Sweden--
    Commercial Office
European Business
    Community
Federation of Bankers
    Associations of Japan
Japan Automobile
    Importers' Association
Japan Automobile
    Manufacturers Association,
    Inc.
Japan Chemical Exporters'
    Association
Japan Chemical Importers'
    Association
Japan Chemical Industry
    Association
Japan Development Bank
Japan Electronic Industry
    Development Association
Japan External Trade
    Organization
Japan Industrial Robot
    Association
Japan Machine Tool
    Builders' Association
Japan Machinery Exporters
    Association
Japan Machinery Importers
    Association
Japan Pharmaceutical
    Manufacturers Association
Japan Tariff Association
KEIDANREN
Machine Tool Importers
    Association of Japan
Ministry of International
    Trade and Industry

REFERENCES

Abegglen, J. C. "The fast pace of Asian change." *Venture Japan.* 1, no. 4, Asia Pacific Communication, Inc., San Francisco, 1989.

Abegglen, J. C., and Stalk, G. *Kaisha--The Japanese corporation.* New York: Basic Books, 1985.

ACCJ (The American Chamber of Commerce in Japan) and A. T. Kearney, Inc. *Trade and investment in Japan: The current environment.* Tokyo: ACCJ, June 1991.

ACCJ and Towers, Perrin, Forster and Crosby. *Employment practices of American companies in Japan.* Monograph No. 2. Tokyo: ACCJ, 1991.

Ballon, R. J. *Foreign competition in Japan--Human resource strategies.* London: Routledge, 1992.

Bank of Japan. *The Bank of Japan Monthly Bulletin*, no. 12, Tokyo, December 1993.

Bartlett, C. A., and Ghoshal, S. "Tap your subsidiaries for global reach." *Harvard Business Review*, Boston, November-December 1986.

Brull, S. "Second city, first in property bargains." *International Herald Tribune*, Tokyo, August 24, 1992.

Commission of the European Communities. *Guide for European investment in Japan.* Tokyo: Delegation of the Commission of the European Communities, 1991.

Czinkota, M. R., and Woronoff, J. *Japan's market: The distribution system.* New York: Praeger, 1986.

Delphos, W. A. *Inside Washington and Tokyo--A business guide to U.S. and Japanese government assistance.* Washington: Venture Publishing, N.A., 1993.

"Does Japan play fair?" *Fortune*, September 7, 1992.

EBC (European Business Community). "A position paper on European investment in Japan." *Investment Committee of EBC*, Tokyo, May 1992.

Economic Planning Agency. *National Economic Accounts Quarterly*, no. 98, Tokyo, September 1993.

EIAJ (Electronic Industries Association of Japan). *Facts and figures on the Japanese electronics industry*, and *Perspective on the Japanese electronics industry--1993 Edition*. Tokyo: EIAJ, 1993.

Emmott, B. *Japan's global reach: The influences, strategies and weaknesses of Japan's multinational companies*. New York: Random House, 1992.

Encarnation, D. J. *Rivals beyond trade: America versus Japan in global competition*. Ithaca, New York: Cornell University Press, 1992.

Gemini Consulting (Japan). *Top 100 foreign firms*. Tokyo: Gemini Consulting, 1991.

Hamel, G., and Prahalad, C. K. "Creating global strategic capabilities." In Hood, H., and Vahlne, J-E., eds., *Strategies in global competition*. Kent: Croom Helm, 1988.

Huddleston, J. N., Jr. *Gaijin Kaisha: Running a foreign business in Japan*. New York: M.E. Sharpe, 1990.

Hymer, S. H. *The international operations of national firms: A study of direct foreign investment*. Cambridge, MA: MIT Press, 1976.

IMF (International Monetary Fund). *International financial statistics yearbook*. Washington: IMF, 1992.

------. *Direction of trade statistics yearbook*. Washington: 1993.

JAIA (Japan Automobile Importer's Association). *Imported car market of Japan--1993*. Tokyo: JAIA, 1993.

JAMA (Japan Automobile Manufacturers Association, Inc.,). *Automobile statistics--monthly report*, 27, no. 2, Tokyo, May 1993.

Japan Industrial Robot Association. *Current status and perspectives of industrial robots*, Tokyo: Japan Industrial Robot Association, October 1993 (in Japanese).

Japan Machine Tool Builders' Association. *Monthly statistical report*, Tokyo, September 1993 (in Japanese).

Japan Tariff Association. *The summary report on trade of Japan*. Tokyo: Japan Tariff Association, September and October 1993.

JCIA (Japan Chemical Industry Association). *Graphical outlook of Japan chemical industry*. Tokyo: JCIA, 1993.

JETRO. *Investment in Japan--facts and figures*. Tokyo: JETRO, 1992.

------. *Business facts and figures--Nippon 1993*. Tokyo: JETRO, 1993a.

------. *JETRO white paper on foreign direct investment--1993*. Tokyo: JETRO, March 1993b.

Johansson, J. K., and Nonaka, I. "Market research the Japanese way." *Harvard Business Review*, Boston, May-June 1987.

JPMA (Japan Pharmaceutical Manufacturers Association). *Data book 1992*. Tokyo: JPMA, December 1992.

KEIDANREN. *Review on Japanese Economy*, Special Issue, Tokyo: KEIDAN-REN, 1993.

Keizai Koho Center. *Japan 1993--An international comparison*. Tokyo: Keizai Koho Center, 1993.

Khan, S. *A study of success and failure in exports--an empirical investigation of the export performance of 165 market ventures of 83 firms in the chemical and electronics manufacturing industries*. Stockholm: Akademilitteratur, 1978.

------. *Success and failure of Japanese companies' export ventures in high-tech industries--a comparative study of Japanese and European manufacturing companies' export marketing and investment strategies in ASEAN, the NIEs, and the People's Republic of China*. Stockholm: Almqvist & Wiksell, October 1988; Japanese edition, Tokyo: Nihon Keizai Hyoron-sha, August 1990.

------. "Case study: Three Swedish companies' strategy and performance in Japan--Nihon Tetra Pak, Fujisawa-Astra, and Sandvik." To be published during 1994 (in English and Japanese).

Kotler, P., Fahey, L., and Jatusripitak, S. *The new competition--Meeting the marketing challenge from the Far East*. Englewood Cliffs: Prentice Hall, 1985.

Management and Coordination Agency. *Report on the survey of research and development--1992*. Tokyo: Statistics Bureau, April 1993.

Mansfield, E. "Industrial innovation in Japan and the United States." *Science*, 241, Washington, September 30, 1988.

Ministry of Finance. *The fourth survey research on business activity overseas: General survey of foreign investment statistics*. Tokyo: MITI, International Business Section of the Department of Industrial Policy, Printing Bureau, 1991 (in Japanese).

MITI. *Guidebook for the law on extraordinary measures for the promotion of imports and the facilitation of foreign direct investment*. Tokyo: MITI, July 1992.

------. *Census of manufacturers 1991--report by industries and report by commodities*. Tokyo: MITI, 1993a (in Japanese).

------. *Newly adopted import promotion measures*. NR-403(93-1). Tokyo: MITI, March 1993b.

------. *The 22nd survey on Japanese business activities abroad*. NR-406(93-4). Tokyo: MITI, June 1993c.

------. *The 26th survey on business activities of foreign affiliates in Japan*. NR-407(93-5). Tokyo: MITI, June 1993d.

Morgan, J. C., and Morgan, J. J. *Cracking the Japanese market*. New York: Free Press, 1991.

Nevins, T. J. *Taking charge in Japan*. Tokyo: The Japan Times, Ltd., 1990.

Ohmae, K. "Managing innovation and new products in key Japanese industries." *Research Management*, 27, no. 4, New York, July-August 1985a.

------. *Triad power--the coming shape of global competition*. New York: Mckinsey & Co., 1985b.

Oppenheimer, M. F., and Tuths, D. M. *Non-tariff barriers: The effects on corporate strategy in high-technology sectors*. Boulder, Co: Westview Press, 1987.

Ouchi, W. *Theory Z*. Reading, MA: Addison-Wesley, 1982.

Porter, M. E. *Competitive strategy*. New York: Free Press, 1980.

------. *Competitive advantage*. New York: Free Press, 1985.

Pucik, V., Hanada, M., and Fifield, G. *Management culture and the effectiveness of local executives in Japanese-owned U.S. corporations*. New York and Ann Arbor: Egon Zehnder International and University of Michigan Press, 1989.

Saito, M. *A study of technology transfer*. Tokyo: Bunshindo, 1979 (in Japanese).

Sakakibara, K., and Westney, D. E. "Comparative study of the training, careers, and organization of engineers in the computer industry in the United States and Japan." *Hitotsubashi Journal of Commerce and Management*, 20, no. 1, Tokyo, 1985.

Sakurai, K. *An analysis of foreign direct investment in Japan*. Research Report No. 27. Tokyo: The Japan Development Bank, March 1992.

Takeuchi, H., and Nonaka, I. "The new new product development game." *Harvard Business Review*, no. 1, Boston, January-February 1986.

Takeuchi, H., and Porter, M. E. "Three roles in international marketing in global strategy." In Porter, M. E., ed. *Competition in global industries*. Boston: Harvard Business School Press, 1986.

Toyo Keizai. *Directory of foreign affiliated companies in Japan*. Tokyo: Toyo Keizai, August 1991.

Vernon, R. "International investment and international trade in the product cycle." *Quarterly Journal of Economics*, 80, no. 2, Cambridge, MA, May 1966.

------. *Sovereignty at bay: The multinational spread of US enterprises*. New York: Basic Books, 1971.

Vernon, R., and Wells, L. T., Jr. *The economic environment of international business*. 5th ed. Englewood Cliffs: Prentice-Hall, 1991.

Yakugyo Jiho Co., Ltd. *Pharma Japan Yearbook--1992*. Tokyo: Yakugyo Jiho Co., Ltd., 1992.

Yoshihara, H. "Japanese production management abroad." In Monden, Y., et al., eds., *Innovations in management: The Japanese corporation*. Georgia: Industrial Engineering and Management Press, 1985.

------. "Foreign subsidiaries as contributors to parent companies--a new paradigm of multinational enterprises." *Kobe Economics and Business Review*, no. 35, Kobe, 1990.

------. "Foreign companies in Japan--key factors for success and failure." *Management Japan*, 24, no. 1, Tokyo, Spring 1991.

------. *Miracle of Fuji Xerox*. Tokyo: Toyo Keizai Shinposha, October 1992 (in Japanese).

------. "Questionnaire on local presidents and internationalization within Japanese parent companies." To be published during 1994 (in Japanese).

Zenginkyo (Federation of Bankers Associations of Japan). *Japanese Banks '93*. Tokyo: Zenginkyo, 1993.

INDEX

About the Authors

SIKANDER KHAN is an Associate Professor in International Business at Stockholm University, specializing in industrial strategies and policies and technology transfer. He has published over 40 papers and frequently lectured on these topics worldwide. Other assignments include UNIDO (United Nations Industrial Development Organization), a three year term at Kobe University, Japan, and consultant to various international organizations.

HIDEKI YOSHIHARA is Professor of International Business and Director of the Research Institute for Economics & Business Administration, Kobe University, Japan. Specializing in diversification strategies and Japanese and foreign multinationals, he has published numerous books, articles and case studies, conducted empirical research in Asia, Europe and the United States, and acted as adviser to and coordinator of the Osaka Industrial Association, Kansai Productivity Center and Kansai Economic Center.